ULTIMATE GUIDE TO

CREATIVE
HOMEOWNER®

FURNITURE
REPAIR & REFINISHING

RESTORE, REBUILD, AND RENEW WOODEN FURNITURE

2ND REVISED EDITION

CREATIVE
HOMEOWNER®

ULTIMATE GUIDE TO

FURNITURE
REPAIR & REFINISHING

RESTORE, REBUILD, AND RENEW WOODEN FURNITURE

2ND REVISED EDITION

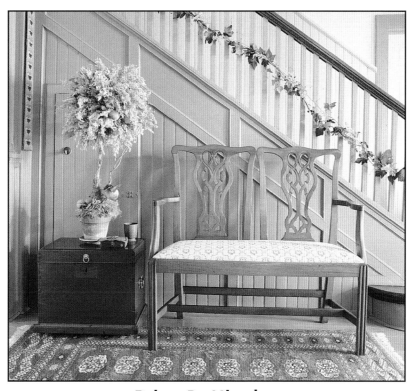

Brian D. Hingley

I dedicate this book to my parents, Albert Parker Hingley
and Phyllis M. Hingley.

Special thanks to my wife, Audrey, for assistance with the
manuscript and to my son, Robert, for illustration assistance. Also, thanks to the employees of Hingley Furniture
Restoration, Inc., especially Bob Lane and Mary Bishop,
whose dedication to our craft and clients helped me greatly
in the completion of this book.

Brian D. Hingley
Richmond, Virginia

CRE▲TIVE
HOMEOWNER®

Ultimate Guide to Furniture Repair & Refinishing, 2nd Revised Edition is an original work, first published in 2021 by Creative Homeowner, and is a revised and updated edition of *Furniture Repair & Refinishing*, originally published in 1998 by Creative Homeowner, an imprint of Fox Chapel Publishing.

ULTIMATE GUIDE TO FURNITURE REPAIR & REFINISHING
ORIGINAL EDITION
Editorial Director: Timothy O. Bakke
Art Director: Annie Jeon
Copyeditor: Robin White Goode
Proofreader: Raymond Marchand
Technical Reviewer: R. S. Wilkinson
Graphic Designer: Michelle D. Halko
Illustrators: Rodney Stokes, Paul Schumm, Vincent Allessi

2ND REVISED EDITION
Technical Editor: Jeff Almich
Cover Photography: Freeze Frame Studio [TK check]
Inside Photos: H. Howard Hudgins, Jr., Richmond, VA, except as noted below
Additional Photos: p. 1: Steven Mays, New York, NY; p. 2: Marc Samu, Bayport, NY; pp. 12, 24, 40, 46, 66, 106, 122, 164, 174, 188, 196, 202, 210, 228 (bot.): Lance Patterson, North Bennet Street School, Boston, MA; pp. 50, 51, 54, 55, 56, 59: Jim Roberson [TK check all page refs]

ISBN 978-1-58011-843-9

Library of Congress Control Number: 2021940915

We are always looking for talented authors. To submit an idea, please send a brief inquiry to acquisitions@foxchapelpublishing.com.

Printed in China

Current Printing (last digit)
10 9 8 7 6 5 4 3 2 1

Creative Homeowner®, *www.creativehomeowner.com*, is an imprint of New Design Originals Corporation and distributed exclusively in North America by Fox Chapel Publishing Company, Inc., 800-457-9112, 903 Square Street, Mount Joy, PA 17552, and in the United Kingdom by Grantham Book Service, Trent Road, Grantham, Lincolnshire, NG31 7XQ.

SAFETY FIRST

Though all the methods in this book have been tested for safety, it is not possible to overstate the importance of using the safest procedures possible. What follows are reminders—some do and don'ts of work safety. They are not substitutes for your own common sense.

- Always use caution and good judgment when following the repair and refinishing procedures described in this book.

- Always be sure that the electrical setup is safe; be sure that no circuit is overloaded and that all power tools and electrical outlets are properly grounded. Use GFCI-protected circuits whenever possible.

- Always read container labels on paints, solvents, and other products; provide ventilation, and observe all other warnings.

- Always read the tool maker's instructions for using a tool.

- Always use hold-downs and push sticks whenever possible when working on a table saw. Avoid working short pieces if you can.

- Always remove the key from any drill chuck (portable or press) before starting the drill.

- Always know the limitations of your tools. Do not try to force them to do what they were not designed to do.

- Always make sure that any power-tool adjustment is locked before proceeding.

- Always clamp small pieces firmly to a bench or other work surface when using a power tool on them.

- Always wear the appropriate rubber or work gloves when handling chemicals.

- Always wear a disposable face mask when you create dust by sawing or sanding. Use a special filtering respirator when working with toxic substances and solvents.

- Always wear eye protection when using power tools or striking metal on metal.

- Always be aware that there is seldom enough time for your body's reflexes to save you from injury from a power tool in a dangerous situation; everything happens too fast. Be alert!

- Always keep your hands away from the business ends of blades, cutters, and bits.

- Always hold a circular saw firmly, usually with both hands so that you know where they are.

- Never work with tools when you are tired or under the influence of alcohol or drugs.

- Never cut very small pieces of wood or pipe using a power saw. Cut small pieces off larger pieces.

- Never change a saw blade or a drill or router bit unless the power cord is unplugged.

- Never work in insufficient lighting.

- Never work while wearing loose clothing, hanging hair, open cuffs, or jewelry.

- Never work with dull tools. Have them sharpened, or learn how to sharpen them yourself.

CONTENTS

INTRODUCTION

Furniture restoration has long been a popular pastime for do-it-yourself enthusiasts. During my years of working on furniture, I've discovered that people with all kinds of backgrounds, from students to homemakers to professional people, have either restored or tried to restore a piece of furniture.

There are myriad reasons for such wide appeal. The reason I hear most often is simply that furniture restoration is enjoyable. Retreating to the sanctuary of a home workshop to work on a furniture project provides not only satisfaction, but relaxation and stress relief. Often your efforts will bring immediate, rewarding results. There's great personal satisfaction in taking a piece of furniture previously destined for the trash and transforming it into a useful, beautiful piece to grace your home for years to come.

People with artistic talent find that furniture projects offer opportunities for creative expression: While many repair techniques in furniture restoration are basic and standard, you can put your creativity to work in the later stages of refinishing as you strive to achieve just the right look for your piece. Others discover that the challenge of problem-solving—or just fixing something that's broken—can be satisfying.

One of the most obvious reasons to do anything yourself is to save money. Learning to

This restored walnut rocker, *which originally cost the author less than $20, remains a bargain, even when you include the expense of a professional upholstery job. Note the handsome hand-carved grape cluster (inset).*

restore furniture allows you to turn that yard sale or auction bargain into something of value for your home at a fraction of the cost of a comparable fully restored piece.

One of the first pieces of furniture I ever acquired and transformed was an old walnut Victorian rocker. The upholstery and springs were missing, but I knew the wood rocker and its frame were redeemable. The top of the rocker featured a beautiful hand-carved grape cluster, and I knew the chair could be a true thing of beauty once I refurbished it. I paid less than $20 for the chair, restored it, and had a professional upholsterer add springs and fabric. Even including the price I paid for a professional upholstery job, the antique rocker was a great bargain. Today that chair continues to occupy a place of honor in my living room more than 20 years after I first brought it home. Guests never fail to comment on its beauty and comfort.

Restored wood furniture usually has a value equal to—and in many cases greater than—a comparable new piece available in today's furniture stores. Much of today's manufactured furniture lacks quality construction, making wide use of plastics and other non-wood materials. Restoring old furniture that is not truly "antique," but all wood and built solidly, still makes sense in terms of practical use and value.

Even though your piece may not be worth thousands, restoring it can produce a useful and beautiful addition to your home, as in this restored pine chest of drawers.

Another money-saving aspect of restoring furniture yourself is that when problems develop in your own household furniture, you can repair them. Keep in mind, however, that you need to know how to do the job correctly before attempting your own repairs. As a professional furniture restorer, I've had to salvage many botched repair attempts. Trying to fix a piece after it's been improperly repaired is more difficult and expensive than simply doing it right the first time.

Yet another reason for furniture restoration is sentimental attachment. Your mother's china cabinet or foot-pedal sewing machine may not be a true antique or worth thousands, but you may never be able to replace its value as a family heirloom.

I once restored a 40-year-old nightstand that was in terrible shape, with water damage and a broken top, for a customer. The piece was not monetarily valuable, but it had been part of the first bedroom suite of the customer's parents, and their daughter, my client, had it restored for them as a surprise Christmas present. That client later wrote me a thank-you note, commenting, "You did a beautiful job

Simple hand tools *are often all that's needed for successful furniture restoration. Bottom of page: a furniture restorer's box.*

Whether you want to lovingly restore a treasured antique or you just want to be able to solve practical furniture problems around the house, the following pages will provide a wealth of information to help you. Before you begin a project, read over the material. Then keep this book on hand for quick, easy reference while you work on your piece.

Each step-by-step project in the book begins with a suggested list of the tools and materials necessary to complete the work. Each task also begins by rating the level of difficulty of the work to be done on the furniture. The level of difficulty is indicated by one, two, or three hammers:

Easy, even for beginners.

Moderately difficult. Can be done by beginners who have the patience and willingness to learn.

Difficult. Can be done by the do-it-yourselfer but requires a serious investment of time, patience, and money in specialty tools. Consider consulting a specialist.

These difficulty ratings should help you gauge whether you want to tackle a project or not. This way, you won't be well into a project before discovering that you're in over your head.

It's important that—as a hobby—furniture restoration is able to be enjoyed. It is my hope that this book will help you have many hours of enjoyment as you set your hand to the task of furniture repair and restoration.

on the nightstand. As you know, the restoration was a gift for my parents. The expression on their faces when they saw it was worth three times the money I spent on the restoration." Doing your own restoration projects on furniture with personal sentimental value can provide you with similar—or even stronger—feelings.

Restoring furniture is something you can do in the setting of your own home, without a workshop full of expensive tools and equipment. If you have a basement, a garage, an extra room, or even an enclosed porch, you can make room for a furniture project. And although many professional furniture shops accumulate expensive tools and equipment, often you can do the work required using only simple hand tools and a few small power tools. If you have limited resources, you can buy your tools only as needed.

While it's true that some aspects of furniture repair and restoration require more ability than others—and there are projects best left to the hands of a skilled furniture professional—don't allow this to discourage you from starting your own furniture projects. If you are patient and determined to learn, you can undertake the majority of restoration projects without having a high level of skill, as long as you have knowledgeable sources to which you can refer as you work.

PART I
HOW TO BEGIN

1

GETTING STARTED

In this chapter you'll learn how to determine whether a piece of furniture is worth restoring. You'll also learn how to check for what exactly needs to be done to restore it. This examination involves not only the obvious things like the condition of the finish but also such items as loose joints and veneer, splits in wood, worn interior drawer runners, and even run-down hardware and mirrors. After you've learned what has to be done to restore the piece, you'll find out how to prioritize the work. Lastly, you'll learn about the kinds of wood (both hardwood and softwood) commonly used in furniture construction so you can identify them as you work on your various furniture projects.

FURNITURE EXAMINATION

As a professional furniture restorer, I've examined thousands of pieces of furniture over the years to determine their condition and to provide repair cost estimates. After carefully inspecting a piece and presenting a cost estimate, it's not unusual for me to hear a customer exclaim, "I didn't pay that much when I bought it!"

Many times, after discovering that the customer had recently acquired the piece at a yard sale or flea market at a bargain price, I'm tempted to reply, "That explains why it needs so much work." In other cases, I might find out that the customer bought the piece 20, 30, or even 40 years ago—when it cost a fraction of what a comparable piece would cost today.

If you're considering a piece of furniture for restoration, whether you're thinking about buying it or you already own it, you must know beforehand what to look for and how to inspect the piece. Some questions to consider before making the decision are listed in "Evaluating the Piece of Furniture," page 14. Once you know that you definitely want to restore the furniture, you must decide on your course of action.

Determining What Needs to be Done

What should you look for to determine the kind of work a piece needs? Some things, like broken legs or missing veneers, are obvious. Other problems, however, such as previous bad repairs, missing or damaged drawer runners, or loose veneer, will show up only under

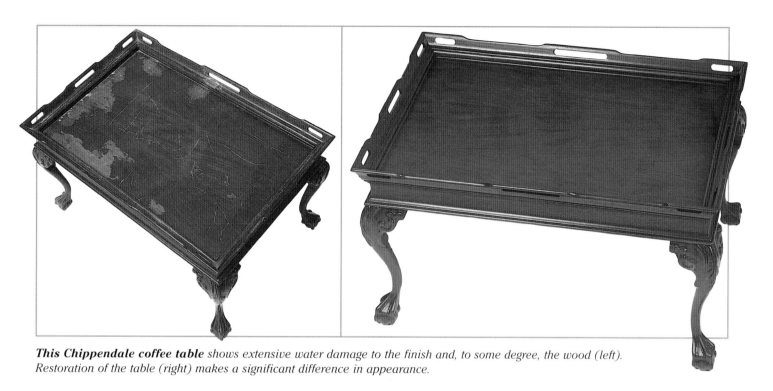

This Chippendale coffee table shows extensive water damage to the finish and, to some degree, the wood (left). Restoration of the table (right) makes a significant difference in appearance.

This slant-top desk is from the early nineteenth century. Any restoration work will need special care by a knowledgeable professional. The open lid reveals the detailed interior of the antique desk (inset).

careful examination. Look over the piece closely from top to bottom and make a list, if not on paper at least mentally, of what restoration work you'll have to do on the piece.

Finish Quality. First, consider the piece's finish condition: Does it need refinishing—which involves totally stripping off the old finish, preparing the wood, and putting on a new finish—or can you clean, preserve, or rejuvenate the existing finish? Except for modern furniture, most pieces will hold their value better if they retain their original finish.

This rule is especially true for antiques—loosely defined as pieces that are at least 100 years old. The strict definition of antique furniture adhered to by many purists, however, includes only furniture made before 1830, the year mass production began. Many antiques have been significantly devalued by refinishing or restoration work.

If you think your piece fits this category, don't do anything to it until you consult with a professional furniture conservator or antique appraiser to determine its value and what, if anything, should be done to it. If something needs to be done, this type of work is best left to a knowledgeable professional. To find qualified furniture conservators or appraisers, call museums, historical societies, or The American Institute for Conservation of Historic and Artistic Works in Washington, D.C., and ask for recommendations. Not all furniture restorers are qualified to do this type of work.

EVALUATING THE PIECE OF FURNITURE

Ask yourself the following questions to help you decide whether you want to undertake a furniture-restoration project:

• Do you like the piece? You'll probably enjoy working on something only if you really like it or want it in your own home, or if you're doing the work for someone else and you know he or she likes the piece.

• How much will the piece be worth once it's restored? To familiarize yourself with furniture values, visit antique furniture stores, used furniture shops, and even new furniture stores, and note the prices on furniture comparable with the piece you are considering restoring. Even if the piece won't have much monetary worth, you may still want to restore it for its sentimental value.

• Do you have a place or use for the piece? No matter how fine a piece that needs restoration may be, it will be of little or no use if you have no place to put it.

• Do you have the time to do the work? At a minimum, you'll need occasional weekends and perhaps one or two nights a week free to work on the furniture. Otherwise, you probably shouldn't consider restoring your own furniture.

• How much time will you need? If you've never restored furniture before, it may be difficult to estimate the amount of time a project will require. I've found that most projects require more work than is apparent at first glance. Sometimes even after a care-

Though not extremely valuable, *this old trundle sewing machine, when restored, would provide an interesting conversation piece for any room.*

ful evaluation, a project will be more time consuming than you first realized. The important thing is not to rush; take as much time as necessary to do the job right and enjoy the work. Even if you only have one night a week free or perhaps a weekend now and then, you can still complete a project by working step by step over a period of time.

• Is the piece worth restoring? This question immediately leads to several others, chief among them: How much work do you need to do? (See "Determining What Needs to Be Done," page 12.)

Most furniture, however, does not fall into this category, so you can approach it with less reverence. The finish may look so bad that you're unwilling to live with it. If water or heat has damaged the furniture extensively, for example, it's likely that you'll have to remove the finish. Sometimes you can greatly improve a poorly finished (or refinished) piece by refinishing it yourself. If you can determine that the current finish is not original, and the color or shade is objectionable to you, consider refinishing it. An original finish will usually show natural wear and aging. This aging is called patina. Chair arms and rungs or stretchers, for example, may show wear in the finish; scratches and stains will have affected the surface of the finish rather than just the wood underneath as in a refinished piece. (See "Is the Finish Original?" page 164, for more on how to determine an original finish.)

Structural Repairs. Next, examine the furniture closely for any necessary repairs. Look at the structure or main joints of the piece. Sometimes loose joints aren't obvious; exert some firm pressure on a joint to see whether it moves. With chairs, for example, grasp the top back rail with one hand while firmly holding down on the front seat rail with the other. Push back and forth on the back to determine whether the joints move at all. Next turn the chair up, grasping two legs at a time, and exert pressure to move the legs back and forth. If you feel any movement in the joints, you'll probably need to reglue them. You can check table legs in similar fashion. Grasp chests and cabinets at the top and firmly rock them from side to side to

When checking for loose joints in chairs, grasp the top back rail with one hand and hold down on the front seat rail with the other while pushing back and forth on the back.

Water damage to the finish of the drop-leaf table top above makes it a candidate for refinishing. The damage is severe enough so that the finish cannot be saved.

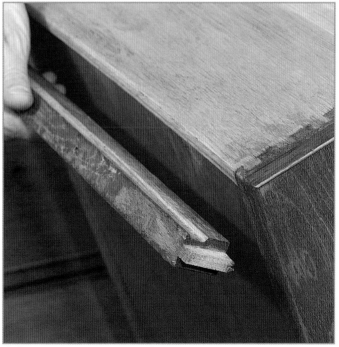

A drawer runner removed from a cabinet has been grooved by the drawer. The runner will have to be replaced or reinstalled upside down to provide a smooth surface for the drawer.

determine whether joints are loose or backs need repairs or reattaching. Take drawers out of chests and desks to make sure the drawer joints are tight.

When examining joints on a bed, be sure to set the bed up and look at the side-rail joints at both the headboard and footboard. If these joints are loose or broken, the bed will never be stable.

Chest Drawers. A dresser or chest may be beautifully restored on the outside, but if you don't repair drawer problems, your patience will be tried each time you open and close the drawer. Check to see whether drawers work smoothly. Do they stick? If so, the drawer sides or runners may need to be planed or waxed. Look for missing drawer stops. Also make sure existing stops will stop the drawer front flush with the front of the cabinet. Examine drawer runners both under the drawer and inside the cabinet to make sure they're not missing or excessively worn or split.

Mirrors. If the piece has a mirror or glass, check to see whether any of it needs replacing. If the glass is old—indicated by the presence of waviness or bubbles—you might have trouble finding comparable replacement glass, and you'll have to settle for new glass. If the silvering on the backside of the mirror glass has deteriorated, you may want to have the glass resilvered, or replace the mirror altogether.

Splits. Look for splits in chair and table legs, cabinet sides and tops, and table tops. On some older pieces,

The cracks in this top are caused by natural seasoning of the wood and are generally acceptable.

season cracks look natural and are acceptable, but sometimes cracks or splits, particularly those not caused by natural seasoning of the wood, look bad and can even affect the structural integrity of the piece.

Warped Wood. Also check for warps in the wood. As with season cracks, some warping is acceptable on old pieces but may be objectionable on newer furniture. Sometimes warping is easy to correct; other times it can

Loose veneer is not always obvious, so check the veneer by tapping it with the fingernail side of your fingers. If you hear a hollow sound, the veneer needs to be reglued.

This table leg has been repaired incorrectly by installing a screw from the outside. To correct the repair, the screw and leg must be removed and the joint cleaned, reglued, and clamped until dry.

be challenging, if not almost impossible, to fix permanently.

Bad Repairs. Next look for bad repairs. Often, old repairs are best left alone, but sometimes they demand attention because they detract from the piece or are not structurally sound. It's not unusual to see home repairs made on chairs or table legs that threaten to give out at any moment and need special attention.

Missing Parts. Are there any missing parts, such as stretchers or rungs on chairs or tables? If the furniture has a carving, look for damaged or missing pieces. It's always wise to look inside—and even under—drawers for these pieces, which previous owners may have stashed away for future repair. I've spent much time and effort replacing missing pieces only to discover them later, hidden in the bottom of a chest. A repair that would have taken 10 minutes ended up taking much longer, not to mention the missed opportunity of using the original part.

Loose Veneer. Don't forget to look for loose veneer. Veneer can often appear intact when in reality it's loose and ready to pop off. Test a veneer's integrity by lightly tapping it, using the back, or fingernail side, of your index and middle fingers and alternately lifting them up and down. If the tapping sounds solid, the veneer is OK; if it sounds hollow, the veneer is loose and will need to be reglued.

Hardware. Lastly, examine all hardware and casters. If any components are broken or missing, find a replacement that matches. If it's not possible to find a match, you may have to replace all the hardware on the piece.

This oak desk (above) *will need extensive restoration work, including the regluing of many loose and disassembled joints, stripping, and refinishing. After restoration (right), the desk is a solid, functional, and attractive piece of furniture.*

If the piece has steel hardware with brass plating, you can upgrade by installing solid-brass hardware. Order brass hardware from woodworking or furniture-repair websites or through local hardware stores. Check the old hardware with a magnet: If it sticks, it's plated; if not, it's solid brass, and you can clean and polish it to a beautiful luster.

Planning the Work

After examining the piece and determining what you need to do, schedule the work process. Make a list of everything that needs to be done, and put each item on your list in the order you'll follow when doing the work. If you neglect this step, you may end up redoing things you've already completed. If you complete the finishing part of the project, for example, and then go on with repairs, you may find that you've damaged the new finish while doing the repairs. You'll then have to go back and touch up the finish. The following is a general guideline you can use for work scheduling:

An old wooden console radio (left) *and coffee table* (below) *are examples of collectible furniture that can be well worth restoring.*

Repair Work. First you should complete the necessary structural work on the furniture.

• Remove all hardware, glass, and mirrors. The glass in

A painted piece of furniture, such as this kneehole desk, can take on a whole new look when it's stripped and refinished in a natural wood finish.

some kinds of furniture may have been installed using glazing compound, a hardened putty used around the edge of the glass to hold it in place. Unless the glazing compound is damaged extensively, you should leave the glass in place and mask it off using a low-stick adhesive masking tape. If any of the glass or hardware needs replacing, now's the time to find or order a replacement so it's ready to install when the restoration process is complete.

• Make all the structural repairs. Reglue all loose joints and repair all breaks, cracks, splits, and warps. Make or replace any missing large structural parts, such as chair stretchers.

• Repair the drawers and doors. Fit all drawers and doors so they work smoothly. Repair or replace any drawer runners and drawer stops, if necessary.

• Repair the veneer. Replace any missing veneer, and reglue any loose veneer. Replace any missing small parts, such as applied carvings.

Original Finish Restoration. At this point you will have completed the repair schedule and should have decided whether you want to restore the original finish or refinish the piece. If you're restoring the finish, follow these steps:

• Clean, touch up, and rejuvenate the existing finish.

• Clean and polish all glass and hardware, and reinstall it.

Finish Removal and Replacement. If you decide to remove the old finish and refinish the furniture, follow these steps:

• Remove the old finish by using a chemical stripper or some other stripping method.

• Prepare the wood surface. Sand the wood, taking care of blemishes in preparation for the final finish. Fill, stain, or bleach the wood—you'll do one or more of these steps only when appropriate.

• Finish the wood. Apply the finish you've chosen, following the step-by-step instructions.

• Clean and polish all glass and hardware, and reinstall it.

WOOD IDENTIFICATION

Before restoring a piece of furniture, you'll want to know what kind of wood you're working on: solid or veneered, hardwood or softwood, open grained or closed grained. These factors can sometimes determine whether the furniture is worth restoring, as well as the type of repairs and finish the piece will require if you do restore it.

Identifying wood can be tricky because stains, finish, and aging can disguise wood by altering its original color and look. Light-colored wood, such as poplar, birch, or pine, is often stained and finished to look like more expensive walnut, cherry, or mahogany. Much modern manufactured furniture falls into this category. When you buy new furniture, read labels carefully to determine whether the wood is really what it seems. "Cherry finish" or "walnut finish" labels do not signify cherry and walnut wood—only that the piece is finished to look like those woods.

Older furniture can also fool you if you don't inspect it carefully. Certain parts of a piece, such as the top or drawer fronts, may be made from a hardwood like

A variety of types of wood have been used in furniture construction. These woods (from left) can usually be identified by their color and grain pattern: heart pine, mahogany, walnut, cherry, pine, white oak, maple, red oak, poplar, birch, bird's-eye maple.

mahogany or mahogany veneer, while other parts, like the legs or frame, may be made of inferior wood stained and finished to match. Side rails on many beds, both old and new, may be constructed of a less expensive wood like poplar or butternut, stained to match mahogany or walnut headboards and footboards.

Most wood exposed to sunlight for long periods will lose its characteristic color and become much lighter. Some woods, such as cherry, can darken with exposure to light or from treatment with oils, waxes, and polishes. In cases where a piece's original wood has been altered, you will have to rely on your ability to recognize the grain, texture, and figure (grain patterns and other markings) rather than color. The more you work with furniture and become familiar with commonly used wood species, the easier it will be for you to identify them.

Wood is generally categorized into two groups: hardwood and softwood. Hardwood comes from deciduous

trees, which have broad leaves that shed during a certain season of the year. Softwood comes from coniferous, or cone-bearing, trees with narrow leaves or needles that remain on the tree year-round.

The terms "hardwood" and "softwood" can be misleading. Although many types of wood in the hardwood category are indeed hard and dense, such as maple, oak, or walnut, there are others, like poplar, that are not. Most quality furniture uses hardwood in either solid or veneer form as a primary wood; a softwood like pine is used as a secondary wood for the inside of cabinets, drawer sides, backs, or bottoms.

Probably because of its availability, pine was used to build many early American furniture pieces. As hardwoods have become more expensive, pine has once again increased in popularity as a primary wood in furniture building and manufacturing. The following woods are commonly used to make furniture.

Hardwoods

Birch. Common in the United States and Canada, birch is a strong, hard, even-textured hardwood. In its natural state the wood appears white or creamy yellow to light brown with a tinge of red. Often, birch is stained to match other kinds of wood in furniture. Much of the clear, cabinet-grade plywood is produced from birch, which takes stain nicely and finishes well. In addition to being used in furniture, birch is often chosen to make interior doors and cupboards.

Cherry. American black cherry is another popular furniture hardwood. Cherry grows primarily in the eastern United States and is a light reddish brown to brown color, which deepens into rich color as it ages. Cherry has a closed grain and is softer than birch. Much cherry lumber is narrow and has been used to produce many beautiful traditional furniture pieces.

Mahogany. Furniture makers have used mahogany for centuries. A strong, relatively hard wood that works and finishes well, mahogany is also used for decorative woodwork and was widely used in shipbuilding. Found in Africa, Central and South America, the West Indies, and south- ern Florida, mahogany falls into three basic categories: American mahogany (West Indian),

This antique Empire sideboard has been constructed using several types of wood to add to its beauty. The primary wood is mahogany (including crotch mahogany grain patterns for door and back panels) while bird's-eye maple is used on the columns and in several center panels. The cabinet's interior is constructed primarily of poplar, a practice common even in fine furniture like this.

African mahogany, and Honduran mahogany. Lauan, which resembles mahogany and comes from the Philippines, is often referred to as Philippine mahogany, although it's not a true mahogany species.

In mahogany's natural state the open-grain wood has a light pink to reddish brown color with a fine texture. In addition to straight grain, mahogany can have interesting patterns, including the crotch grain pattern often used as a veneer face for cabinet doors and drawers. Many people think of a harsh red color when they think of mahogany, but this is a result of dyes or stains that have been applied to the wood. Although you may find true mahogany finished in various tones of red, it can also be finished in beautiful warm brown or even golden tones.

Maple (Sugar Maple, Rock Maple). Maple, an exceptionally hard, dense, close-grained wood, is abundant in the United States. In its natural state the wood has a white or off-white to amber color. The grain is tight and subtle, except in the case of burl, curly, fiddleback, and bird's-eye maple. These grain patterns offer a variety of interesting, beautiful configurations and are often used for decorative purposes in table tops, drawer fronts, or door panels, in both solids and veneers.

This hall tree is *an American piece that relies heavily on the use of quartersawn oak for its decorative beauty.*

Because of the absence of a grain pattern in most maple, however, sometimes it can be hard to tell whether a piece of furniture is made of this wood. If so, lift the piece and judge it by weight. Because it's so dense, maple is heavier than most other furniture-quality wood.

Oak. Common varieties of oak used in furniture include white oak, red oak, and English, or brown, oak. Oak has a pronounced open grain with a rough texture. It is quite hard, sometimes making it difficult to work. White oak has a slightly gray-brown color; red oak is similar except that it has a reddish brown tinge. English oak tends to be a deeper brown color.

During the late nineteenth and early twentieth centuries, oak furniture began to be mass-produced in America, and so became popular and affordable. Many of the pieces manufactured at that time still exist today and have become even more popular as true antiques have become more expensive and difficult to find. Quartersawn oak is a distinctive and sometimes beautiful oak grain pattern used for decorative purposes on much of the late nineteenth- and early twentieth-century manufactured furniture. Quartersawn oak is milled by cutting the oak log into quarters lengthwise and then slicing the quarters into boards.

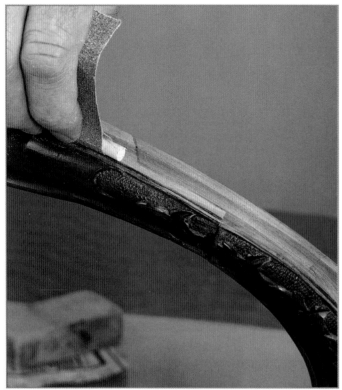

Walnut has been used in many American furniture pieces and has a gray to chocolate brown color.

Poplar. Another American hardwood, poplar has a straight, even, closed grain, but it is fairly soft, making it easy to work. Poplar is white or yellow, sometimes with a green caste and an occasional dark streak running through it. Poplar accepts stain and finish well and often is colored to resemble mahogany or walnut. It is widely used as a secondary wood for the insides of cabinets, chests, and drawers.

Rosewood. Grown in Brazil and India, rosewood is a distinctive-looking hardwood. The wood is naturally brown or reddish brown with dark or ebony grain figuring, but it can sometimes have a creamy color in it. Often used in musical instruments like pianos or guitars, rosewood, unlike most kinds of wood, is resistant to shrinking.

In furniture, rosewood appears primarily in veneer form and was used generously on Empire- and Victorian- style furniture during the nineteenth century. Because of its hardness and density, rosewood can easily be finished to a high luster.

Teak. A yellowish brown open-grain hardwood, teak comes from India, Burma, and Thailand. This naturally oily wood is popular for both interior and exterior woodwork, especially on boats. In the world of furniture, you're most likely to find teak in Scandinavian-style pieces, usually with a rubbed oil finish.

Walnut. Found in the eastern United States, American black walnut has been used extensively in furniture. The wood has a gray to chocolate-brown color, sometimes with purple streaks or light-colored sapwood on the edges of its boards.

Not as hard as maple or oak but harder than mahogany, walnut works well in furniture building and can be finished in warm wood tones. Walnut usually has interesting and beautiful grain patterns ranging from straight grain to swirl patterns to distinctive burl grains, depending on the cut of the wood. Because it's an open-grain wood like oak, walnut must be treated with a grain filler to obtain a traditional smooth finish.

Another kind of walnut used in furniture construction, European walnut, is scarce and expensive. You'll find this wood most often in veneer form. While American walnut darkens with age (though if exposed to UV light it will lighten), European walnut becomes lighter.

Other Hardwoods. Other kinds of hardwood used in furniture include ash, basswood, beech, butternut, and chestnut.

Ash and chestnut have a regular texture and open grain like oak. Ash is often used for garden tool handles and baseball bats but is occasionally used for furniture. Chestnut, valuable and well-known for its worm holes, has enjoyed some popularity in the form of wormy chestnut furniture.

Basswood and beech are both light-colored woods with tight, closed grains. These wood species can be stained to match other kinds of wood, such as cherry, mahogany, or walnut.

Similar in grain to walnut but light-colored, butternut may be stained to mimic walnut in furniture.

Softwoods

Familiar softwoods include pine, cedar, hemlock, fir, redwood, and spruce. Of these, pine, cedar, and redwood are most often used in furniture, including outdoor furniture.

Pine. Comprising a variety of species, pine may appear to have either a white cream to tan color or a yellow color with a brown grain figure. You'll also see knotty pine, known for prominent and abundant knots in its boards, which has enjoyed some popularity, particularly in Colonial-style reproduction furniture.

Found in abundance in America, pine has been widely used for many purposes besides furniture, including the construction of buildings and boats. Many early

American furniture makers used pine as a primary wood, and it can be found in some finer furniture as a secondary interior wood for drawer sides, bottoms, and runners. Pine, which can be finished attractively, continues to be a popular wood for some types of furniture today. You should note, however, that because pine has a tendency to accept liquid wood stain unevenly, producing a blotchy appearance, you should normally seal the wood before staining. (See "Washcoat," page 206.) This does not apply to gel stains.

Cedar. Cedar is a pink-to-brown close-grained wood used for exterior as well as interior woodwork, owing to its resistance to decay. Because cedar has an aroma that is disagreeable to insects such as moths, it's commonly used to line chests and closets used for garment storage. Cedar wood produces a distinctive, pungent fragrance.

Redwood. Like cedar, redwood is also used for exterior work because of its resistance to decay and insect infestation. As its name implies, this natural wood is red in color; manufacturers use it to produce exterior furniture, such as picnic tables or deck furniture.

Inlays and Veneers

There are many wood varieties that are not used as the primary wood in furniture construction but are frequently used as inlays and decorative pieces in the form of veneer. These wood species include satinwood, boxwood, holly, and ebony. While some are extremely distinctive in appearance, others are harder to identify. These exotic types of wood have been used for centuries to enhance the beauty of furniture.

Wood veneers have been used in furniture construction for centuries and their beautiful distinctive colors and grain patterns can often beautify or accent an otherwise plain piece of furniture. Clockwise from left, the ones shown here are crotch mahogany, Honduran mahogany, Brazilian walnut, white oak, walnut, red oak, cherry, burl walnut, and rosewood.

2

TOOLS AND EQUIPMENT

When you consider setting up a work area to begin your project, you might immediately think of a particular part of your home: the garage, the basement, an unused room, even a spot out in the backyard. All of these and more have been successfully used as home furniture-restoration workstations, but only when certain conditions are met. Once you've chosen the work area, you'll need certain tools and equipment to complete your projects successfully. Here's a look at what creates a favorable work environment for a home workstation and how you can stock it properly and safely.

THE WORK SPACE

For most furniture pieces, such as chairs, small tables, chests, or dressers, you'll need an area that measures about 100 square feet (10x10 feet, for example). If you plan to work on larger pieces like wardrobes, large dressers, or banquet-type dining tables, however, you'll need to expand the work area accordingly to fit the piece. Keep in mind that you may have more than one piece in your work area at a time. The best work area is one you can isolate from other areas of activity so that it can be kept as dust-free as possible when doing finishing work. You'll also need both work space and storage space for tools and supplies.

Ventilation. Although you'll want to keep your work area closed off from other areas, you'll still need a fresh-air supply. Some furniture restoration work, such as repairs, can be done without concern for ventilation. Other phases of the work, such as stripping and finishing, which generate strong fumes, must have proper ventilation. To deal with hazardous fumes you'll need at least two windows or doors, one on each side of the work area.

Temperature. Temperature control in your work space is also important. Ideally, you should maintain a temperature range of 65 to 75 degrees F, with a low humidity level, particularly during the finishing process. Temperature considerations aren't as crucial while doing repairs, sanding, or stripping, although some glues may not work well or dry properly if temperatures are too cold.

Power. Don't forget electricity accessibility as you plan your home work space. Have at least two electric plug outlets, which will enable you to plug in a small power tool and an electric light source at the same time. If wall receptacles are not available, look for overhead light-bulb sockets. These can be fitted with a screw-in adapter, providing a plug-in receptacle and light-bulb socket combination. You may also be able to run a heavy-duty extension cord with two outlets to your work area. If you're running a cord outdoors, use one rated for exterior use.

Lighting. Lighting is a crucial consideration for your work area. Basements and garages typically have just enough light to see but not enough to see well when performing detailed repair work or furniture finishing. During daylight hours, you may have enough windows to provide adequate light, but night work means you'll need as much light as possible. You can buy pre-wired

fluorescent fixtures with a plug-in cord and mount them on the ceiling to provide additional lighting. You can also buy portable floodlights that hold standard light bulbs. These portable lights come equipped with spring clamps, so they can be easily moved and mounted wherever you need them while working.

Storage. Don't forget about your work-space storage needs. You'll need storage for tools, materials, and any parts or hardware disassembled from your furniture project. All solvents, chemicals, and finishes must be stored according to safety instructions that come with each product. Most, if not all, will need to be kept away from heat, sparks, and flame, so consider this as you plan your storage space.

You'll need tools and equipment to be as accessible to your work area as possible. You can tuck other items, like stripping materials, finishing materials, and hardware, which you'll use only from time to time, safely away in less convenient areas, even completely out of the work area.

Fluorescent Light Fixture over Work Area

Air Flow

Air Flow

¾" Plywood

Sawhorses

Storage Cabinet with Lock

The Work Space. *Requirements for an ideal work space include good ventilation, access to power, good lighting, and safe, secure storage for chemicals and other materials.*

The Workbench

You can create a simple, compact work surface using a 3x4-foot sheet of ¾-inch plywood resting on a set of sawhorses. A setup like this provides an ideal work surface to tackle small pieces, such as chairs, drawers, and bed parts, because it brings them up to a convenient working height.

You can also set a larger piece of furniture, such as a chest of drawers, on the horses without using the plywood. When you need to work on table tops or a large, freestanding item, you can quickly dismantle the workbench by leaning the plywood against a wall and then stacking the horses and setting them aside.

If you don't have a set of sawhorses or don't want to build them from scratch, you can buy a sawhorse kit at a hardware store, home center, or building supply center. Another possibility for a more permanent, stable workbench is to use an old library table, buffet, or flat-top desk.

SAFETY

In my years as a furniture restorer I've witnessed many accidents—and even experienced a few myself. Most of the accidents I've seen resulted in only temporary injuries, although a few were more serious. You can avoid harm or injury by following some simple safety precautions. The tips listed here should help in making your home workshop a safe place, but remember that it's your responsibility to ensure your safety and the safety of those around you.

Preventing Fires

Fire prevention is a primary consideration. Many of the materials used in furniture restoration are either flammable or combustible. Even wood sanding dust is highly flammable.

Avoid Smoking. First and foremost, establish a "no smoking" rule in your work area. If you are a smoker, remember that even if you leave the work area to smoke,

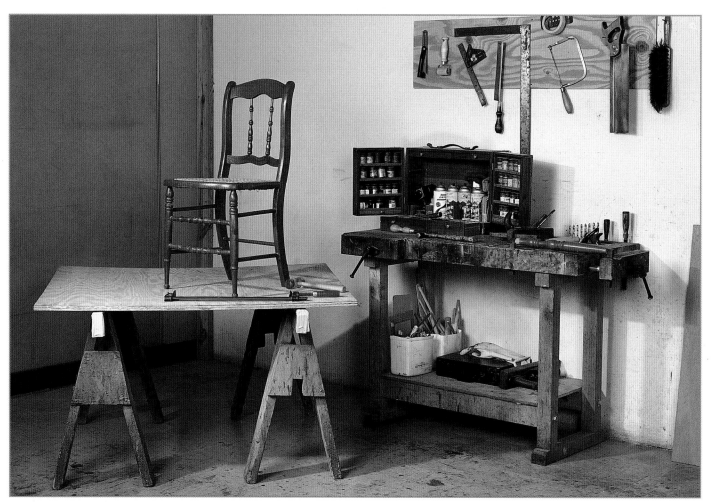

You can make a good workbench surface for working on smaller items, such as chairs, by using 3x4-ft. sheet of ¾-in. plywood resting on a set of sawhorses. If necessary, you can use the sawhorses by themselves for larger pieces, or you can remove them, stack them, and set them aside to make room for freestanding furniture.

you may still have flammable chemicals or solvents on your hands or clothing that could easily ignite. This happened once to a co-worker who had been using paint stripper. He lit a cigarette, and his shirt, splattered with stripper where he had inadvertently wiped his hand, caught on fire. Fortunately he was able to put out the fire quickly without injury. He was, however, inducted into the furniture-repair shop's "Hall of Flame" as its first—and fortunately only—member.

There are other, more subtle, fire hazards. Check stoves and furnaces for open-flame pilot lights. Consider any electric motors or equipment that could produce sparks: If excessive levels of vapor, mist, or dust build up, these could be fire-ignition sources. Be careful not to create sparks with metal tools, or even static electricity.

Dispose of Used Rags Properly. Rags used for stripping, cleaning, staining, and finishing are ideal candidates for spontaneous combustion. Oil-soaked rags—especially those containing quick-drying oils—are particularly susceptible to this hazard. Spontaneous combustion occurs when heat generated by the chemical reaction of volatile materials in, say, rags containing finish builds to a point where it causes the rags to ignite and burn. This can occur in chemical-soaked rags that are simply left lying around, balled up or lying on top of one another. The safest way to get rid of used rags is to unfold and hang them to dry completely before discarding them in a closed metal container.

Buy a Fire Extinguisher. Invest in a good fire extinguisher that's rated for both type A (trash, wood, and paper) and type B (chemical) fires, either of which can occur in a workshop environment. Mount the extinguisher in an area that's easily accessible in case of an emergency, and check it annually to be sure it's charged and ready to use.

Assemble a First-Aid Kit. In case of a fire-related, chemical, or tool-handling accident, make sure you have a first-aid kit stocked with plastic bandages, gauze, scissors, first-aid cream, and eye-flushing solution.

Protecting Against Chemicals

Wear Breathing Protection. Another important safety consideration is how to protect yourself from toxic fumes and dust. Besides making sure you have an ample fresh-air supply, wear a respirator around fumes and a dust or particle mask when doing heavy or prolonged sanding.

Important safety items for any furniture workshop include a closed metal container for used rags, an appropriate fire extinguisher, and a well-equipped first-aid kit.

When sanding a piece of wood that has been stripped or bleached, use a respirator because you may be breathing not only wood dust into your lungs but also all the chemical residues left from the old stripper, the old finish, or the bleach. Ordinary dust masks don't protect you from dangerous chemicals and finish fumes. Respirators have special disposable organic cartridges for this purpose. When the cartridges need to be replaced, you'll begin to smell the fumes from solvents while wearing the mask.

Store respirator masks in sealed plastic bags to make the cartridges last longer. Respirator masks, although considerably more expensive than dust masks, are a worthwhile investment if you plan to do stripping or finishing work.

Protect Your Eyes, Skin, and Ears. When you're using solvents, chemicals, and finishes, eye and skin protection are also important. Protect your eyes by using safety goggles or glasses, preferably glasses with enclosed sides, whenever you do work that could pose any danger to your eyes. Keep an eye-flush bottle in your first-aid kit in case a chemical splashes into your eyes.

You should use gloves whenever your hands will be in finish remover, or any solvents, such as mineral spirits, alcohol, lacquer thinner, and stain. Although failure to

Safety equipment, such as gloves, safety glasses, hearing protectors, respirators, and dust masks, can provide you with appropriate protection when doing various aspects of furniture restoration.

Never store finishes, paints, or thinners in drink containers like cups, soft-drink bottles, and milk cartons. Children associate cups and bottles with food and drink. Keep all solvents, chemicals, and finishes locked away from the reach of children or pets. If you are unable to lock them in cabinets, lock up your entire work area when you're not present.

Check containers at least once a year for rust, corrosion, or swelling. If any of these things occur, discard the item properly or transfer contents into a new, properly labeled container.

Be Environmentally Responsible. Most home-workshop applications don't pose major environmental safety problems because of the small amounts of hazardous materials used. But keep in mind that finishes applied with spray guns or aerosol cans can affect air quality. Disposing of old thinners by pouring them down a sink drain or on the ground can pollute ground water. If possible, try to use up all chemicals. If you must dispose of leftover chemicals, consult your local waste management department or consult the Environmental Protection Agency (EPA) website at https://www.epa.gov/hw/forms/contact-us-about-hazardous-waste.

TOOLS AND EQUIPMENT

Before you begin a project, turn to the section of this book dealing with your particular project and read over the material to see what tools you'll need. If you don't have a particular tool, consider whether you can substitute something that will work just as well. (See "Improvising Tools," on page 29.) Before you buy a new tool, determine whether it will be something you can use frequently. If it's an expensive item that you'll rarely use after you complete your project, you might be able to borrow or rent it instead of buying it.

Hand Tools

Hammer. A claw hammer is essential for most furniture jobs. Claw hammers are designed not only for hammering and nailing, but also for extracting nails from wood. Unlike finish claw hammers, which usually weigh 16 ounces, and framing hammers, which weigh 20 ounces or more, furniture claw hammers range from 7 through 13 ounces. You may also use an upholstery tack

wear gloves may not be a health hazard, wearing them will keep your hands clean. Vinyl or latex gloves are fine for most jobs, and they're inexpensive and disposable. They are also thinner, so you can get more of a feel for what you are doing. If you want more protection for jobs like stripping finish, use industrial-type gloves made from neoprene, which resists virtually all chemicals. These gloves are available in long-length versions, which protect not only your hands but your wrists and forearms. Rubber gloves will protect your hands from most stripper stains and solvents. After prolonged use the gloves may weaken, so keep several pair available in your workshop. Protect your clothes with a chemical-resistant bib apron.

You may need ear protection if you plan to use loud power tools, such as a circular saw or electric sander. Use industrial ear plugs or earmuff-type hearing protectors.

Store Chemicals Safely. Storage is also a safety issue. Many solvents, chemicals, and finishes need to be stored away from heat, sparks, and flame, in properly labeled, sealed containers. Caustic materials should be kept in their original containers with the original label.

THE PROS KNOW

IMPROVISING TOOLS

Start your furniture restoration "career" by buying only what you need, and increase your equipment collection piece by piece. If you have a limited budget, look for ways to improvise.

Make Do. Use a claw hammer and a piece of softwood in place of a rubber mallet to knock loose joints apart or to tap them together when regluing. Sometimes you can use a large nail in place of a nail set or scratch awl. Use a ruler or yardstick instead of a measuring tape or folding ruler. You can substitute a clamp for a vise when you need to lock a workpiece to your bench. Try using a household grapefruit knife in place of a small spatula. Glue a piece of felt, cork, or leather to a block of wood as a sanding block for hand sanding.

Clamp Ingenuity. If you need a few small clamps but you have only one or two, use a pair of vise-type pliers as a small clamp. Create a tourniquet clamp for regluing joints using a piece of sturdy clothesline and a paint paddle or wooden dowel to replace a band or strap clamp. (See the "Tourniquet Clamp" drawing.) Another inexpensive idea for some clamping jobs is to make a clamp using wedges and a wood block or two. (See the "Wedge Clamp" drawing.) Because some glue-up jobs require extra long clamps—which can be quite expensive—you can sometimes hook two shorter clamps together to do the job. (See the "Double Clamps" drawing.)

No Substitutions, Please. Although you can improvise creative substitutions similar to the above examples, some aspects of furniture restoration require the right tool for the job to guarantee success. You'll need a good natural-bristle brush to apply solvent-based finishes like varnish or brushing lacquer, for example. Natural-fiber brushes apply these

Wedge Clamp

finishes more evenly than brushes with synthetic fiber, and they won't break down or melt when exposed to strong solvents such as those in lacquer. You'll also need a natural-bristle brush if you use a paint and varnish remover to strip an old finish, although for this purpose a cheap brush will do. Chemical removers can soften and melt synthetic bristles. Synthetic-fiber brushes such as nylon, polyester, or nylon/polyester blends work best when applying water-based finishes, however. Natural bristles tend to splay and lose their shape when exposed to water, making them awkward to use.

Wooden Dowel

Sturdy Clothesline

Tourniquet Clamp

Double Clamps

hammer for replacing upholstery. Lightweight and narrow, upholstery tack hammers have a magnetic tip on one end of the head for picking up and starting tacks while using only one hand.

A rubber mallet is good for knocking loose furniture joints apart and banging them together when regluing. The rubber head minimizes damage to the furniture's finish and wood. Use a wooden mallet to tap a wood chisel when you need more force behind it. The wooden head doesn't damage wooden chisel handles.

Measuring Tools. You'll need to make accurate measurements when doing repair work on furniture. A steel measuring tape works well for this. You can also use a folding wooden carpenter's rule, although it's difficult to measure inside dimensions of drawers and cabinets with a wooden rule unless you get one that's equipped with a small sliding brass rule at one end.

Squares also come in handy for precise furniture work. You can use a large carpenter's framing square to check the squareness of drawers and cabinets or a sliding T-bevel (also known as a bevel gauge) to copy odd angles. Other kinds of squares you might want include try squares, adjustable combination squares, and large T-squares, which are especially good for use as a straightedge.

Hammers used in furniture repair include (from top) an upholstery tack hammer, mallets (wooden and rubber), and a lightweight claw hammer.

Handsaws. Handsaws are a must for cutting and shaping wood on the small scale needed for furniture work. A backsaw, a small square-ended handsaw with a rigid back and fine teeth designed to do precise cutting, is best for working on furniture.

If you have to make small scroll, or curved, cuts in thin wood, consider using a coping saw. The coping saw has a thin, narrow blade attached to a bowed metal frame with a wooden handle. You replace the blade much as you would a hacksaw blade.

When you need to cut veneer, use a sharp utility knife or, better yet, a veneer saw, a small, unusual-looking saw with an angled handle that's offset.

Although you'll rarely use a hacksaw, you should include one in your workshop. An occasion is likely to arise when at least the blade by itself can be used to cut through old nails or screws that must be cut close to the surface.

Measuring tools such as these, including various types of squares for checking the accuracy of angles, are often required for furniture work.

Chisels and Planes. The wood chisel is a vital tool for a furniture workshop. You'll find yourself reaching for it frequently, to do anything from installing mortise hinges on doors to cleaning old glue from joints. Remember to keep wood chisels sharp. A sharp chisel is easier to use and less likely to cause an accident. Dull cutting tools require more force and are more likely to slip. When a tool slips with a lot of force behind it, the results can be disastrous.

Chisels come in a number of blade widths. A common range of sizes is $1/8$-, $1/4$-, $3/8$-, $1/2$-, $3/4$- and 1-inch-wide blades. A $3/4$-inch chisel can handle most work, although you'll probably need smaller chisels, down to $1/8$ inch, from time to time.

For heavy-duty chiseling jobs, such as cutting out a mortise in a piece of wood, mortise chisels are available. Firmer chisels—a term given to certain chisels because of their sturdy build—can also be used for heavier chisel work, including cutting mortises. For lighter, more delicate hand chiseling work, paring chisels are available.

Another type of chisel, which is similar to the paring chisel except that it's built for heavier work, is the bevel-edge, or bench, chisel. If you're going to own only one

Handsaws *are important tools, the backsaw being the most commonly used. Counterclockwise, other saws are the crosscut saw, gent's saw, hacksaw, coping saw, and veneer saw.*

type of chisel, bench chisels are the best, because they can be used for all-around work including mortising and paring.

Although a hand plane is not essential, you'll find that at least a block plane can be helpful when doing small wood repairs like fitting a wood patch to repair a damaged table top corner. The plane lets you smooth the patch, as well as the edge of the top where the patch will be applied, allowing them to fit together precisely and accurately. For most furniture-restoration projects, a block plane will suffice. You can buy a larger smoothing plane to handle any larger projects you may want to do. Always keep plane blades sharp for easy use and best results.

Another small but useful tool is the utility, or hobby, knife. You can use it in many ways, from cutting veneer patches to cleaning old glue from joints. Wood rasps and files are also helpful tools. A rasp is especially beneficial for roughly forming wood that needs to be shaped because it cuts away wood quickly. A wood file allows you to cut away wood, or shape it, with greater precision than a rasp provides.

Wood planes, bench chisels, paring chisels, wood rasps, wood files, and even a utility knife are commonly used in addition to handsaws to cut.

Screwdrivers. Sooner or later you'll need both flat-blade and Phillips screwdrivers. There are two important things to remember about screwdrivers: Have several sizes on hand so you can use the right-size blade or tip for the screw you're working on, and buy high-quality screwdrivers that won't wear out quickly. A good screwdriver will make your work easier and should last indefinitely—if you don't abuse it.

Pliers. Include three kinds of pliers in your toolbox: standard pliers, diagonal or straight cutting pliers (end nippers), and needle-nose pliers. You'll probably use the cutting pliers most often to pull out old nails embedded in wood and to cut off nailheads.

Small hand tools,
such as (clockwise from right) a palette knife, pliers, nail sets, phillips screwdrivers, a scratch awl, flat-blade screwdrivers, and a veneer roller, are indispensable when repairing furniture.

SHARPENING A CHISEL OR PLANE BLADE

Tip Edge
90°
Side Edge
Grinder

Belt-Disc Sander

1 Hold the chisel at the correct angle when grinding a bevel. You can use a grinding wheel or a bench-top belt-disc sander. Keep the tip edge of the chisel square with the side edge when you grind it (inset).

The secret to using a chisel or plane successfully is to keep the blade sharp. Although the steps below describe how to sharpen a chisel, the same steps apply to sharpening a handplane blade after removing it from the tool.

Grind the Bevel. If the blade is new or already has a clean and straight beveled tip, go on to Step 2. If there are chips on the edge or the edge is not consistent, start with this step.

You can use a bench grinder or a belt sander with an 80-grit sanding belt to grind the bevel. Lay the chisel on the tool rest of the bench grinder with the beveled side of the tip flat against the wheel. If you're using a belt sander, lay the beveled side of the tip flat against the platen area of the sander.

After you determine the bevel angle, maintain the angle while applying light pressure, holding the chisel on the grinding wheel or belt sander. If you think you need it, attach a grinding jig to the chisel to help maintain the proper bevel angle. Keep the tip edge squared with the side edge of the chisel blade. When you're grinding the bevel, keep a cup of water nearby into which you can dip the chisel tip every few seconds. This will

keep the tip from burning, which will draw the temper from the steel.

If you have deep nicks in the tip, mark a line across the blade just below that nick or chip using a square and a marker pen. Put the tip straight into the grinding wheel at a right angle with the wheel until you grind back to the line. Then use the grinder to regrind the proper bevel.

Hone The Edge. For this step you'll need a honing stone and oil. Buy a stone that has a coarse side and a fine side. Use the coarse side first; then turn the stone over and finish with the fine side.

Other Hand Tools. Other tools you may need include a scratch awl, a small spatula or palette knife for patching holes and working with different kinds of wood putty, a nail set for setting finishing nails below the surface, and a small veneer roller for pressing freshly glued veneer. You can also use a wallpaper seam roller to press newly glued veneer.

Clamps

Clamps are among the most basic and useful tools in the furniture shop and are essential for any gluing or regluing job. You'll need several basic types for the majority of your furniture work. Using the right clamp for the job can make the difference between a permanent repair and a temporary one.

C-Clamp. Perhaps the best-known kind of clamp, the C-clamp is shaped like the letter "C" and works well for many purposes. Use C-clamps for small-size projects; switch to bar or pipe clamps for any work spanning more than 4 or 5 inches.

Bar and Pipe Clamps. Particularly helpful for gluing large panels or for spanning distances of 6 inches or more, bar and pipe clamps consist of a bar or pipe fitted with two jaws. The jaw on one end has a crank or handle you use to screw the clamp down for final tighten-

Apply a small puddle of honing oil on the coarse side of the stone, and lay the flat side of the chisel across the face of the stone. Put your fingers on top of the blade to ensure that it stays completely flat while rubbing it back and forth on the stone. Next, turn the chisel over with the beveled side down, laying only the bevel flat against the surface of the stone.

Keep the beveled edge flat against the surface of the stone while rubbing it back and forth.

Turn the stone over to its fine side and apply a small puddle of honing oil. Lay the face, or flat side, of the chisel blade flat against the stone and draw it across with a few strokes. Then turn the chisel over with the beveled side against the stone, allowing the beveled surface to rest flat against the stone. Raise the handle of the chisel slightly to increase—by a minute amount— the angle of the bevel at the tip, creating a micro bevel. Rub the chisel back and forth on the stone as before.

Finish the Edge. For this step you need a piece of leather called a strop to touch up the sharpened edge. Some woodworkers mount the strop on a flat piece of wood

2 Using a honing stone that has a coarse and a fine side, apply honing oil to the stone. Rub the chisel back and forth on the coarse side as shown, first on the flat side and then on the bevel side. Repeat the procedure on the fine side of the stone, lifting the chisel slightly on the bevel side to create a mirobevel.

Leather Strop

Leather Strop

3 Touch up the sharpened edge on a piece of leather by moving the chisel in a trailing stroke, first on the flat side and then on the bevel.

and use a stropping compound on the leather.

Lay the face of the chisel flat on the surface of the leather, and pull the chisel toward you in a trailing, not a leading, stroke. After a few strokes, turn the chisel over, laying the beveled edge flat against

the leather. Again draw the chisel toward you. When you're finished, you'll end up with a razor-sharp edge, so be careful. To touch up a chisel edge after use, repeat this last step or buff the beveled edge on a felt wheel installed on your bench grinder and charged with polishing compound.

Several types of clamps will be required for gluing projects. Cushion the jaws with wood blocks (left). A bench vise (top center) is also useful to hold a small workpiece stationary, freeing your hands.

Hand Screw. A hand-screw clamp has two wooden jaws with two threaded rods running through them. The rods have wooden handles that you use to tighten or loosen the jaws. The jaws can be adjusted quickly to fit a particular job by grasping both handles, one in each hand, and moving them as though you were peddling a bicycle.

Hand screws work well for certain gluing projects because the jaws can cover a large area, distributing even pressure over that area when adjusted properly. Because the jaws are made of wood, rather than metal, they minimize damage to the project.

When clamping with a hand screw, you can keep the jaws parallel with one another or angle them to accommodate the work. For most jobs you'll probably use a medium-size hand screw—about 8 to 10 inches—and possibly a smaller one for more delicate tasks such as gluing small veneer patches.

ing. The other jaw is made for quick adjustment by sliding it up and down the length of the bar or pipe so it fits your particular work. These clamps come in lengths from 12 to 96 inches. You can also purchase pipe-clamp jaws and assemble your own clamps to create whatever length you need. Pipe is available from hardware stores or plumbing-supply centers. Just make sure to have the ends of the pipe threaded to accommodate the threaded jaw parts.

When considering the sizes you'll need, remember that long bar clamps can also be used to glue short jobs, but short clamps are limited and can't accommodate large projects. On the other hand, if your clamp is too large it can be awkward to operate. Start out with a few medium-size clamps (48 inches long) and if you can afford it, a few 12-inch-long clamps for small jobs.

Strap Clamp. Another basic clamp, the strap (or belt) clamp, consists of a strap that fits around the work to be glued. The strap has hardware that enables you to tighten it like a seat belt and then use a crank, wrench, or screwdriver to do the final tightening. Strap clamps work well for jobs such as holding chair joints together after you've glued them.

Spring Clamp. Used for jobs requiring firm holding power but not as much pressure as other clamps might provide, spring clamps work like a clothes pin. The clamps usually have protective plastic over the jaw tips to keep them from damaging wood, and they come in a number of sizes.

Bench Vise. A bench vise is an extremely useful piece of clamping equipment to have in your workshop. A vise will hold a small workpiece stationary, freeing your hands to work on it. Without a bench vise, you'll find many woodworking tasks frustrating, dangerous, and sometimes impossible. You can mount a bench vise to any workbench or table, as long as the surface is solid and stable. Depending on the vise type, you'll mount a bench vise to the top surface or to the side of a bench-top. Top-surface bench vises have a swivel, allowing the vise to turn in different directions.

Most bench vises have steel jaws, which can be damaging to wood, so it's a good idea to attach wooden pads to the inside of the jaws as a cushion and to prevent furniture damage. Cut softwood blocks to fit the inside of the vise joints, and use contact cement to attach the blocks to the jaws.

Woodworker's benches usually come equipped with special woodworking bench vises. These vises, which are also available separately to be mounted to an existing workbench, have wooden jaws.

Power Tools

Thinking of power tools for furniture work or woodworking may bring to mind a number of large, expensive pieces of equipment: table saws, wood lathes, radial-arm saws, band saws, shapers, planers, and jointers. To this list you could add drill presses and scroll saws.

Although some of these tools can be helpful, they are necessities only if you plan to construct your own furniture from scratch. You can do most furniture restoration and repair with just a few power tools. Remember, you may not need all the tools listed below for your particular project. Unless you're setting up a permanent repair shop, look ahead to the instructions for the project and check on what tools are required.

Electric Drill. Electric drills are available in corded and cordless models. Cordless models come with recharge-able power packs and a recharger. You can get a drill kit with two power packs, one of which you can recharge while you're using the other. If you don't get such a kit, buy a second power pack anyway; it will come in handy. Cordless drills have been greatly improved over the last few years and work well for just about any job, depending on the power level of the unit. You'll pay more for a cordless drill, but you won't need access to electricity in the immediate work area. Buy a minimum 12-volt model to ensure that you'll have enough power for your work.

Regular electric drills come in horsepower ratings from $1/3$ hp to $1^1/2$ hp. Electric drills come in standard sizes of $1/4$-, $3/8$-, and $1/2$- inch models. These measurements refer to the size of the chuck opening, which is the part of the drill that tightens to hold the drill bit or attachment you're using. A $1/4$-inch drill will probably handle most furniture repair jobs, but occasionally you might need the larger $3/8$-inch size. If you don't already own a drill, purchase a $3/8$-inch-chuck model. For the majority of furniture-restoration projects—and most household uses for that matter—a drill with a $1/2$-inch chuck generally will not be worth the extra expense.

Look for a drill with all the following features:

• Variable speeds. Lets you control the speed of the drill, slowing it down or speeding it up while drilling or driving screws. This feature is necessary for screw-driving.

• Reversing switch. Enables you to reverse the direction of the bit or attachment you're using.

• Double insulation. Provides insulation between the wiring of the drill and the drill casing to protect against electrical shock without using a three-prong plug.

Some corded and cordless drills have an adjustable clutch system that enables you to adjust the torque so you don't drive screws too deeply into wood. This feature also lets you drive screws without stripping or breaking off the heads. Many drills also have a keyless chuck, which allows you to loosen and tighten the chuck without using a chuck key.

Electric drill accessories include drill bits, screw-driver bits (Phillips and flat-blade), sanding and grinding attachments, a wire brush wheel, and a lamb's-wool buffing and polishing attachment. Drill stands are also available that can turn your drill into a small drill press.

An electric drill *is often necessary for furniture repair. A large variety of accessories, including a doweling jig (top left), a portable drill stand (top center), and buffing, grinding, and sanding attachments (left), can make a drill an even more useful power tool.*

Lastly, a doweling jig allows you to align dowels when joining two pieces of wood; it also allows you to drill out old broken dowels accurately and install new dowel pins in the exact location as the originals. Because much furniture uses dowel joinery, a doweling jig will be a useful addition to your home workshop.

Power Sander. Sanding by anyone's definition is a mundane, arduous task. Electric power sanders can save you many hours of monotonous labor.

Small power tools, such as (from left) a router, a circular saw, and a saber saw, can make cutting or shaping wood quick and easy when properly used.

There are many kinds of widely used electric sanders. Orbital sanders move the sandpaper in a circular motion. Oscillating sanders move the paper back and forth. Disc sanders spin the paper, and belt sanders turn a continuous-loop sanding belt. Most of these sanders are good for general-purpose work, but they must be followed up with hand sanding to remove the scratch marks they leave behind. Also available are random-orbit sanders and detail, or triangle, sanders. Random-orbit sanders are so named because of the random circular pattern of the sanding pad and thus the sandpaper. The sanding pad incorporates an orbital as well as a back-and-forth movement. When used correctly, random-orbit sanders are noted for removing and smoothing wood quickly with barely noticeable sanding marks.

Detail sanders, which usually have a small triangular pad, are good for sanding tight areas, including inside corners and edges. The pad moves in an orbital fashion, producing arc-shaped oscillations that in turn sand and smooth the wood.

You should invest in a random-orbit sander and a portable belt sander before investing in any other sanding equipment. You can use the random-orbit sander to prepare and smooth wood for finishing. Use the belt sander when you have to cut down an area of wood quickly. The belt sander is not used for most finish-sanding work because it can leave deep sanding marks that are difficult to remove.

Because sanding marks often aren't visible until the wood is finished and it's too late to remove them, wipe the wood with mineral spirits or denatured alcohol before finishing to reveal the marks. You can then sand them out before you begin applying the finish.

Circular Saw. If you have straight cuts to make, you can use a regular handsaw or, for long or repetitive

cuts, a circular power saw. A circular saw is also useful for cutting multiple kerfs when you need to notch wood or for cutting slots—in a side rail of a bed, for example. For cutting wood up to $2^{1/2}$ inches thick, buy a $7^{1/4}$-inch circular saw with a minimum of 10 amps. If, however, you'll be using the saw for much heavy cutting, buy at least a 13-amp model.

Saber Saw. Another versatile saw you may want on hand is the saber saw, or portable jigsaw. You can use the saber saw to make rough cuts in wood up to 3 inches thick and smoother cuts up to 2 inches thick. Although saber saws are primarily designed for making curved cuts, including totally enclosed hole cuts of any shape, you can also use them to cut short straight-line cuts if necessary.

Saber saws are usually rated according to amperage, blade speed, and the stroke length of the blade. The more amps a saw has, the greater its power. Blade speed is measured by strokes per minute (spm). The stroke length is the distance the blade moves up and down while operating; it can range from $^{1/2}$ inch to 1 inch.

You can buy saber saws with a single speed, two speeds, or variable speeds. They are also available with a mechanism for rotating the blade while cutting. Called scrolling, this feature enables you to exercise more control when making small cuts. The base on most saber saws is adjustable for making angled cuts. You may also want to check out the cordless models now available.

If you think you'll be using the saw often, get a model with plenty of power and variable speeds. A 3.5-amp-or-greater saw should be sufficient. Also consider a saw with the scrolling mechanism.

Router. The router is an excellent, versatile tool for making quick work of cutting and shaping wood. A great variety of bits is available to suit almost any requirement you'd have. You can use a router to make groove cuts in wood, as well as furniture-joint cuts such as dadoes, rabbets, mortise-and-tenons, and dovetails. (See "Types of Joints," page 66.) Router bits are also available for cutting rounded and molded edges in wood.

If you want to transform your router into a small shaper, you can buy a table to mount the router upside down, making it a stationary machine and allowing you to pass the wood through the router blade rather than move the router through the wood. This method gives you the added control needed to make delicate cuts.

You can buy routers in sizes from 1 to 3 horsepower (hp); a 1-hp model will more than suffice for most furniture repair work. If you're considering turning your router into a stationary shaper, consider getting a more powerful 2- or 3-hp model.

Because routers can cut and shape wood quickly, you should practice on scrap wood to master your technique. Make sure you've firmly clamped the piece you're cutting in place and you've tightened the router bit before beginning your cut.

Bench Grinder. Although you wouldn't classify bench grinders as strictly a woodworking tool, the vast majority of furniture builders and restorers have at least one permanently mounted somewhere in their shops. Bench grinders accommodate two wheels, usually a grinding wheel and a cloth buffing wheel, and include features like adjustable tool rests, wheel guards, spark deflectors, and eye shields.

Make sure you mount the bench grinder on a sturdy workbench or table. You can use the grinding wheel for shaping the bevel on a chisel or plane blade prior to honing, or whenever grinding metal is necessary in the furniture shop, such as when shaping a metal mending plate. The cloth buffing wheel is excellent for cleaning metal, particularly old brass hardware. Different grades of polishing and buffing compounds produce varying degrees of luster on the metal. (See "Cleaning and Polishing Hardware," page 228.) You can also substitute a wire wheel for those times when you need to remove heavy rust, scale, or paint from any kind of metal.

Electric Appliances. Even though electric irons and electric burn-in knives are electrical appliances rather than power tools, they appear here because of their usefulness in furniture repairs.

A bench grinder can be outfitted with a cloth buffing wheel on one side and a grinding wheel on the other for shaping the bevel on a chisel tip. You'll use polishing and buffing compounds with the buffing wheel to clean and polish furniture hardware.

You might be tempted to use your own household iron, but you'd be better off buying a separate iron—perhaps a used thrift-shop iron—for your furniture workshop. The main purpose of the iron is to steam dents out of wood surfaces. You can accomplish this by using the hot iron along with a damp or wet rag. (See "Steaming Out a Dent," page 198.)

Electric burn-in knives, which you can buy from furniture-restoration supply websites, have a metal tip that heats to a temperature hot enough to melt a hard lacquer or shellac resin stick. (See "Repairing Damage with a Burn-in Knife," page 180.) You can also buy a plug-in rheostat control for an electric burn-in knife. The rheostat has a heat control knob that enables you to maintain a constant knife temperature for melting and

A household iron is useful for steaming dents out of wood and attaching heat-activated veneer to furniture surfaces. Use an electric burn-in knife (right) to melt lacquer and shellac sticks and smooth the material for repairing nicks in finished surfaces.

smoothing the burn-in stick. The melted resin from the burn-in sticks fills scratches and dents in a finished surface without disturbing the surrounding finish. The resin hardens as it cools, then you sand and smooth it to blend in with the surrounding surface.

Stripping and Finishing Tools

Tools that are useful in the stripping process include square-tipped putty knives or paint scrapers and brass-bristled brushes. When using either tool, be careful, and use a light touch whenever possible to keep from damaging the wood.

It's best to use tools with wood or metal handles instead of plastic because remover can soften and dissolve plastic. Use a wide putty knife to scrape the finish off the piece's surface after the remover softens or dissolves it. For small areas, you'll need a narrow putty knife. Grind the sharp corners of the knife to keep it from accidentally gouging the wood surface as you scrape.

Use a brass-bristled brush to remove finish from carvings, cracks, and crevices after a chemical remover has dissolved the finish. Brass bristles are softer and easier on wood than steel, and they won't corrode. Other tools to help you pick stubborn finish out of nooks and crannies include an awl or ice pick, a knife with a sharp point, and a pointed wooden dowel.

Natural-Bristle Brushes. When you're ready to strip or finish, brushes are a necessity unless you're dipping furniture in a stripper vat or spraying the finish. There are numerous brushes available for these tasks, and they come in a variety of sizes and styles. For finishing with solvent-based finishes like varnish, alkyd urethane (polyurethane), or shellac, use a natural-bristle brush, which is made from animal hair. The bristles are finer than synthetic bristles, and they hold solvent-based finishes well so that the finish material flows evenly. Unlike the synthetic types, natural bristles also stand up to any strong solvents that are used in some solvent-based finishes like brushing lacquer.

A common, readily available natural bristle is called China bristle. Bristles are identified on the brush handle. China bristle is made from hog hair. Other natural-bristle brushes use horse, sable, badger, or ox hair. The finer the hair, the better the brush. A fine badger-hair brush, for example, is an excellent tool for applying shellac or an oil-based finish such as varnish.

Synthetic-Bristle Brushes. If you're using water-based finishes, buy a brush with bristles made of synthetic fiber, such as nylon or polyester. Nylon bristles

Useful tools for stripping off old finishes include a natural bristle brush (for applying the remover), nylon abrasive pads and a spatula-type putty knife (for scrubbing and scraping the old finish from the surface), and a brass-bristled brush and sharpened wooden dowel (for removing old finish or paint from crevices).

are good for thin, water-based coating; polyester bristles are better for heavy-bodied latex finishes. Natural bristles do not work well with water-based finishes because the bristles splay and lose their shape when exposed to water. Although synthetic-bristle brushes work well with water-based coatings, they usually aren't good to use with strippers because the strong chemicals in some finish removers can dissolve the bristles. For applying finish removers, use an inexpensive natural-bristle brush. When using wood bleach, however, a natural-bristle brush won't hold up, and you can substitute an inexpensive synthetic-bristle brush instead.

Artists' Brushes. Excellent tools for touch-up work when refinishing or for touching up an existing finish, artists' brushes are available with various types of tips and bristle materials in a variety of sizes. For touch-up work using artists' brushes, use a natural-bristle material. As for size, it's usually a good idea to have on hand small, medium, and large brushes. The brushes are sized according to number: #2 (fine) through #10 (broad).

Brush Buying Tips. When buying a brush for finishing work, get the best one you can find. Although it's not true with everything, brush quality usually has a direct correlation with price. The more expensive the brush, the better it is.

The brush should have a tapered tip, rather than a squared-off tip. When you look at a cross section of the tip, the bristles should come to a point, similar to the A-shape of a roof. Known as a chisel trim brush, it works well for the final tipping-off process, which you do to remove brush marks and bubbles while the finish is still wet.

Brushes vary greatly in size. A good brush for finishing is 2 to 2½ inches wide. You can go larger than this, but if you encounter any tight areas, larger brushes can be awkward to use. You can also finish a large surface well with this size brush and maintain good control in the process.

Another thing to look for when judging general brush quality is long bristle length. This does not mean that all short-bristle brushes are inferior. There are some natural-bristle brushes, such as those made from badger hair, that have relatively short bristles because the hair is so flexible. These fine-haired, flexible brushes are good for applying thin, solvent-based finishes.

Check the thickness or density of the bristles by wrapping your thumb and forefinger around them to bunch them together. The amount of bristles on the brush should not be too sparse, otherwise, the brush won't hold much material. Also, check the tip to make sure it's trimmed evenly. Check the straightness and uniformity of the bristles, and push them against the palm of your hand to make sure they will spring back in place and that no bristles come loose.

Brushes are important for finishing work. These brushes include artists' brushes used in touch-up work, natural-bristle brushes, and synthetic-bristle brushes.

One more sign of a quality brush is that the individual bristle tips will be flagged or split, much like the split ends on your hair when it's been damaged. These flagged ends help hold and spread the finish.

THE PROS KNOW

MAINTAINING BRUSHES

To get the longest life from your brush, here are some recommendations.

• Soak the brush before each use just beyond the top of the bristles at the bottom of the metal ferrule in the appropriate thinning solvent for the finish you are using. After soaking for a few minutes, remove the brush from the solvent and shake out any excess. The brush is now ready for use. Soaking the brush like this will protect the bristles and make the brush easier to clean after you use it.

• To clean the brush, wipe any excess finish from the bristles into the container or brush the finish out onto a scrap surface until the brush is as dry as possible. Clean the bristles well in the appropriate solvent, and shake out any excess. Then wash the entire brush with warm water and a sudsy soap, and rinse out all the soap with water.

• To store the brush, shake out any excess water, and wrap the brush in kraft paper or paper-bag paper. When you wrap the brush, make sure the paper extends well beyond the top of the bristles onto the metal ferrule. Next, fold the paper over several inches below the tip of the brush and back up onto the brush above the bristles. Use a rubber band to hold the paper in place until your next use. Hang the brush or lay it flat so you don't put pressure on the bristles and cause them to lose their original shape.

Kraft Paper

Fold below the tip of the bristles.

Rubber Band

3

REPAIR MATERIALS

This chapter covers the materials needed for repairing furniture, including instructions on the selection and use of wood screws, nails, dowels, and various types of wood glue. Look for valuable tips to make your regluing project easier and to ensure its success. Lastly, we'll look at what's necessary for the repair shop with regard to solid wood and veneer.

The materials you'll need for repairing specific pieces of furniture will depend on the project you're preparing to tackle. If you're dealing with a one-time project, follow the instructions and buy only the materials you need for that piece. If you plan to collect old furniture and do most of the repairs yourself, however, you may eventually need all or most of the materials mentioned in this chapter.

MECHANICAL FASTENERS

Most good wood furniture is held together by joinery and glue. When that furniture breaks and you're faced with repairing it, you sometimes need the help of fasteners like dowels, nails, and screws to strengthen weak areas.

Wood Screws

There are many ways to join wood in making furniture, such as mortise-and-tenon joints, dowel joints, and dovetail joints. Wood screws are not a substitute for this kind of joinery, but they still have many applications in furniture and its repair. Corner glue blocks on many chairs and table frames are attached with wood screws to reinforce leg joints and make them strong and stable. Many tops are attached to bases with wood screws in pieces like tables or chests of drawers. Some dining room chairs use wood screws to attach arms to the frame and back.

Other uses of wood screws in furniture include attaching hinges for doors, desk drop lids, and table leaves. In some cases wood screws may even be useful when repairing splits and breaks in wood.

Selecting Screws. Wood screws are categorized according to head shape (flathead, oval-head, round-head); diameter, indicated by the gauge numbers 0 through 24; and length, indicated by the distance from the top of the screwhead to the tip of the shank, usually $1/4$ to 6 inches. You'll most commonly use #6 through #14 flathead screws in furniture repair, from $3/4$ inch to 2 inches in length. You might sometimes use oval- or round-head wood screws when the head is to remain visible rather than countersunk and covered.

Mechanical fasteners, like mending plates, screws, nails, and dowels, are not the primary methods of holding furniture together, but they can be useful for some aspects of furniture repair.

A good rule for determining the length of screw necessary for a job is to choose a screw that will sink about two-thirds of its length into the base, or primary, piece of wood. When you use large screws, rub a little hard wax or soap into the threads to make driving the screw easier. Other lubricants may stain wood.

Using Screws. It's important to match the correct size screwdriver with the screw. Make sure the screwdriver tip fits the thickness of the screw slot and the width of the screwhead. The better fit you have, the easier your job will be and the less chance you have of damaging the screw, the surrounding wood, or even yourself.

When applying pressure to drive or remove a screw, make sure the screwdriver tip is aimed away from you in case it slips from the screwhead. If you're installing a screw in wood that has not been previously drilled for the screw, be sure to drill a pilot hole. The hole must be large enough to allow the screw to go into the wood without splitting it, but not so large that the screw won't tighten securely. When you install screws for hinges, make the pilot hole the same diameter as the screw shaft minus the threads. In softwood, drill the hole to about one-half to two-thirds the length of the screw; in hardwood, drill to the full depth.

When you use a wood screw to attach one piece of wood to another, drill a pilot hole in the bottom piece of

When installing a screw, make your job easier by matching the screwdriver tip size to the screwhead and slot size

wood so that the screw will tighten in the hole. Next, drill an oversize hole in the top piece of wood so that the screw shank moves freely in it. This allows the screw to tighten in the bottom without tightening in the top piece. In this way, the screw acts as if it were a clamp, pulling the two pieces of wood tightly together.

Nails and Brads

Contrary to apparent popular belief (based on many "repairs" I've had to fix), the answer for most structural problems in furniture is not to drive a large nail into it. This approach to repair usually just complicates matters at best. Nails do, however, have some appropriate uses in furniture restoration.

Common nails have a head and can be used to secure backs to cabinets, chests of drawers, or dressers. They can also attach a drawer bottom where it joins the drawer back. Finishing nails and brads have virtually no head and can be countersunk, or set, with a nail set, thus hiding the nail. You can use finishing nails for attaching molding, such as around a drawer front or to hold glass in a cabinet door frame, or for attaching drawer stops. Sometimes they can be used for other small repairs in conjunction with glue.

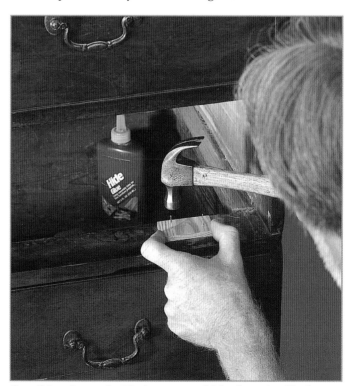

Small brads, used with glue, are useful for fastening blocks or other attachments to furniture in inconspicuous spots.

Nail Sizes. Nails are denominated by the term penny, which is abbreviated *d*. The *d* stands for denarius, an ancient Roman silver coin, the penny of the New Testament. In a system developed in England many years ago, the penny number of a nail referred to the cost of 100 nails of that size, but today it indicates the nail's length. A 2*d* nail, for example, is 1 inch long, and for each increase in penny size the nail length increases by $^1/_4$ inch. Therefore a 3*d* nail is $1^1/_4$ inches long, a 4*d* nail is $1^1/_2$ inches long, and so on.

Wire brads come in lengths of up to 3 inches. Small wire brads (less than 1 inch) are particularly useful for doing delicate work such as attaching small moldings.

Using Nails. When using nails in wood that is exceptionally hard, like maple or oak, drill a pilot hole to keep from splitting the wood or bending the nail. Sometimes you can snip the head from the nail and use the nail as a drill bit for the pilot hole. Drill the hole a little less than the full length of the nail so that when you drive the nail into the wood, it will tighten securely.

Another simple method that sometimes works to keep wood from splitting when driving a nail is to clip off the sharp pointed tip. This allows the nail to enter the wood and crush wood fibers without pushing them apart at the grain line, which can cause a split. This method works well when using tiny nails or brads to attach small, delicate pieces of wood.

Dowels

Dowels are cylindrical rods that are used to attach pieces of wood to one another and to strengthen furniture joints. Although you may see plastic or metal dowels, the vast majority of dowelled furniture joints employ wooden dowels. You can also use dowels to add strength and support when repairing splits and breaks in wood.

Dowel Sizes. Dowels are readily available at home centers and hardware stores in 36-inch lengths and in diameters from $^1/_8$ to 1 inch. The most common diameter sizes for dowels used in furniture applications are $^1/_4$, $^5/_{16}$, $^3/_8$, and $^1/_2$ inch.

Using Dowels. To use a dowel in a joint you must cut it to size, chamfer the ends, and cut a groove in its side before installing it. The chamfer makes the dowel easier to insert into a hole, and the groove allows excess glue to escape from the hole and prevent wood around the hole from splitting as a result of pressure. To groove a dowel, clamp it lengthwise in a vise and cut the groove with a backsaw. Some stores stock pre-cut, ready-to-use grooved dowels in an assortment of diameters and sizes. Some general rules about using dowels include the following:

Before installing a dowel, *chamfer the end that will be inserted and cut a groove in its side lengthwise to allow excess glue and air to escape as the dowel is being forced into the hole.*

• If possible, use a dowel with a diameter not larger than one-half the thickness of the wood it is entering. A large dowel could weaken the wood. In a $^3/_4$-inch piece of wood, for example, the dowel should measure $^3/_8$ inch in diameter or less.

• When using dowels in a joint for strength, use at least two dowels if you can.

• Cut dowels about $^1/_8$ inch shorter than the length of the hole they're meant for in order to leave room for glue and to allow you to pull the joint tight.

Mending Plates and Corner Braces

Mending plates and corner braces are flat metal plates and angles, usually with countersunk holes so they can be attached with screws. You'll rarely, if ever, find these plates on old handmade furniture; if so, they've been added as a repair. Some antique furniture employed the use of wrought-iron plates where necessary to add strength not provided by the wood itself: An example is the use of a spider-shaped plate on the underside of a pedestal table base to reinforce and lock leg joints at the central column. As long as the iron plate remains attached, these old pedestal base legs seldom become loose.

Try not to use metal plates. Professionals and purists oppose their use, but in some instances they are the only means of providing strength to an otherwise weak repair. If you must use mending plates, install them where they won't show.

ADHESIVES

There are many kinds of adhesives on the market with just as many claims for their abilities. Glues used for furniture repairs are not as varied and fall into one of the following categories.

Polyvinyl Glue

Probably the most popular and useful general-purpose wood glue available, polyvinyl glue is sold in plastic jugs or squeeze bottles in liquid form. It is colored either white or creamy yellow and is often called carpenter's glue. Solvents include vinegar and warm water.

When using polyvinyl glue, clamp the work tightly after gluing for at least an hour but preferably overnight. You can clean up any excess with plain water while the glue is still wet. It's important to clean excess glue from unfinished wood thoroughly, otherwise, the glue spots will show up as white or light splotches when you stain and finish the wood. If the piece you're gluing is a finished piece, you can usually let the excess glue set up for 30 minutes to an hour, then peel or lift it off the finished surface. Be careful not to allow the excess glue to dry too long if the finished surface is at all porous; the glue may become difficult to remove or may even lift the finish off with it.

Use a plunger to inject glue into a small hole drilled into a joint if it's impractical to disassemble the joint.

Polyvinyl glues were originally developed as non-waterproof glues, and because most furniture is not subject to water, these glues work well. If you need to glue up an outside piece, such as a porch rocker or garden bench, you can get polyvinyl glues in a waterproof version.

Hide Glue

Hide glue dates back to early Egyptian times and is so-named because it's made from the hides and hoofs of animals. The hide and hoof material is processed and cleaned, and boiling water or steam is used to extract the proteins that form the glue. This protein material is then clarified with alum, bleached, and dried.

The glue of choice for furniture makers before 1900, hide glue is reversible, meaning that joints glued with it can be undone by applying heat and water. This reversibility makes the glue ideal for use on genuine antiques.

Originally, hide glue came in dry or flake form, and heat was required to liquefy it. Although a dry form is still available, today you can also get it in a ready-to-use liquid form. This liquid form is also made from natural animal proteins and is reversible, but it offers the advantage of a longer open working time.

When you use hide glue, make sure the joints are clean, dry, well-fitting, and under clamp pressure for about five hours. After you remove the clamps, allow the glue to cure overnight before using the piece of furniture.

Epoxy

You may have to work quickly when using some epoxies (the 5-minute variety, for example), but it's an excellent glue for certain jobs. Epoxy works well on nonporous material such as metal or glass. It's waterproof, solvent-proof, and heat resistant. Epoxy remains somewhat flexible over time and fills gaps well when you don't have tight-fitting joints.

Epoxy is a two-part formulation consisting of a resin and a hardener, which must be mixed together according to label directions. Many manufacturers sell epoxy in a dual-cylinder plunger that doles out just enough of each ingredient. It's important to mix the two parts thoroughly to ensure that the epoxy will set up and dry completely.

Epoxy is convenient if you have a small repair job that needs to be ready quickly. Clamp the parts together until the epoxy sets or according to label instructions. One way to be sure the epoxy has set is to save some excess from your original mixture and check to make sure it's hard before you remove your clamps. When clamping, don't squeeze all the adhesive out of the joint, as its strength depends on some epoxy remaining. Once epoxy cures, solvents won't affect it.

Contact Adhesive

Although contact cement is used most commonly to apply sheets of plastic laminates to tables or countertops, you can also use

There are a variety of glues available for furniture work, each with different properties. The glue you choose will depend on your project.

this adhesive to apply wood veneer to solid wood surfaces. You apply contact cement evenly to both surfaces and allow them to become dry to the touch, usually within 10 to 15 minutes. You then put the two surfaces together, starting at one edge and working across the piece, lowering and pressing the veneer or laminate to the solid surface it's joining.

Once the two surfaces make contact, they become instantly bonded and cannot be separated, so you'll need to align them exactly right the first time using a slip sheet or wooden dowels as spacers for the surfaces until you have them lined up. Contact adhesive is available in both solvent- and water-based formulas.

Other Kinds of Glues

There are several other kinds of glues that are not as popular for furniture repair as those mentioned, but they may still come in handy.

Cyanoacrylate. Perhaps better known as CA glue or Super Glue, this adhesive does not have wide application in woodworking and furniture repairs. It's good for small-application jobs such as accidental splinters or splits because it can flow into cracks and joints. It comes in varying viscosities and in gel form, and hardens in minutes—or in seconds with use of an accelerator.

The glue I've used and recommend for furniture applications comes with a bottle of spray accelerator. You simply apply the glue, hold the pieces together, and spray on the accelerator, which follows the glue into the crack with a chemical reaction that results in almost instantaneous bonding.

A word of caution about using cyanoacrylates: Your fingers can be glued together as quickly as wood can, so be careful any time you use this kind of glue. And because cyanoacrylates can have a shelf life as low as 6 to 12 months, buy only the quantity you believe you can use in that time period.

Polyurethane Glue. The word polyurethane probably conjures up images of a durable finish for wood. But several polyurethane glues are used by woodworkers.

Polyurethane glue is a one-part, ready-to-use formula that you apply to one surface of the two surfaces you want to join. After you assemble the parts, use clamps to apply pressure until the glue sets—from 1 to 4 hours, depending on temperature and humidity. The glue usually takes about 24 hours to become fully cured.

An advantage of polyurethane glues is that they are

waterproof and fairly ease to use. A disadvantage is that they foam up, and cleanup can be messy and requires a solvent.

Urea-Formaldehyde Glue. This glue is made by mixing a powder with water according to label directions. It is a strong, highly moisture-resistant glue and can be used for joints that will be under high stress. Joints should be clean and well-fitting. Because this type of glue contains formaldehyde, which has been shown to cause cancer in laboratory animals, be sure to read and follow to the letter individual label precautionary measures for the use, handling, storage, and disposal of the product. Mix only what you can use immediately, and clamp the joint for 5 to 12 hours. Allow a minimum of 24 hours before you use the piece.

Resorcinol. Resorcinol glue has excellent resistance to moisture and has even been used by boat builders. The adhesive contains two parts: a powder and a liquid catalyst that are mixed according to label directions. Apply pressure for about two hours to the pieces being joined by the glue.

One consideration when using resorcinol is that it dries to a dark reddish-brown color and could possibly stain light-colored wood.

SOLID WOOD AND VENEERS

Unlike furniture making, furniture repair does not require large stockpiles of expensive lumber. Many times you can get by with small sections of veneer and scraps of wood that a furniture maker would use as kindling to start a fire in a wood stove.

Solid Wood. Small pieces of solid wood, like scraps and cutoffs, work fine for jobs like replacing glue blocks, doing small patch repairs, and replacing small pieces of molding. Other repair tasks, such as replacing a rocker runner, will require larger pieces of wood. You can usually buy what you need from specialty lumberyards in whatever size and quantity you require. Eventually you'll end up with an ample supply of small pieces useful for many repairs.

Wood Veneer. You'll need to keep only small amounts of veneer on hand for furniture repair. Buy what you need from a local wood specialty store or online through a woodworking supplier. Sometimes veneer suppliers will offer sample sets of veneer. These sets, which contain a variety of veneers in small quantities, can be useful for repairs. Also, check with woodworkers in your area; they may sell you small amounts of what you need in both veneers and solid wood.

THE PROS KNOW

TIPS FOR DOING GLUE REPAIRS

Working with glue can sometimes be more challenging than it first appears. I learned this quickly when I made my first solo attempt at furniture repair by regluing a dining room chair, a job I envisioned as quite simple.

Everyone in the furniture shop had gone home, and I stayed late to do the job. After disassembling the chair and cleaning each joint, I applied glue and began to reassemble the parts. The difficulty arose when I discovered that many of the parts of the old, handmade Hitchcock chair I was working on wouldn't fit properly unless you fitted them into their original holes. I had interchanged several stretchers, so I couldn't get the chair back together properly. After much frantic trial and error—and having to revive the glue by reapplication in several joints after it had become stiff—I finally got the chair back together and in clamps.

The following are some tips that may help you avoid some of the same trials in your gluing projects:

• Read and follow the directions for the glue you are using. Some glues emit fumes, which require adequate ventilation or the use of a respirator. Don't ignore directives about temperature; most glues require normal room temperature to dry properly.

• Clean all mating surfaces of old glue, finish, and the like. If you disassemble joints, label them with masking tape and a marker to ensure proper reassembly.

• Assemble all joints on a flat surface without glue using the clamps you'll use when gluing the piece. Check for fit and alignment of all joints before removing the clamps, and then remove all the clamps and place them out of the way but within reach.

• Disassemble the joints and apply glue, reassembling them one by one.

• Reapply the clamps, check for fit and alignment of the joints again, clean off any excess glue, and leave the clamps on for the specified time.

One final note about gluing projects: It's sometimes easier to do the job in stages rather than all at once. Some styles of chairs, for example, can be glued up by first gluing and assembling the legs and seat. After this part of the chair is dry, you can remove the clamps, and then glue and assemble the chair back to the chair base. You can determine whether this method is best after test-fitting the joints.

Some of the more commonly used wood veneers you might want on hand include a couple types of mahogany (straight grain and crotch-cut grain), some walnut (straight-grain and burl-cut grain), a few varieties of oak (regular and quartersawn), rosewood, and some maple (regular and bird's eye).

Small pieces of wood like this one, which is being prepared as a patch for a crushed corner on a desk top, come in handy in the furniture-repair shop.

Small veneer pieces that a furniture builder may throw away can often be put to good use in repair work. You can also buy sample sets of different varieties of veneer.

4

REFINISHING SUPPLIES AND MATERIALS

Restoring a piece of furniture may mean trying to repair and revive the original finish in some way. More often it means removing the original finish and preparing the bare wood for a new finish. This chapter covers materials for removing finishes and sanding, preparing, and finishing the bare wood. If you're planning to stock your home furniture shop with supplies, consider the shelf life of any volatile liquid materials you buy. Strippers, stains, and finishes don't last indefinitely and can sometimes go bad before you have a chance to use the entire amount. Always check labels carefully to see whether they contain information regarding shelf life, and only buy what you can use in the prescribed amount of time. Because there are so many different products and brands available with varying degrees of shelf life, it is difficult to give guidelines on individual materials. If shelf life is going to be an issue when you buy a particular product and it's not mentioned on the label, consult your supplier or call the manufacturer for additional information, and label your own products.

MATERIALS FOR REMOVING FINISHES

Old-timers used a caustic solution of lye and water to strip paint from furniture, and because this solution is so strong and effective in removing hard-to-strip paints and finishes, it can still be found in some strippers' dip tanks today. The problem with this method is that because the solution is so strong, it can also loosen glue joints, discolor wood, and burn the user's skin and eyes. The water-based solution also raises wood grain, creating a fuzzy texture.

Other, easier-to-use strippers have become available in the past 30 to 40 years, many of which contain an effective solvent called methylene chloride. These strippers are fast-acting on most finishes and should be relatively safe to use as long as you read and follow all directions. Note, however, that methylene chloride is a suspected carcinogen. Also, anyone with a history of heart problems should not use methylene chloride. Keep in mind that you'll need to work in a well-ventilated area and wear protective clothing, gloves, an apron, and safety glasses.

Materials for Removing Finishes

You can buy chemical-based paint and varnish removers in liquid or semi-paste form in various strengths, depending on other solvents used. The solvents in both forms evaporate quickly, which is why they have such strong fumes, so manufacturers add paraffin wax to slow down the evaporation somewhat. Because the strippers contain wax, it's important to rinse or wash the piece down after stripping, better preparing the piece for the

Using a chemical stripper (at top right in photo) is the easiest way for a do-it-yourselfer to remove a finish. You'll also need a brush, a scraper, an abrasive (steel wool, abrasive pads, and/or a brass brush), and rags. Lacquer thinner cleans the wood surface when you've finished stripping.

next step in the refinishing process. Lacquer thinners work best for this cleaning, but you can also use mineral spirits or denatured alcohol.

Liquid Remover. Liquid remover is thinner than semi-paste and begins to act immediately on the old finish. Because the liquid is thin and runny, it doesn't cling and therefore works better on horizontal surfaces. Liquid removers are available in a water-wash or no-wash form. After you've removed the finish with a water-wash remover, you're supposed to wash or rinse the piece with water to remove any residue. Washing with water raises the wood grain, however. The no-wash variety claims it doesn't need washing. I prefer using lacquer thinner to clean up the piece after stripping, even with no-wash removers.

Semi-Paste Remover. Semi-paste has a thicker consistency than liquid remover, allowing it to cling to vertical surfaces much better than liquid products. The resulting thicker coat also allows the remover to work a bit longer.

Reduced-Hazard "Safe" Strippers

Of course no stripper is safe, but recently a number of strippers have been developed without the use of methylene chloride or other harsh chemicals. Some of these

strippers are nonflammable and can be used without gloves.

Because of the safety claims of these products, it may be worthwhile to check into them for your particular project. Check the label to make sure the one you buy is formulated to strip the kind of finish you're removing. You'll find that there are trade-offs with most, if not all, of the reduced-hazard strippers: They tend to be more expensive and much slower-working than methylene chloride-based chemical strippers.

Solvent Wood Refinishers

Another kind of stripping product is a wood refinisher. Refinishers are made up of solvents consisting of a mixture of chemicals much like those used in lacquer thinner. These solvents dissolve finishes from the top down, enabling you to soften the finish, taking it off a little at a time or even redistributing it on the wood without totally removing it. Sometimes this can be useful, as in the case of an old cracked or crazed finish that you just want to rejuvenate rather than totally strip.

Because refinishers are basically pure solvent, they will work only on evaporative finishes such as shellac and lacquer, which form a film simply by the evaporation of the solvent and can be redissolved by the same solvent. Other finishes, such as oil-based varnishes, are called reactive finishes. These finishes, which form a film as the resin goes through a chemical change, require conventional strippers to be removed.

If you're stripping a shellac or lacquer finish and you want to remove it completely, remember that, although refinishers do a good job, they're slower and more expensive than paint and varnish removers. Refinishers are also flammable and tend to create strong fumes during use, and they require adequate ventilation, protective clothing, and gloves.

Bleach and Vinegar

It is rarely a problem to darken wood color, which you can easily do by using wood stains. Reversing the process and lightening wood, however, usually requires bleach.

Some wood bleaches also come in dry crystals (oxalic acid) and must be mixed with hot water before use. You'll find wood bleach in paint or hardware stores. Wood bleach comes in two parts; when the two parts combine, a chemical reaction takes place and bleaches the wood. Pay close attention to label directions when using wood bleach. Be sure to wear a dust mask when sanding to keep from breathing possible caustic sanding dust from the bleach solution.

Household, or chlorine, bleach is a less potent form of bleach. You can use chlorine bleach, but it may require several applications to lighten the wood sufficiently. When you use bleach, remember that

To lighten wood (left side of wood sample), you need bleach. Use regular household bleach (left) or two-part wood bleach, followed by a neutralizing solution of vinegar and water.

you must remove all finish, oil, and wax from the wood to allow the bleach to penetrate and work.

Let your first application work overnight before you decide to do any more. After the final bleaching application is dry, wash the wood with a water and white vinegar solution to neutralize the bleach. Once the wood is dry, sand it with fine sandpaper (220- to 280-grit) to smooth the wood. Don't apply too much pressure, or you'll cut through the bleached surface of the wood. The wood is now ready to be stained or otherwise prepared for finishing.

Steel Wool

For nonprofessionals, the most available form of steel wool is the fist-size or smaller pad, which comes in seven different grades, from #0000 (the finest) to #3 (the coarsest). You'll use several grades for furniture work. The #3, #2, and #1 steel-wool pads work well for removing old finish after you've softened or dissolved it using finish remover. Dip the pad in the solvent, and scrub with the grain of the wood to remove the old, softened finish.

Use #000 or #0000 pads to rub out dust particles from finish coats before applying the next coat. You can also use them to rub down the final finish coat to achieve a satin, hand-rubbed look. Sometimes you can do this final rub using oil or wax to give the finish even more luster. These fine steel-wool pads are also useful for cleaning dirt, grime, oil, or old wax from existing finishes. You can do this on most finishes by dipping the wool in mineral spirits and rubbing down the old finish, followed by a wash-down then a wipe-down using a clean rag. After the piece dries, apply a new coat of

wax. The #0 and #00 pads are rarely used because they tend to be too fine for removing a finish and too coarse for rubbing one out.

Abrasive Pads. In some applications you can use a modern substitute for steel wool: the nylon abrasive pad, which is not as hard on wood but is as durable and can accomplish the same results. If you're stripping old finish from wood, for example, and are concerned about unnecessary scratches, nylon abrasive pads work well. Use them just as you would steel wool.

Rags

Whether you're stripping, cleaning, or waxing an old finish, regluing a loose joint, or staining, filling, or finishing wood, rags are a necessity in the furniture shop.

For some purposes, like stripping old finish or cleaning excess filler from wood, almost any old rag will do, as long as it doesn't contain any oils or silicones that can get into the wood. But for staining and finishing, it's important to use clean, soft, lint-free, smooth rags, such as those torn from an old white cotton T-shirt. White rags ensure that no fabric dyes or color will stain the wood, and cotton, unlike synthetic fabrics, tends to absorb stains or finishes well. Using a smooth, rather than ribbed or textured, fabric is also important in preventing streaks in your stain or finish during application.

Boxed rags are readily available at paint, hardware and home improvement stores. Be sure to use caution when you get rid of old oily rags. (See "Dispose of Used Rags Properly," page 27.)

Masking Tape

Masking tape works well for some aspects of furniture restoration, such as protecting a portion of furniture during the stripping or finishing process. If you want to refinish the top of a table but not the legs or base, for example, use masking tape and paper (doubled or tripled old newspaper) to protect the area you're not finishing. Masking tape is also useful for taping off glass areas that can't be removed during the refinishing process. When doing repairs, you can also use masking tape to hold small pieces of veneer or wood in place while regluing.

If you've ever applied masking tape to a surface and left it on for more than a day or two, I'm sure you know that removing it can be tedious and difficult. To make such removals easier when the job is done, manufacturers have developed a masking tape with less adhesion. This kind of tape often comes in a color that's different from regular masking tape—usually blue. You can find it in well-stocked paint and hardware stores.

Automotive paint-supply stores usually stock a thicker, better grade of masking tape in a variety of widths. Although this automotive-grade tape is more expensive, it's a superior tape that works much better than the average grade of masking tape.

Masking tape is useful for covering areas that need to be protected during refinishing. The blue tape is a special quick-release type.

SANDPAPER

Sandpaper, which is basically nothing more than sand or another abrasive glued to a paper backing, is essential in furniture work. Sandpaper is used not only to prepare the wood's surface but also in the finishing process itself to give you superior results.

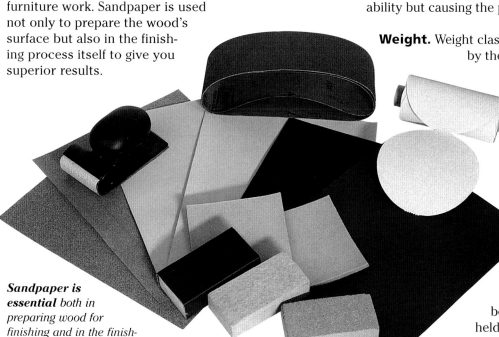

Sandpaper is essential both in preparing wood for finishing and in the finishing process itself. Use sanding blocks for any large flat surfaces.

Today most sandpaper is made from abrasives other than sand, which may be attached to cloth or even polyester film instead of paper. These coated abrasive sheets come in a variety of grits, or grades, which refer to the size of the abrasive particles. The sheets also come in a variety of types, which refer to the kind of abrasive material used. The type and grit of sandpaper you need will vary, depending on the project you're undertaking.

"Open Coat" or "Closed Coat." These terms refer to the amount of abrasive material applied to the sandpaper's backing. "Open coat" means the abrasive grit is spread out on the backing sheet, covering only about 40 to 70 percent of the area, to prevent friction-generated heat while sanding and to keep the abrasive surface from clogging. "Closed coat" means 100 percent of the backing surface is covered with abrasive, providing more cutting ability but causing the paper to clog more easily.

Weight. Weight classes of sandpaper are determined by the thickness of the backing paper. The weights are rated by the letters A, C, D, E, and F, with A representing the lightest weight and F the heaviest. For furniture woodworking purposes, A, C, or D are appropriate weights; E and F papers usually have extremely coarse grit, such as that used on a belt sander or on a power sander, like the type used to remove finish on old wood floors. The thicker woodworking papers (C and D weights) are better for power sanders and hand-held sanding blocks because they will last longer. They are not as good for hand sanding without a block in tight spots or on rounded surfaces like turnings or spindles because they are stiff and tend to crack more easily. An A-weight paper can be folded or even crumpled easily and works well in tight areas.

Sanding Blocks. You can buy various kinds of sanding blocks at paint and hardware stores, or you can make your own. (See "Improvising Tools," page 29.) You can also buy solid felt or cork sanding blocks, which work especially well, from finishing-supply websites. The size of your block should enable you to wrap one-quarter or one-half of a sheet of sandpaper around the sides firmly enough to grip and hold it in position while sanding. When the paper becomes worn in one area, shift and reposition it on the block so you can use a fresh area.

Make your own cork sanding block by gluing ⅛-in.-thick gasket cork to a softwood block measuring 2¾ x 3⅞ in. Chamfer the top of the block.

Types of Sandpaper

Garnet. This paper uses the natural mineral garnet as an abrasive. It's usually reddish-brown in color and sands just about any type of wood well. Since the development of aluminum oxide, a synthetic abrasive with excellent cutting ability, garnet paper has become less popular among woodworkers, but it still does an excellent job.

Aluminum Oxide. This synthetic abrasive is usually brown, white, or pale gray in color. It's tough and durable and has excellent cutting ability. Often called production paper, aluminum oxide is widely used to smooth and prepare wood but can also be used for sanding during the finishing process.

A relatively new aluminum oxide "sandpaper" employs a polyamide mesh backer instead of paper. It is more durable than paper-backed aluminum oxide, and allows for superior dust collection on powered sanders, and it doesn't clog when hand sanding. It is, however, more expensive.

Silicon Carbide. Silicon carbide, another synthetic abrasive, is waterproof and extremely hard. This paper is dark gray, brown, or black and is used for wet sanding with a lubricant like water or oil. Silicon carbide works well for sanding finishes between coats or for sanding the final finish to produce a desired sheen.

Stearated silicon carbide paper comes in a grayish-white color, which indicates it's been manufactured with a lubricant (stearate) included in its abrasive surface. The lubricant minimizes "gumming up" of the paper while sanding between coats of finish. Excellent for finish sanding, silicon carbide paper can also be used to sand wood.

Grits and Grades

The standard method for grading sandpaper is to label the back of each sheet according to grit size. The lower the number, the coarser the grit. There are other ways to grade sandpaper, though, one of which is simply to label it with a description such as fine, medium, or coarse. Another method identifies the grit size by using zeros or numbers. The more zeros, the finer the paper; the higher the number (up to 4½), the coarser the grade. (See "Choosing the Right Sandpaper," below.)

Choosing the Right Sandpaper

Grit	No.	Description	Purpose and Comments
12	4½	Extra Coarse	Rough sanding and shaping; rust and
16	4		paint removal; not recommended for
20	3½		furniture
24	3		
30	2½		
36	2		
40	1½	Coarse	Rough sanding and paint removal;
50	1		shaping wood; rarely used on furniture
60	½	Medium	Rough sanding to remove deep scratches;
80	0		shaping wood; must be followed by finer grit before finishing wood
100	00	Fine	Preliminary sanding and preparation of
120	000		wood before applying finish
150	0000		
180	5/0	Very fine	Preparation of hardwoods for finishing
220	6/0		and occasionally sanding between coats
240	7/0		
280	8/0	Extra fine	Sanding and smoothing finishes between
320	9/0		coats
360	*	Superfine	Sanding and smoothing finishes between
400	10/0		coats
500	*	Ultrafine	Sanding final finish coats, usually with
600	*		water or another lubricant like oil, to
and above			produce various sheens

THE PROS KNOW

SANDING TIPS

• Divide sandpaper into quarters, cutting it with scissors or tearing it on the edge of a shop table or bench.

• Use a sanding block (preferably cork, felt, or rubber) for sanding flat surfaces. Use straight strokes and even pressure.

• You can make a shaped block to get into the contours of molding and other shaped wood. Sometimes a piece of dowel will work.

• Use folded paper to get into cracks, corners, and crevices.

• Sand with the direction of the wood's grain to prevent cross-grain scratches. When sanding burl, swirl, or crotch grained woods, use the finest paper available. Use masking tape to protect an adjacent piece of wood with the grain running in a different direction. (See the photo below.)

• Never use a grade that's coarser than necessary.

• Work progressively through coarser to finer grades. When using coarse paper, your next step should be under 100 points. For medium grade paper, you can step up to 100 or more points, and for finer papers, 200 or more.

• When hand sanding without a sanding block, you can trifold a quarter-sheet of paper (use a half-sheet for larger areas), which will give you a better grip while sanding. When one side of the paper is worn, fold out a new section of paper, and continue until all three sides are used up.

• If the paper is stiff (C and D weights) and you are not using a sanding block, you can make the paper more flexible by pulling the back side over a benchtop edge.

• Clean your paper when it starts to clog by using a stiff-bristled brush or by tapping the paper on a hard surface.

WOOD-PREPARATION MATERIALS

Once you've stripped and rough-sanded a piece of furniture, you need to prepare it for final finishing. You may see that the wood has imperfections, like nicks and cracks, that need to be fixed with wood putty. Or you may notice that the wood has an open grain that must be filled. When you've done those tasks, you'll probably want to stain the furniture before putting on a clear-coat finish.

Wood Fillers

Wood Putty. Wood putty is available in a variety of forms and under a number of names, including wood dough, plastic wood, wood patch, water putty, and the like. Basically, there are three kinds of putty: nitrocellulose-based wood putties, which clean up with lacquer thinner; acrylic-based putties, which clean up with water; and gypsum-based putties, which come as a powder.

Apply wood putty by pressing it into a hole with a putty knife or dull screwdriver (top). Leave a little excess, which you can sand flush when the putty dries. Note that putty doesn't absorb stain like wood but takes on a solid color without grain or figure.

Because there are so many brands and types from which to choose, it's important that you read labels to see how various kinds of wood putty work. Items to consider include drying time of the putty, whether it shrinks when dried, whether it is stainable, and how it sands. As you work on furniture, you'll probably find yourself experimenting with different brands until you find the one that satisfies you most.

Wood putty works best when used to fill smaller blemishes like nailholes, nicks, or cracks. If possible, small scratches and dents should be either sanded or steamed out and large problem areas patched with matching wood, but there are certainly times when wood putty becomes necessary in furniture restoration.

You can buy wood putty in such generic wood-tone colors as mahogany, walnut, or maple, but the only accurate way to match it with your project is by direct sight comparison. Wipe raw wood with mineral spirits and match the wet wood putty to this color as closely as possible. You can mix dry powdered stain with the wood dough if needed to adjust the color for a closer match. Dry powdered stains are available in small quantities from finish touch-up supply houses or woodworking suppliers; they are dry, concentrated colors that will go a long way.

If the wood putty you use shrinks as it dries, you may need to make a second application to build it up so that you can sand it even with the wood's surface. If you're not satisfied with the way the putty looks after you've applied it and sanded it smooth, you can fine-tune the color match using an artist's brush and artist's colors or pigment from wiping stains. You can even paint in grain lines to

To match wood putty with the finished color of natural wood, wet the raw wood with paint thinner, then compare it with the color of the wet putty.

continue the grain pattern of the wood through the patched area.

Two-Part Epoxy Sticks. These are double-barrelled syringes with pre-measured amounts of colored epoxy and hardener. The colored sticks can be mixed to match the color of wood or stained to be filled. To get the best color match, colored epoxies are best used after wood has been stained. When matching heavily grained wood, match the lightest color then use graining pencils or pens to add the darker grain.

Two-Part Fillers. Another handy item for patching or repairing wood is two-part auto-body filler and a variation of this product developed (and colored) especially for use on wood. The fillers are thick, creamy substances to which you add a catalyst that causes them to heat up and harden in minutes. The cured filler can then be cut, carved, shaped, or sanded to any form you need. The two-part filler materials adhere well as long as the wood has been cleaned of other materials like finish or wax; they become extremely hard, making it easy to build up and shape large areas like corners and edges; they dry fast; and they do not shrink. You shouldn't use these materials for some pieces—particularly antiques—but for many applications they can yield wonderful results. These fillers work well, for example, if you have an area on a piece of furniture that your dog has chewed.

You can patch wood defects with standard wood putty (center), available in a variety of colors, or with two-part fillers (right), including auto-body filler (left). Two-part fillers need to be tinted before application, using dry powdered stains, or touched up to match the surrounding wood during the finishing process.

Two-part fillers don't absorb stain readily, so you'll need to add color to come close to the desired finished wood color. You can color the filler by using dry powdered stain then touching it up with an artist's brush. Use artist's colors or pigment from wiping stains to match the wood tones and the surrounding grain lines.

Paste Wood Filler. When wood filler is mentioned, the first thing that comes to mind for most people is the kind of wood putty mentioned above. Paste wood filler, also known as grain filler or pore filler, is not the same as wood putty or two-part filler. Paste wood filler is a creamy product used for packing into the pores of open-grain woods like oak, walnut, or mahogany. It provides a smooth, even surface on which a finish can be built. If you don't want a glassy-smooth, closed-grain look to your finish, paste wood filler is not necessary.

The paste comes in both water- and oil-based forms, and either will work well provided you follow label directions. Water-based filler dries considerably faster than oil-based. The quick drying time gives you less time in which to work, but it also means less waiting time before the next step in the finishing process. Available in neutral or tinted wood colors, paste filler can be further tinted with a tinting colorant such as Japan colors, artist's oil colors, or universal tinting colors. You should be able to get tinting colorants at a good paint, hardware, or art-supply store. Use Japan or artist's oil colors to tint oil-based filler; use universal tinting colors (UTCs) to tint water-based filler.

Paste wood filler is a creamy substance that's used to fill the pores of open-grained woods before finishing. The material helps produce a smooth closed-grained-looking finish.

Wood Stains

You may be surprised to learn that you won't need wood stain for some refinishing projects—for example, those pieces that have the natural wood color showing through. If you want to match a particular color, give inferior wood an expensive look, or bring out otherwise subtle grain patterns in wood, however, wood stain is a necessity.

To change the color of wood, you can choose from among many available products, including dyes (left half of photo), which come in both dry powdered and premixed liquid form, and pigmented wiping and penetrating stains. Some woods require grain filler (far right) before staining.

Wood stains, generally speaking, fall into two broad categories: pigmented stain, made up of finely ground color particles suspended in a solvent, and dye stain, made up of color particles dissolved rather than suspended in a solvent. There are also some stains that combine both pigment and dye.

Pigmented Stain. The most common form of pigmented stain, called a wiping stain, is oil-based, although you can also find it in water-based form. One of the biggest advantages of pigmented wiping stains is that they're easy to use and readily available in paint or hardware stores. They come in wood tones as well as white or light pastel colors for giving wood a pickled effect. Wood-tone stains work well when you're staining inferior woods such as poplar or birch to make them look like more expensive species. These stains also help to provide uniform color to otherwise uneven wood color. Some woods, such as pine, however, tend to result in a blotchy appearance when they are stained. Uneven wood density causes uneven color penetration.

Stain blotching *is caused by swirly grain or uneven density in wood. Pine (above) is among the woods that commonly blotch when you apply stain.*

Pigmented stains color wood by leaving colored pigment in the grain of open-grained woods (and on the surface of any wood). These pigments tend to settle to the bottom of the container unless they are agitated by stirring or shaking. The stains contain a solvent and a binder. The binder serves to hold the pigment in place so that it adheres to the wood surface. Because of the thick color pigments, pigmented stains tend to be opaque, which allows them to resist fading as a result of sunlight exposure. This opacity also makes them good for staining an otherwise unattractive wood to improve its appearance. On some woods that are naturally attractive, however, the opacity can mask their beauty. A better choice for such woods might be a dye stain.

Dye Stain (Aniline). While pigmented stains tend to be opaque, dye stains are translucent. This is true because the color materials are completely dissolved in the stain solution, allowing the stain color to penetrate into the wood rather than stay on the surface like pigment. Because of this, you can change the color of an attractive wood without masking its natural beauty. These stains aren't as readily available as other types; you may have to order them through woodworkers' or finishers' supply websites.

Dye stains are made from aniline, a derivative of petroleum and other related hydrocarbon compounds, and are often called aniline stains. The medium used for these dyes may be water, alcohol, or oil (mineral spirits or lacquer thinner).

Water-soluble dye stain comes in powdered form to be mixed in warm water. Because water stain will raise wood grain, you need to prepare the wood surface by wetting it with plain water. After the wood dries, sand it with extra-fine paper to smooth the raised grain and prepare it for staining. This will keep you from having to sand the raised grain after staining, thus cutting through the stain color. If you use water stain, allow the piece to dry overnight before finishing it.

Alcohol-soluble stain is much like water stain but uses alcohol as the solvent and does not raise the wood's grain. Alcohol stain can be bought premixed and is fast-drying, a disadvantage if you try to apply it any other way than with a spray gun. You can use alcohol stain for shading, tinting, or touch-up work.

Oil-soluble dye stains are also available in premixed form, although you can get them in powered form, too. The stains dissolve in mineral spirits or lacquer thinner; they are slower drying than alcohol-soluble dye stains and can be applied with a brush and rag much like a pigmented stain. Color penetration of oil-soluble dye stain is not as good as that of water-soluble dye, and the colors are susceptible to fading in sunlight. Oil-soluble dye stain also tends to lack the clarity of water stain.

Another kind of dye stain that is a substitute for water stain is NGR, or non-grain-raising, stain. NGR stains are water-soluble, but they don't contain water. The dye is first dissolved in a glycol ether solvent then thinned with alcohol or lacquer thinner. You can clean up NGR stains with water and add them to water-based finishes. As the name states, NGR stains do not raise the grain of wood as water stains do. NGR stains usually come in premixed form, and although they can be applied like water stain, they don't penetrate the wood as well. They also tend to lack the clarity of water stain.

Ready to Mix (RTM) Stains. These come in 12 water-based colors and can be mixed to match any stain color. Some kits include color chips and formulas.

The same color stain may look different, depending on the wood to which it's applied. Here the same stain was applied to maple (top), mahogany (upper middle), poplar (lower middle), and oak (bottom).

Gel Stains. Gel stains have become invaluable in furniture work, and they're particularly well suited to the novice because they're so easy to use. Gel stains are drip- and run-free, don't make a mess, and provide even, consistent color without showing overlap marks or blotchiness. Because of their thicker consistency, gel stains work well on vertical surfaces, whereas thinner stains present application problems. Gel stains come in an oil-based pigmented and in a water-soluble dye-stain form, which offers a user-friendly alternative to other dye stains. This type of dye gel is an excellent alterna-

tive to mixing up your own water stain, and it makes for easy application. You'll find some gel stains in hardware or paint stores, but you may have to order from a woodworkers' or finishers' supply site to get exactly the stain you want.

Stain Controllers. Stain Controllers can be used before applying a liquid stain to keep the stain from penetrating unevenly. Stain controllers (also called wood conditioner, pre-stain, and grain tamer) are composed primarily of slow-evaporating, petroleum distillate solvents. They work by filling up the pores and less-dense parts of the wood so the stain can't penetrate. The stain just mixes with the solvent near the surface.

To use a stain controller successfully, apply it to the wood with a brush or rag until all parts of the wood stay wet and no more of the liquid is absorbed into the wood. This usually takes successive applications for 5 or 10 minutes, but the number of applications needed will vary depending on the wood and the ingredients used in the stain controller.

When no more dry spots appear on the wood, wipe off all the excess stain controller and apply the stain as quickly as possible—within 30 minutes is best. If you wait too long, enough of the stain controller will have evaporated or been absorbed deeper into the wood so that the stain will again penetrate and blotch the wood.

Tack Cloth

The tack cloth is a rag used to pick up dust and other materials from the surface of bare or finished wood before applying a new coat of finish. You can buy tack cloths at hardware or paint stores; they are relatively inexpensive. Store-bought tack cloths contain a varnish-like substance to make them sticky so that they will attract and pick up dust and other loose particles that could otherwise get trapped in the finish. They've also been chemically treated to keep them from drying out. Using a tack cloth will give you a smooth, more professional-looking finish.

If you want to make your own tack cloth, use a 12-inch square of lint-free cotton rag or cheesecloth. Dip the rag in warm water, wring it out, and then dip it in turpentine or mineral spirits and wring it out again. Drip varnish over the rag's surface, and squeeze the rag into a ball until varnish is distributed throughout the rag, making it tacky enough to pick up dust but not so wet that it will leave varnish on your surface.

To keep your tack cloth from drying out, keep it in a sealed container—a jar or self-sealing plastic bag. If it does dry out, repeat the above process to rejuvenate it.

FINISHES

In furniture restoration, "finish" refers to the material that coats the wood for the purpose of protecting and beautifying it. Although a finish can be tinted or colored, usually it's clear or almost clear. Except for painted finishes, the wood is usually colored using wood stains, wood fillers, or bleaching prior to applying the finish. In furniture restoration, shellac, lacquer, varnish, polyurethane, oil, wax, and paint are commonly used.

Stains, paint, and clear finishes (left to right) are made of just three ingredients: Stains and paints contain colorant (usally pigment), binder, and solvent or thinner; finishes are simply binder and solvent or thinner.

Solvents

There are three basic solvents important in preparing finishes and in general furniture restoration: lacquer thinner, denatured alcohol, and mineral spirits. Keep in mind that these solvents can be dangerous if you don't follow the label directions concerning the use of protective clothing and equipment and safety practices for fire and explosion prevention.

Lacquer Thinner. Lacquer thinner is the strongest of the three solvents; it is so strong that it will quickly dissolve both shellac and lacquer finishes. As its name suggests, its primary use is for thinning lacquer. Lacquer thinners are also good solvents for cleaning up a piece of furniture after stripping off the old finish. Because it's a strong solvent and will dissolve or soften most finishes, it's handy to have in your shop for cleaning out spray guns and brushes.

Lacquer thinners can be formulated differently, and some cheap types that are good for cleanup work may not work well for finishing. Evaporation time may also vary for different lacquer thinners, which will affect lacquer-drying time. If the lacquer dries too slowly, it can slow down the finishing process and allow dust to settle in the finish. If the lacquer dries too fast, other problems, such as blushing, can arise. Moisture becomes trapped in the finish, causing it to "blush," or appear milky or cloudy. Thinner problems are usually associated with spray lacquer finishes because brush lacquers are already formulated for brushing and don't have to be thinned.

If you're using the thinner to thin a lacquer finish, check the label of the lacquer material to see whether a particular thinner is recommended. If no thinner is recommended, it's usually best to begin with a standard lacquer thinner ("medium" or "normal" evaporation speed). Then add lacquer retarder (a slow-drying thinner) to slow the evaporation rate to suit the prevailing temperature or humidity conditions.

Alcohol. Like lacquer thinner, alcohol can dissolve shellac and lacquer finishes, but it is weaker, making it a much slower-working solvent. Denatured alcohol is used primarily for thinning shellac. If you're applying a shellac finish or homemade French polish, you'll need to have denatured alcohol on hand. Sometimes this solvent is also useful for rejuvenating an old shellac finish by dissolving and redistributing the old finish and then reapplying a coat or two of new shellac. This process is called reamalgamation, and it sometimes requires the addition of some lacquer thinner to the solvent mix.

Mineral Spirits. Mineral spirits, or paint thinner, is used for thinning and cleaning up oil-based paint and varnish, but it has additional uses in furniture restoration. It's a good cleaning solvent for washing down old finishes to remove wax, silicones, and oil. Mineral spirits alone will dissolve and remove old waxes and oils, but it will only dissolve silicone, not remove it. To remove the dissolved silicone, follow the thinner by washing the surface using a solution of 1 cup of ammonia mixed in 1 gallon of warm water. You can sometimes then rewax or recoat the old finish to revive it. Mineral spirits also helps remove silicones from raw wood (following the procedure above), preventing problems when applying a finish. Other uses of mineral spirits include cleaning brushes, thinning pigmented oil stains and wood filler, and using it as a lubricant when wet-sanding finishes like shellac or lacquer.

Shellac

The granddaddy of modern "film" finishes, shellac is manufactured much as it was decades ago from a resin secreted by the tiny lac insect in India and Southeast Asia. Shellac was originally sold in dry form as flakes, granules, or buttons, which were dissolved in denatured alcohol to produce liquid shellac. Although you can still buy shellac flakes, at the hardware store you'll most likely find it in premixed form in various "cuts": 1-pound, 2-pound, 3-pound. The pound measurement indicates the amount of dry material that has been dissolved in one gallon of thinner, thus a 1-pound mix would be thinner than a 3-pound mix.

Advantages. Shellac is one of the best finishes for bringing out the beauty of a good piece of furniture. If the wood is attractive to begin with, shellac will enhance that quality and give it a charm hard to achieve with other finishes. This is probably due to several factors. Shellac has no synthetic ingredients or added plasticizers, which can create an artificial look. Each successive coat of shellac melts into the previous coat, bonding with it to form a single layer of finish on the wood's surface. A good shellac finish can be built on most woods in about three or four coats with a scuff sanding between coats (and it dries quickly; you can apply several coats in one day). The last finish coat can be waxed by rubbing it down with paste wax on a #0000 steel wool pad, followed by a buffing with a soft cotton rag. This allows for great clarity and depth, and because of its flexibility, the finish is non-chipping. Also, the natural orange tint of amber shellac imparts a warm glow to the finish.

Shellac was used to produce the classic French polish finish representative of many eighteenth-century European pieces. Modern shellac results in a nice Old World look and is appropriate on many older or antique pieces. Although this time-honored material may be outdone in some ways by synthetic finishes that are more durable, it's difficult to surpass the natural beauty of shellac.

As mentioned, natural shellac has a distinctive orange tint, which helps achieve a warm depth in the finish. White shellac, which is just bleached orange shellac and is actually clear, is also available. White shellac is a good alternative if you're finishing a light-colored or bleached wood and want to maintain the wood's original color. You can also buy flakes in blonde (lighter than orange but not quite clear) and darker colors, including garnet. Flakes are also available dewaxed—needed if you're planning to use polyurethane as a topcoat (poly and some other clear finishes won't stick to natural shellac, which has some wax in it).

Shellac was originally applied with a soft pad, or "rubber," as it is called in the method known as French polishing, but shellac can also be sprayed or brushed on, drying quickly for sanding and recoating. Shellac is often used as a sealer coat to prepare

Common finishes include shellac (bottom left), oil-varnish (bottom right), and various kinds of paints and varnishes (middle row). For most finishes, you'll need sandpaper and steel wool (top left), as well as a tack cloth (top right) for rubbing between coats.

wood for other finishes. This sealer coat acts as a barrier, locking and sealing contaminants in so that they do not produce adverse reactions such as fish eye in lacquer, small areas where the finish separates on the surface, resembling the eyes of a fish. To use shellac as a sealer, you apply what's called a "wash coat" of shellac to raw wood and then scuff-sand the surface before applying the other finish.

Disadvantages. After considering the many good characteristics of shellac you might think, "Why use any other finish?" But shellac, like all finishes, has some drawbacks, including a short shelf life—about six months—after it's mixed. Once its shelf life has expired, "old" shellac won't dry after application, and you'll have to strip the finish from the wood. Because old shellac doesn't look any different, you won't know whether a questionable finish is bad until you apply it to the wood and wait to see whether it dries. If you have time, you could coat a sample piece of wood before applying shellac to your furniture.

The best way to make sure the shellac is still good is to mix it from flakes, granules, or buttons, or to buy liquid-form shellac in amounts corresponding only to your current project. This may seem troublesome, but it will save you extra work in the long run. Shellac finishes get scratch marks more easily and are not as durable as some other finishes, such as lacquer and varnish. White water rings, stains, and other blemishes are also a common problem because shellac is not as resistant to water or alcohol as lacquer and varnish.

Lacquer

If you talk to a professional furniture finisher about finishes, before long lacquer will come up, and with good reason. Lacquer dries quickly, picks up few dust particles between coats, can be recoated quickly, penetrates wood well, adheres to previous coats by melting into them, is more durable than shellac, and can produce any number of sheens from matte to high gloss. Lacquer is a good, practical, attractive finish that can be built up to many coats in a short amount of time.

Since the 1920s, lacquer has become the most widely used furniture finish. Most new furniture has a lacquer finish. Two common types of lacquer for woodwork are nitrocellulose and cellulose acetate butyrate (CAB). There's not much difference between these formulations, except that CAB lacquer is more resistant to chipping and does not yellow with age, making it a good choice as a clear coating over white finishes.

Another type of lacquer, available in several forms, is called catalyzed lacquer. One kind of catalyzed lacquer contains a catalyst that is premixed during manufacture; another kind is a two-part version that has a catalyst you add just prior to applying the finish. This type should be mixed only as needed because it has a short shelf life once mixed.

Catalyzed lacquer produces a tough, durable finish. The secret to it's toughness is the catalyst. After the finish dries through solvent evaporation, the catalyst causes a chemical reaction to take place that continues to harden, or cure, the lacquer for up to a few days. The following information applies to all lacquer except that catalyzed lacquer is harder and considerably more resistant to scratching, heat, water, and solvents.

Water-based lacquer has also been developed as an alternative to solvent-based lacquers in order to avoid some of these pollution and flammability. (This is also addressed on page 61 under Water Based Finishes).

Advantages. Although conventional lacquer is not highly resistant to either solvents or heat, it offers more water resistance than shellac. A lacquer finish also offers good clarity and depth as long as you apply it properly and the finish doesn't blush. (See "Lacquer Thinner," page 56, for a description of the blushing problem.) You can rub out or polish lacquer to produce just about any type of sheen.

An evaporative finish, lacquer requires only about 15 to 30 minutes to dry. Because lacquer is quick-drying, you can apply several coats in the time it takes to apply one

Fish eye *will occur in a lacquer finish if any wax, oil, or silicone is left on the surface when finishing. The effect is exaggerated here by applying a dark finish over a white substrate.*

coat of a finish like varnish. Fast drying also helps prevent dust and other particles from settling into the finish surface. Lacquer is similar to shellac in that each coat softens and bonds with the previous coat, forming a single layer of finish on the wood's surface.

Problems. Despite all its pluses, lacquer still has some negatives. Because it dries so fast, lacquer is considered a spray-on finish. To spray a lacquer finish you'll need a professional spray system including spray gun, air compressor, air lines, and filter, not to mention a safety-approved exhaust system that can run into thousands of dollars in expense. This is an investment for the professional finisher that pays for itself over time, but for most do-it-yourselfers it's impractical.

Lacquer dries so fast because it requires a high percentage of volatile thinner to maintain the solids in solution. The large amounts of thinner evaporate quickly, and that causes the main problem with lacquer: air pollution. Many parts of the country restrict the use of lacquer. Lacquer is also highly flammable and toxic. You need to be careful when you use lacquer, and you should wear a respirator.

Spray lacquer's quick-dry feature can sometimes cause blushing. You can control blushing by using a slower-drying lacquer thinner in the lacquer mix and by adding a retardant. The retardant further slows the drying time and allows moisture to escape from the surface before the finish dries. It also allows the lacquer to flow out better.

Fish eye is another problem associated with lacquer. If the wood surface has any wax, silicone, or oils left on it when you apply the finish, these areas will appear as crater-like fish eyes. Rather than use shellac as a sealer coat to prevent fish eye, as mentioned earlier, you can add fish-eye eliminator to the lacquer mix (according to label directions) to solve the problem. Once you add fish-eye eliminator to the lacquer, each successive lacquer coat must also include it.

Variations. Lacquer sanding sealer can be used as the first coat or two when finishing with lacquer. The use of a sealer can improve adhesion between the finish and the wood. It also provides a barrier coat to seal in any contaminates that may remain on the wood's surface. Lacquer vinyl sealer is recommended for this purpose, but a wash coat of shellac will accomplish the same thing. Sanding sealer also works well to build up a smooth, even surface in preparation for the lacquer top coats. To aid in this, sanding sealer contains stearates. These stearates are soft, powdery soap-like substances that act as a lubricant for ease in sanding and add body to the finish, enabling it to build more quickly.

Sanding sealer *contains a lubricant that causes the finish to powder easily when you sand it.*

Although most lacquer finishing is done with a spray gun, lacquer is also available as a brushable finish. Because lacquer dries so rapidly, brushable lacquer contains special solvents to slow down drying so you have time to brush it on, although you have to work quickly. Even with these added solvents, brushable lacquer still dries fast and requires a little more practice than some other brush-on finishes. Once you get the hang of it, though, you can produce a good-looking, durable brush finish.

Because the solvents in lacquer are so strong, brushing can disturb some stains, particularly pigmented stains. To avoid this, seal the stain first with a coat of shellac. Some brush-on lacquers are self-leveling, meaning you can apply them generously to horizontal surfaces and brush marks will all but disappear. Two or three coats of brush lacquer will provide a good water- and alcohol-resistant finish.

Lacquer is also sold in aerosol cans. Don't try to do a total refinishing job with aerosol cans of lacquer, but you can use them with excellent results for touch-up work or spot finishing. You can also use them for spraying a finish that has been cleaned to revive it, particularly on smaller items like chairs. The important thing about aerosol lacquer is to make sure to get a brand that has a good spray nozzle, as this will affect how the finish goes on the piece, which determines the final look. Finding the best spray nozzle is a matter of trial and error through trying several different brands.

Lastly, aerosol lacquers release a lot of material into the air. This produces a lot of overspray (a dry, rough, powdery form of lacquer), so you'll need good ventilation for safe use of any spray lacquer.

Varnish

Varnish is one of the toughest, most durable wood finishes, standing up well to heat, moisture, alcohol, and wear. The biggest drawback to finishing with varnish is its slowness in drying. This makes varnish a good brushable finish but also allows it to collect dust particles while drying. You'll need to sand between coats, with rubbing and polishing on the last coat to remove these particles. It also means your finishing schedule will have to last two or three days or more, depending on the varnish type and the number of coats desired.

Oil-based varnishes have been used for centuries. They are made up of resins, drying agents, oils, and thinner solvents like turpentine or mineral spirits. Before the twentieth century, varnishes used natural resins, usually fossilized pine sap. Since then, synthetic resins have been developed that are cheaper, more available, more consistent in quality, and more durable than natural resin varnishes. Alkyd, phenolic, and polyurethane are three types of synthetic resin varnishes.

Alkyd Varnish. Alkyd resin varnish, although slow-drying, produces a highly durable, attractive interior finish. It's available in gloss or satin sheen, and can be sanded and rubbed out on the last coat. Alkyd varnish is flexible and not as hard as polyurethane, so it's less brittle and will not chip as easily.

Phenolic Varnish. Phenolic resin varnish is usually called spar varnish and is excellent for exterior finishing work such as boat woodwork. Phenolic varnish is usually only available in a gloss sheen. It's flexible, allowing wood to expand and contract in exterior conditions without cracking the finish, and it also resists the sun's ultraviolet rays. The finish sometimes contains ultraviolet absorbers to help prevent it from yellowing or darkening with age. Because of its flexibility, phenolic varnish is not as resistant to abrasions as some finishes and can sometimes show worn areas with time and use.

Polyurethane Varnish. Polyurethane is highly resistant to water, alcohol, abrasions, and heat; it is available in gloss, semigloss, satin, or flat versions. It can be applied by spraying or brushing. It's the clearest of the varnishes and rubs out well on the last coat. It also tends to be faster drying than other varnishes, thus eliminating some of the problem of dust particles settling into the final finish.

Because polyurethane will not dissolve or melt into previous coats as will lacquer or shellac, it's important to scuff-sand the finish between coats to provide for proper adhesion. Polyurethane is a tough, durable, practical finish, but you may want to consider its appropriateness for your piece, especially if it has historic or collectible value. Some furniture experts and collectors consider the look of polyurethane, especially waterborne formulations, to be too artificial or plastic. In truth, all modern film finishes contain plastic; it's just that polyurethane tends to be a little more cloudy in appearance, giving it a slightly more artificial look. Film finishes without plastic would include those used prior to the twentieth century, including shellac and natural resin varnishes.

Advantages. Varnish is especially good as a furniture finish. It has excellent water and alcohol resistance, and it's more solvent-, heat-, and abrasion-resistant than lacquer or shellac. It also brushes well, so it's easier for a nonprofessional to use.

Disadvantages. Varnish brushes well because it cures slowly, and this presents a quality-control problem: The surface can collect dust before it dries, resulting in a poor finish. It has a short shelf life because it easily skins over. The finish is hard to rub out to an even sheen, and it doesn't repair well, owing to its solvent resistance.

Oil Finish

Oil finishes have been used for years and work well to enhance the natural beauty of wood. They are some of the easiest finishes to apply; it's hard to make a mistake. Oil finishes can even be applied without using a brush or any special equipment: You just wipe them on, let them soak in, and wipe them off. All you need for the work are a few rags. Be sure to dispose of all oily rags properly. (See "Dispose of Used Rags Properly," on page 27.)

Oil finishes are usually extremely thin, so they don't offer much protection for the wood surface. Because oil finishes penetrate deep into the wood, they tend to darken and intensify the wood's natural colors. Also, oil finishes can be extremely difficult—or impossible—to totally remove from wood if this ever becomes necessary.

Also consider your stain type if you plan to use an oil finish: Highly pigmented stain may restrict the penetration of an oil finish into wood. Basic types of oil finishes include linseed oil, tung oil, and penetrating resin, or Danish oil.

Linseed Oil. Linseed oil was the oil finish used by many old-time wood finishers and is still used by some people today. It's exceptionally slow to dry and never really gets completely hard. Because raw linseed oil is so slow-drying, manufacturers add dryers to speed up the process. This form of linseed oil, known as boiled linseed oil, is best for finishing work.

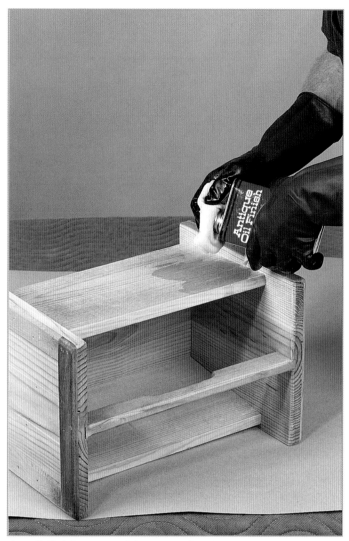

An oil finish *is one of the easiest finishes to apply: You just wipe it onto the wood surface and then wipe it off. Some oils take a long time to dry completely, however.*

Although linseed oil is easy to apply, it must be applied in multiple coats, with rubbing between them, to build up the finish to any degree. Some finishers say you must apply the oil twice a day for a week, twice a week for a month, twice a month for a year, and twice a year for life. Others say the schedule should be once a day for a week, once a week for a month, and so on. Although this kind of diligence in the finishing process can provide beautiful results, it still doesn't offer the wood much protection because of the softness of the oil and its inability to resist heat, wear, and moisture. Linseed oil, then, can make a fine finish for wood not subjected to any of these conditions, but more modern oils and finishes may still be a better choice for most furniture.

Tung Oil. Tung oil is derived from the nuts of the tung tree, which is native to China, and dries faster than raw linseed oil but slower than boiled linseed oil. It also produces a finish slightly more durable than lin-

seed oil. Tung oil usually comes in a thinned-down form for ease of finishing. The finishing process is similar to that of linseed oil, in that it requires multiple coats to produce a satisfactory finish. The number of coats needed depends on the type of wood and the look you're trying to achieve.

Unlike linseed oil, tung oil does not necessarily require continued, year-after-year coating; but if the finish begins to wear or dull, a new coat of tung oil will always renew it.

Oil-Varnish Finishes. These penetrating resin finishes are more-modern versions of oil finishes, producing excellent results with less time and effort. Often sold under names like Danish Oil and Teak Oil, these finishes are essentially a mixture of oil and varnish. Manufacturers claim that the finishes "toughen the fiber of the wood," but because this type of finish tends to be relatively soft when dry, it's doubtful that it adds any real strength to a substance that is already as hard as wood. With multiple coats, the finish will eventually build above the wood's surface and produce a thin film. You can rub the surface down with #0000 steel wool between coats and after the last coat to produce a good-looking satin finish.

Penetrating resin finishes are available in clear or in various stain colors with the idea of accomplishing the staining and finishing processes in one step. In addition to the standard liquid variety, pentrating resin finishes are available in a gel form. Still an oil-varnish combination, sometimes using polyurethane as the resin, the gel is also a wipe-on finish, making for easy application.

Water-Based Finishes

Finish manufacturers developed water-based finishes primarily to address air-pollution problems created by solvent-based finishes like lacquer. Water-based lacquer, for example, has a much lower volatile or-ganic compound (VOC) level and is less toxic and much less combustible than solvent-based lacquer. Its higher solids content allows the finish to build more quickly, too.

Some professionals were slow to adopt water-based finishes when they were first developed, but they've come a long way since. Water-based finishes can now be sprayed, brushed or padded on, and can be polished to a high-gloss sheen. A primary advantage is that if you need to do a repair in your home, there is very little smell to deal with.

Water-based polyurethane can be applied much like an oil finish by generously brushing it onto the wood, allowing it to penetrate, and then wiping off the excess. After several coats, with light sanding between coats, you can paste-wax the finish, producing a thin oil-finish look.

Paint

Some people may consider paint an unacceptable option for furniture finishing. I agree that many beautiful woods have been hidden under the stroke of a paint-laden brush, all in the name of giving the piece a new look. When you finish—or refinish—a piece with wood originally meant to be seen, you should always use a transparent finish. Some pieces were created to be painted, however, such as many of the old Hoosier kitchen cabinets. Often many different types of wood were used in one cabinet, with the idea that they would be covered by paint.

Opaque, or solid-colored, finishes are available in pigmented shellacs and lacquers, pigmented oil varnishes or oil paints, and pigmented water-based finishes or latex paint. These opaque finishes work basically like their transparent counterparts with the same preparation, application techniques, and drying times.

When applying paint to raw wood or over a previously painted or finished surface, follow label directions for undercoating and sealing prior to the final top coats. Just as clear finishes reveal and amplify surface imperfections, a painted finish will do the same, sometimes more so. Be sure to give preparatory work necessary attention to produce a professional-looking finish.

Paints are basically opaque versions of the clear finishes already discussed, with corresponding applications and characteristics. Opaque lacquer, for example, is a spray-on rather than a brush-on finish. If you have a spray system set up for refinishing, it works great and produces a tough, durable furniture finish. A wide variety of colors are available from auto paint supply stores. Lacquer paints are also available in spray cans for small finishing jobs.

If you don't have the necessary equipment to spray a lacquer, you can use one of the brushable paints available. The most common ones are either oil-base paints (alkyd resin enamels) or latex paints (latex enamels). Oil-based paints are considered pigmented varnishes, and they handle basically the same. As with varnish, thinning can be done with mineral spirits. Latex paints are like water-based varnishes, with thinning and clean-up done with water. These paints come in flat, satin, semi-gloss, or high-gloss sheens in an almost unlimited variety of colors. Some paints are designed for interior use and some are designed for either interior or exterior. This will be indicated on the label, and

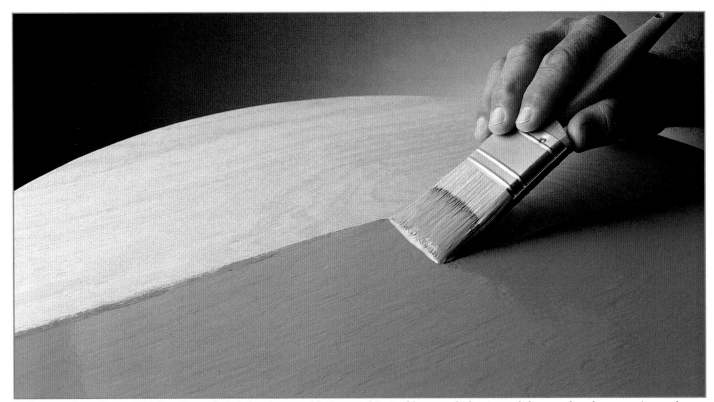

Paint can be a beautiful furniture finish *for chairs, table tops, cabinets. It's a good idea to seal the wood and use a primer when applying paint.*

of course the finish surface characteristics will vary accordingly. Interior-exterior rated paints are formulated to withstand moisture and sunlight much better than coatings designed only for interior use.

When using paints to finish wood, you'll usually need to use an undercoat (primer) before applying the paint. This will provide a good foundation for the final finish coats. The primer coat can usually be tinted to more closely match the final paint color, making it easier to cover with the paint coats.

An alternative to using a primer coat is to use a thinned-down version of the paint itself as an undercoating. As with primer, sand this coat with very fine sandpaper when it dries in preparation for the top coats. Usually you can do a painted finish with three coats, one primer coat, and two top coats. Shellac can also be used as a sealer when painting raw wood or when painting over other finishes or paints left on the wood. Shellac works as a good barrier coat, sealing in resins from woods like knotty pine, which would otherwise bleed into the paint. It also forms a barrier between the paint and otherwise incompatible finishes which may already be on the wood.

When choosing paint for furniture, keep in mind that the higher the sheen, the greater the reflectivity of the surface and the more it will show any surface imperfections. Although a flat sheen may not be appropriate for most furniture, a satin or semigloss can offer excellent protection and hide many surface blemishes.

FINISHING TOUCHES

Once you've applied the finish to a piece of furniture, you're almost done restoring it. All that's left to do is to put some finishing touches on the piece, such as waxing the finish, adjusting the sheen with abrasives like pumice or rubbing compounds, polishing the hardware, or cleaning any glass.

Wax

You can add protection and sheen to many film finishes, especially glossy ones, using wax. A good furniture wax is a paste wax containing at least some percentage of carnauba wax. It's important that it contains carnauba wax because this is the hardest furniture wax available. Furniture paste wax is available in various amber, dark, and clear shades.

A wax finish is an easy-to-apply, wipe-on finish but it is usually not suitable by itself because it offers so little protection for the wood. Wax is normally used only as a top coating for other finishes such as shellac. It's a good idea to replace wax every year or two by washing the surface down

You can coat furniture with paste wax (far left) or liquid wax (far right rear) for a high-gloss sheen once you've applied the finish. You can also give the finish a satin or semigloss look by rubbing it with a premixed rubbing compound (left and center rear, right front) or an abrasive like pumice or rottenstone (center), followed by a coat of wax.

with mineral spirits using a nylon abrasive pad or #0000 steel wool and then reapplying the wax.

For pieces that will receive little or no wear, paste wax alone can provide a good, thin, natural-looking finish for the wood. Once you apply wax directly to raw unfinished wood, however, it can be extremely difficult to later remove completely if you decide to try another type of finish.

An alternative to applying paste wax alone as a finish is to use it in conjunction with shellac. For heavy-use items such as tables and servers, apply paste wax on top of the cured finish. This will help to repel moisture and stains, and allow for easy clean up. Plus, it can cover up minor scratches.

Pumice and Rottenstone

Pumice and rottenstone are finely ground mineral materials that can be used as fine abrasives, along with an oil or water lubricant, to rub out the final finish coat.

Rottenstone. Rottenstone is a very fine gray powder, used with either oil or soapy water and a felt pad or soft cloth to rub it out. Rottenstone produces a satin to semigloss sheen.

Pumice. Pumice, a white powder, is the coarser of the two, and is usually used with an oil sometimes thinned with mineral spirits to produce a dull to satin sheen. A felt pad or soft rag is used for the rubbing process.

Rubbing Compounds

Rubbing compounds are similar to pumice and rottenstone, in that they are abrasives used to rub out the final coat of finish to get a particular sheen. The difference is that they are premixed in liquid or paste form and you do not need to add additional oils or lubricants.

Although many compounds have been formulated to work on automotive finishes, most will work fine on furniture finishes and will produce various degrees of gloss sheen. Keep in mind if you want to achieve a gloss or high-gloss finish, you'll probably have to sand the surface with a very fine wet-or-dry sandpaper (400- to 600-grit or finer) before polishing out the surface with compound. When you use compound to polish a table top to a gloss sheen, a power buffer with a lamb's-wool or foam pad makes the job go faster.

Burn-in Sticks. Also called shellac or lacquer sticks, you can use burn-in sticks to fill dents and scratches on finished surfaces without damaging the existing finish.

These hard, solid sticks of finish come in a variety of solid, clear, amber, and translucent colors that allow you to repair just about any finish.

You melt the sticks with a hot knife or burn-in iron, dripping the material into the dent or scratch. As the material cools, it rehardens. You then sand the area with a sanding block and very fine sandpaper (usually wet-sanding with 400–600-grit wet-or-dry paper). Sand it to level and smooth the burn-in material with the surrounding finished surface without cutting through it. You can then rub out the surface with #0000 steel wool or recoat it with finish to blend in the sheen with the existing finish.

Burn-in shellac or lacquer sticks are available from finish, repair, and touch-up supply companies. You can find these companies listed or advertised in woodworking magazines and online. You can also call a local furniture shop for information about sources. Be sure to ask about the shelf life of the sticks when ordering so you don't overstock your shop.

Brass Cleaner and Polish

The furniture restoration process often includes cleaning and polishing of brass or brass-plated hardware. You can clean and polish some hardware with an electric buffing wheel, using various buffing and polishing compounds. You can also use ordinary ready-mixed liquid brass polish available at most hardware stores and simply follow the label directions.

If you're feeling really adventurous, you can make your own brass-cleaning solution by adding baking soda to ammonia; the baking soda acts as a mild abrasive and the ammonia acts as a strong cleaner.

Cleaning and polishing hardware becomes part of the furniture-restoration process sooner or later. You can use an electric buffing wheel with polishing compound, premixed brass polish (above), or a homemade solution of ammonia and baking soda.

PART II
FURNITURE REPAIRS

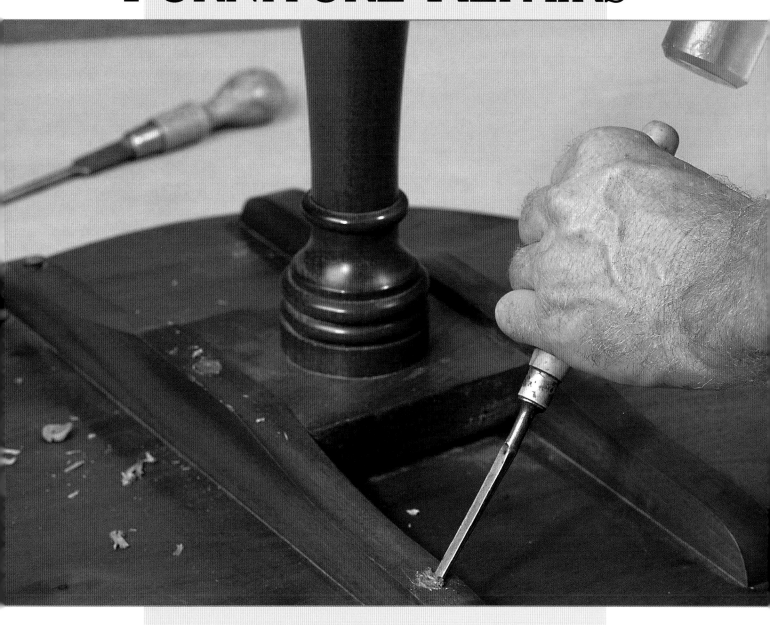

5
STRUCTURAL REPAIRS I: LOOSE JOINTS

A basic knowledge of joints is important in furniture repair for a number of reasons. If joints are loose on a piece of furniture, you'll probably have to disassemble the piece to reglue it. When you look at the exterior surface of a joint, you may only see a line where the two pieces of wood meet. Your knowledge of joints can give you understanding of what's hidden below the surface of that line, enabling you to work the joint loose without breaking it. If you have a broken joint or pieces are missing, knowing the type of joint you're working with allows you to repair it properly.

Recognizing different kinds of furniture joints can also help you determine the quality of a piece. If you discover that a chair is constructed using mortise-and-tenon joints as opposed to dowel construction, for example, you can be sure it's a high-quality chair. The same is true about furniture with dovetail construction on the drawers as opposed to rabbet-joint drawers. Dovetails are a better joint and will last indefinitely.

TYPES OF JOINTS

There are a number of ways to join two pieces of wood, but most are variations of the following basic joints:

Butt Joint. This joint is made when two pieces of wood are butted together and glued. Boards are commonly joined end grain to edge grain, edge grain to edge grain, or edge grain to face grain, although other configurations are possible. When you glue an end-grain surface of one board to another wood surface, the joint won't hold unless it's reinforced with dowel pins or some other reinforcement. The reason for the reinforcement is that the end grain of wood doesn't provide enough solid surface for the bonding process to take place. When magnified, end grain looks much like the end of a group of drinking straws bunched together. Consequently, the open end of the grain fibers absorbs most of the glue you apply to the joint and doesn't leave enough on the surface to provide a good bond.

When you use the butt joint to glue two or more boards side by side, or edge grain to edge grain as when making a wide top for a table, however, the joint can be quite strong. You must make sure that the joining edges are planed smooth to form a perfect fit, though, and that the joint is glued and clamped sufficiently.

Lap Joint. This joint is created when two pieces of wood overlap one another at a right angle.

| Edge to Edge | End to Edge | Edge to Face |

Butt Joint. *A butt joint occurs when two pieces of wood are butted together and joined. The most common—and strongest—butt joint in furniture is edge to edge (also known as long grain to long grain).*

Full Lap

Half Lap

Lap Joint. *When two pieces of wood overlap one another at a right angle, they form a lap joint.*

Usually at least one piece of wood is notched out, allowing the other piece to fit down into it. This kind of lap joint is called a full lap joint. Both pieces may also be notched to half of their thickness, allowing them to fit into each other. This joint is known as a half-lap joint.

Miter Joint. The miter joint is formed by cutting corresponding angles, usually 45 degrees, on the ends of two pieces of wood and joining them together. The most common use of the miter joint in furniture is in mirror and picture frames. The miter joint may be reinforced with pins or dowels or with the installation of a wooden back panel, often ¼-inch plywood.

Rabbet Joint. When you notch the end or the edge of a piece of wood and use that notch to join two boards, you've created a rabbet joint. You can also make a rabbet joint by notching both pieces of wood. The rabbet joint is not a strong joint in itself and is usually secured with fasteners like nails or screws. Sometimes drawer sides are joined to the fronts with rabbet joints. Rabbet joints are used in

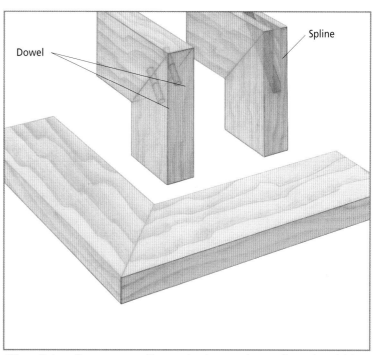

Dowel

Spline

Miter Joint. *Cut corresponding angles in two pieces of wood and join them, and you've formed a miter joint. Miter joints are often reinforced using dowels or a spline.*

casework furniture like chests or in some drawers to join the sides to the front and/or back. Cabinet backs can also be joined to the case with rabbet joints.

Dado Joint. A dado is a groove cut across the grain of a piece of wood. A dado joint is formed by cutting a dado in one piece of wood the exact size as the square-cut edge of another piece. The square-cut edge of the second piece is then inserted into the groove of the first piece to form a tight, secure joint. This type of joint is also usually glued. Dado joints are commonly used to join wood at right angles, as in bookcase shelves.

Sometimes the dado is hidden because the groove is not cut all the way across the board to the front of the bookcase. This kind of dado joint is called a blind dado.

Mortise-and-Tenon Joint. The mortise-and-tenon is one of the strongest furniture joints, and its use usually signifies quality furniture. The joint is normally formed by cutting a square tongue—the tenon—on the end of one piece of wood and an equal-size square hole or slot—the mortise—in another. The tongue of the first piece is then inserted into the slot of the second. Although not necessary, sometimes a pin or peg is also

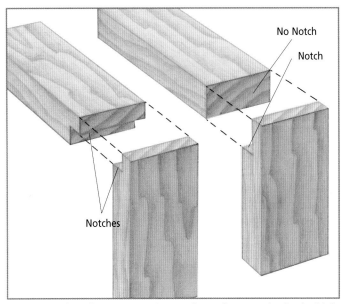

Rabbet Joint. Joining two pieces of wood, one or both of which are notched, creates a rabbet joint.

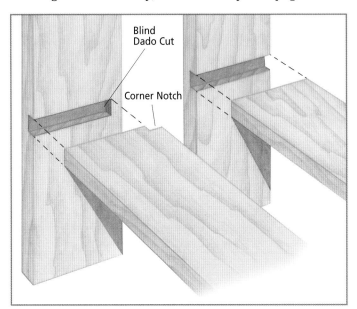

Dado Joint. Cut a cross-grain groove large enough to accept a second piece of wood. Cutting the dado short creates a blind joint.

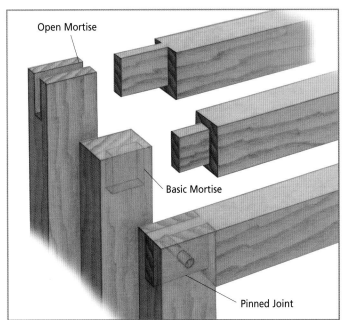

Mortise-and-Tenon Joint. Form a mortise-and-tenon joint by cutting a tongue, the tenon, on one piece of wood and a matching hole or slot, the mortise, in the joining piece.

Mortise-and-tenon joints like these are sometimes locked together by the insertion of pegs through the joint. The pegs are visible on the outside of this table leg.

inserted through the joint, perpendicular to the tenon, locking the joint together. Mortise-and-tenon joints have been used not only in furniture but in the construction of centuries-old wooden bridges, barns, and houses. Many of these structures still stand today, a testimony to the strength and stability of this joint.

Dowel Joint. Dowel joints are basically substitutes for mortise-and-tenon joints. Many modern pieces, particularly chairs, are constructed using dowel joints. A dowel joint is made by fitting a butt joint then drilling corresponding holes in the two pieces of wood to be joined and inserting the dowel pin or pins before joining the pieces. Glue is used in this type of joint, and the dowel pins serve as round tenons, holding the two pieces together. Although dowel joints are commonly used and are easier to make than a mortise-and-tenon joint, they usually aren't as strong.

Dowel Joint. *A dowel joint is fairly strong, but it's basically nothing more than a butt joint reinforced with dowels.*

Dovetail Joint. The dovetail joint is one of the most distinctive and best joints used in furniture construction to join wood at a right angle. Easily distinguishable by its multiple flared tenons, which interlock like fingers and look like doves' tails, the dovetail forms a strong, durable joint. Most commonly used to attach drawer sides to drawer fronts, dovetail joints almost always indicate quality furniture. Antique and handmade furniture was built using hand-cut dovetails created with fine-toothed saws and chisels. Modern manufactured dovetails are cut by machine and are usually distinguishable from the hand-cut type because the interlocking flared tenons, called pins or tails, are exactly the same size and are evenly spaced. Hand-cut dovetail joints usually have tails that differ slightly in size and may vary in spacing. Machine-cut dovetails are excellent, strong joints, but the old hand-cut variety is still hard to beat.

Dovetail joints can be constructed using either "through" dovetails or "half-blind" dovetails. Through dovetails are cut all the way through the thickness of both joining pieces of wood, with the "fingers" visible from two sides. Half-blind dovetails are cut so that the dovetails are visible only from one side. An example of a half-blind dovetail joint would be where a drawer side is joined to a drawer front with dovetails that are not visible on the face of the drawer front.

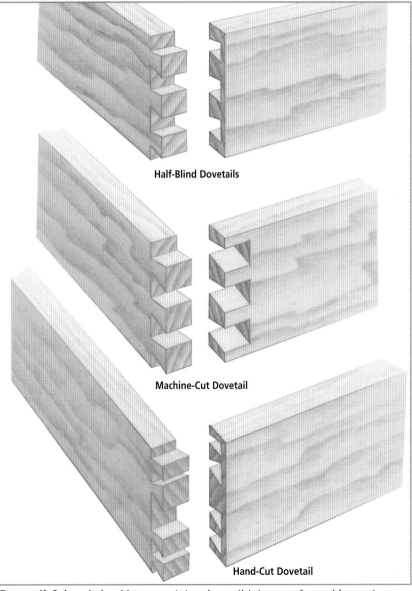

Half-Blind Dovetails

Machine-Cut Dovetail

Hand-Cut Dovetail

Dovetail Joint. *A durable corner joint, dovetail joints are formed by cutting alternating dovetail-shaped tenons called tails and pins in two pieces of wood and joining the pieces by interlocking the two. The cuts may be made by hand or machine.*

LOOSE JOINTS

Loose joints are among the first problems you'll likely encounter as you begin to repair furniture, and they can be a problem on virtually every type of furniture. As you reglue loose joints on your piece using the step-by-step instructions included in this section, you may encounter other problems, such as broken joints or splits and breaks in the wood. (See "Splits and Breaks in Wood," page 129.) If so, incorporate this repair into the regluing process. Because all regluing projects are not as simple as they might appear, I've included some problem areas to look for when regluing joints.

To fix a loose joint, in most cases you'll have to disassemble, clean, glue, reassemble, and clamp it. To take a joint apart, first make sure it isn't pegged or pinned. (See "Removing Pegs from Joints," page 71.)

Taking Joints Apart. Tap the joint with a rubber mallet or a hammer and a softwood or cork block. Begin tapping softly at first, and strike it only as hard as is necessary to break the joint loose but not hard enough to damage or split the wood. If the joint is too tight to break apart, it may not need regluing. If it's still necessary to separate the joint, drill a small hole into the joint and inject a 50-percent warm water and 50-percent vinegar solution into the joint, allowing it to soak for a while to loosen the glue. Tap the joint occasionally to see whether the glue has softened, loosening the joint.

Regluing in Subassemblies. When regluing furniture, some pieces may have too many joints or may be too awkward to reglue all at once. In such cases you can often reglue components of the piece in subassemblies. On frame chairs with the main back post or stile con-

tinuing down in one piece to form the back leg, for example, you can reglue the chair's entire back section independently as one component. After the glue dries and you remove the clamps, you can glue the rest of the chair together with the back section.

With armchairs, sometimes you can add the arms after you've glued the rest of the chair, as long as you check to be sure they fit properly before the rest of the chair is dry. Some platform chairs, such as Windsor chairs, have back support posts that fit directly into the seat, where the base of the chair (consisting of seat, legs, and stretchers or foot rails) can be glued independently. You can then glue and attach the back later.

Joint Reinforcements

In addition to the pegs and pins mentioned earlier, other items to look for when disassembling loose joints are corner blocks, glue blocks, wooden buttons, wood screws, and metal braces.

Corner Blocks. These are angle-cut blocks of wood installed on inside corners of chair frames and table aprons. Corner blocks reinforce corner joints and are usually glued or screwed in place. When you reglue joints, remove and reglue all corner blocks.

Glue Blocks. Similar to corner blocks in that they're used to reinforce joints, glue blocks are small blocks of wood, usually square or triangular shaped, commonly used to help attach chest or table tops to frames or bases. When you disassemble a piece, pay special attention to glue blocks that might be hidden under chests and the like, and be sure to loosen them with a chisel and mallet before trying to take the joints apart.

Corner Blocks. *Often used in chairs and table frames, corner blocks are pieces of wood cut to fit into and reinforce corner joints.*

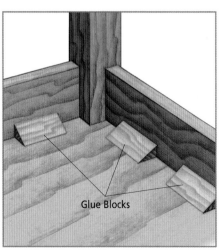

Glue Blocks. *Table and chest tops sometimes need extra gluing surface to hold them in place. That's where small triangular or square glue blocks come in.*

Screws. *Wood screws are often used to reinforce a joint, especially in table tops. The screws are attached through countersunk holes or screw pockets.*

Wooden buttons are decorative covers for countersunk wood screws. You can remove them by prying them out.

Screws. Wood screws and metal brackets are frequently used to assemble or reinforce joints. Many table tops and chest or dresser tops are held on with wood screws. Always look beneath tops for screws or metal brackets when disassembling furniture, and be sure to remove them before knocking joints apart.

Wooden Buttons. Wooden plugs or buttons are sometimes used to cover countersunk wood screws. You can remove these covers by inserting the tip of a scratch awl under the button edge and popping it out. Or you can use two chisels, one on each side of the button, to

pry out the button. The screws can then be removed and the joint disassembled.

Removing Pegs from Joints

When you begin to disassemble a joint, look closely for pegs (small dowels) and pins (tiny brads or nails) that may be inserted through the joint to lock it together, and remove them before taking the joint apart.

Difficulty Level: 𝍦

Tools and Materials

Scratch awl	Drill and assorted bits
¼-inch chisel	Mallet
Needle-nose pliers	Appropriate-size dowel
Backsaw	

1 Drill the peg. If a wooden peg or dowel is inserted through the joint locking it together, hammer it out with a same-size dowel. If the peg won't move, make a center point in the end of the peg with a scratch awl. Choose a drill bit just smaller than the diameter of the peg, and drill out the peg using an electric drill.

2 Remove the peg. After drilling, loosen the remaining bits of the peg by gently tapping a ¼-inch chisel around its perimeter. Grasp the peg shards with needle-nose pliers and remove them. After regluing the joint, replace the peg with a new dowel of the appropriate diameter and cut it flush with the wood surface using a backsaw or a flush-cut saw.

1 Drill out the wooden peg using a slightly smaller drill bit.

2 Loosen the peg shards using a narrow chisel, and then grasp them with needle-nose pliers to pull and remove them.

PINNED JOINTS

Pegs are usually apparent, but sometimes you have to look closely for nails because the nailhead may be countersunk and covered with wood putty. If you discover nails, try one of two removal processes:

• Pull the pin out with diagonal pliers, which may require digging around the head of the nail with a wood chisel. (See "Repairing Loose Headboard and Footboard Joints," page 101.)

• Drive the nail all the way through with a nail set, if possible, and pull it out the other side.

Brad

Stretcher Rail
or Chair Rung   Wedge

Chair Stretcher Rails. *Insert a wedge into the end of a stretcher rail or rung to make it fit more snugly in a loose joint.*

Veneer Shims

Tenons. *You can attach thin pieces of veneer as shims to one or both sides of a loose-fitting tenon to make it fit more snugly.*

Loose Dowels, Rungs, and Tenons

After cleaning a joint and test-fitting it, you may find that it's too loose to form a strong joint. You'll need to take care of this obstacle before proceeding with regluing. Problems sometimes encountered when regluing joints include loose-fitting dowels, chair stretcher rails, or tenons.

Dowels. If dowels fit too loosely, the best solution is to remove each dowel and drill out the hole using a twist bit to accommodate the next-larger-size dowel. To keep the holes aligned you may need to use a doweling jig. (See "Using Dowels to Fix a Broken Joint," page 115, for how to use the jig.) Install the larger dowel pins, making sure you cut them to the correct length (slightly shorter than the depth of the hole to allow room for glue) before proceeding with your regluing schedule.

Chair Stretcher Rails. Chairs often have horizontal members called stretcher rails that run between the legs. A rounded stretcher rail is called a rung. If a stretcher fits too loosely in the joint, remove it from the chair and put it in a vise with the end facing up. Using a backsaw, cut a kerf in the center of the end of the rail

deep enough to accommodate a small wedge, and drill a small hole at the base of the kerf. Cut a wedge from a piece of hardwood the width of the stretcher diameter, and tap it into the kerf at the end of the rail until the rail end expands to the proper size. Cut off the end of the wedge, and then test-fit the stretcher rail into the hole before regluing it.

Tenons. If a tenon is too loose, remove it from the mortise and cut some shims (thin pieces of wood used to fill space) to the same size as the tenon. Veneer pieces will usually work for this purpose. Use as many shims as necessary to widen the thickness of the tenon, placing them wherever the tenon is loose fitting. Glue and clamp the shims to the tenon until the glue is dry. Next, test-fit the tenon into the mortise, sanding or trimming the shims if necessary for a precise fit before regluing.

LOOSE JOINTS IN CHAIRS

Structurally speaking, chairs get the hardest use of any furniture. If you own—and use—chairs for 10 years or more, they will probably need at least some regluing, depending on their construction and frequency of use.

At first glance, chair repair seems simple and straightforward. But don't be fooled by the chair's relatively small size. Chairs generally incorporate at least a dozen—and as many as 20 or more—joints in their basic construction. In addition, despite the fact that chairs are the one category of furniture that's virtually useless if not structurally sound, their design is often weak and fragile. To complicate matters further, chairs tend to break at their weakest point, which can be the most difficult place to repair to its original strength. These weak points are usually where two or more parts intersect to form joints. A back post, for example, that has been mortised or drilled for adjoining seat rails can be weak and may break. Repairing this problem can be difficult because several joints occur in the damaged area, and a back post gets a considerable amount of stress from use.

Fortunately, many times the only problem with chairs is that the joints have loosened. Although chair styles and construction vary, the following procedures are basic and common to most chairs when they need regluing.

Loose Joints in Chairs. *Although they're small, chairs are complicated structures with a large number of joints.*

Regluing Joints without Disassembly

There are times when a joint may be loose, but it's difficult or even impossible to take the joint apart. If a chair has an upholstered, caned, or rush-woven seat that's in good shape, you may not want to remove the seat or ruin it by cutting it out just to reglue a few loose joints.

Other joints that are difficult or impossible to disassemble are the wedged joint and the shrink joint, usually used on older chairs to lock the legs and stretchers or rails together. A wedged joint is formed when a wedge has been inserted into the end of a stretcher rail or rung, expanding the end of the member as the wedge is tapped into the hole. This locks the joint tight, making it difficult to disassemble.

A shrink joint is created when a chair stretcher or leg is turned from dry wood with a knob-type end on it. This knob end is inserted into the hole of the other member while that wood is still green. As the green wood dries, it shrinks, tightening around the knob end of the dry wood

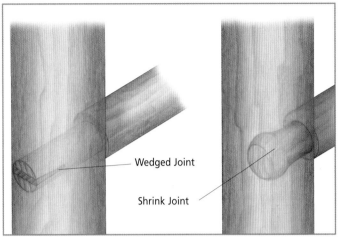

Regluing Joints without Disassembly. *Wedged joints (left), where a wedge locks a chair stretcher or rung in place, and shrink joints (right), where the knoblike end of a chair member is held firmly in place when green wood in the mating member shrinks around it, are difficult to remove, even if they become loose.*

member and locking the two pieces together. This joint is also difficult to separate without splitting the wood.

If you encounter any of these situations, you may want to reglue the joint or joints without taking them apart. This procedure entails getting glue around the mating joint parts without actually being able to get at the parts themselves.

Difficulty Level: 🔨

Tools and Materials

Drill and assorted bits	Clamps
Wood glue and injector	Rag
Appropriate-size dowel	

1 Drill a glue hole. Drill a small hole, about ⅛ inch in diameter, inconspicuously under the joint on a slight angle directly into the mortise, or hollowed-out area, in the wood.

2 Inject glue. Put about an ounce of polyvinyl or hide wood glue in a syringe-type glue injector (available from woodworkers' websites or hardware stores) or in a glue squeeze bottle with a narrow tip. Thin the glue by adding about 25 percent water, and mix it well. Insert the syringe or glue-bottle tip into the hole you just drilled, forcing the glue into the joint. Move the loose joint back and forth, being sure to work the glue throughout the joint.

3 Clamp the joint. Install a clamp on the joint, and then plug the glue hole with a small dowel pin of the appropriate diameter and clean up any glue that's been squeezed out of the joint. Allow the glued joint to dry for several hours.

1 Drill a small angled hole in an out-of-the-way location under the joint.

2 Insert the syringe tip into the hole, and inject the glue into the joint.

3 Clamp the joint tightly, plug the access hole with a same-size wooden dowel pin, and clean up excess glue.

Regluing a Chair

In this case, you're able to take apart the entire chair, clean all the joints, and glue the chair back together.

Difficulty Level: 🔨 🔨

Tools and Materials

Screwdrivers	Masking tape and marker
Rubber mallet	Solvent or rasp, chisels, or utility knife
Clamps	Rag
Mineral spirits	
Wood glue and glue brush or palette knife	
#0000 steel wool, and wax	

1 Check the joints. Take off the seat if it's removable to check the joints. If the chair has a slip seat, a removable upholstered seat that slips out of the chair frame, check under the seat for screws that hold it in place. Remove the screws and put them in a labeled plastic bag so you can find them when you're ready to reinstall the seat.

Some chairs don't have slip seats; the upholstery is attached directly to the chair seat rails. It may not be necessary to remove all the upholstery, only that which is around the loose joint: In this case, carefully remove only the upholstery necessary to work on the joint you want to fix. You can tack the upholstery back in place after you complete the job.

Check all the joints to find out which ones are loose by applying pressure to the joint. If there's any movement at all, you should probably reglue the joint, as it will continue to loosen with use. Also, if possible, determine what kind of joints (usually dowel or mortise-and-tenon) the chair has, and look closely to make sure pegs or nails are not driven through the tenons or dowels. If you find pegs or pins, you must drill them out or remove them before you try to separate the joint. (See "Removing Pegs from Joints" and "Pinned Joints," pages 71 and 72.)

2 Label and disassemble the chair parts. If the chair has corner blocks inside the seat frame, label them and the inside of the seat rails with masking tape and corresponding numbers. Remove the screws, and put them in a labeled bag. Using a mallet, tap the corner blocks loose.

NOTE: After removing corner blocks, check to see whether the screws fit tightly in the block screw holes. If so, enlarge the holes so the screws fit loosely in the block. When you reinstall the blocks to the chair frame, this will ensure that the screws act as a clamp, tightening into the chair frame and pulling the corner blocks up tight.

Label all chair parts with corresponding numbers using masking tape labels so you'll make no mistakes when reassembling the chair. Make sure the finish on the wood is sound before labeling if you're not refinishing the chair. Use blue quick-release tape if you're unsure of the soundness of the finish, and be careful when peeling it off. Beginning with the loosest joint, tap it apart with a mallet. Continue tapping joints apart until you've removed all the loose parts. Be careful not to apply unnecessary force, which could split or break the chair.

1 Apply pressure to each joint to see which ones are loose and need to be repaired.

2 Label all the joints with masking tape, and then knock them apart using a rubber mallet.

3 Clean the joints. Clean old glue from the joints using adhesive solvent or by gently scraping with a rasp, a chisel, or the edge of a utility knife. To clean dowel holes, use an old drill bit of the proper size or a narrow wood chisel.

3 *Clean all old glue from the joints using solvent or by carefully scraping with a rasp, a chisel, or the edge of a utility knife.*

4 Test-fit the parts. After you've cleaned all the joints, assemble the entire chair without glue to make sure everything fits properly. You may be tempted to skip this step, but don't. It's frustrating to get glue on the joints only to find that something doesn't fit properly or you've accidentally mixed up the parts. If this happens, usually the glue will be set by the time you get the problem straightened out, and you'll have to clean the joints again.

5 Glue up the chair. Take the chair apart, and begin to apply hide or polyvinyl wood glue. Cover all the joint surfaces with a thin layer of glue, spreading it with a glue brush, a palette knife, or a small dowel. Assemble the joints as you apply the glue.

6 Clamp the joints. After you've assembled all the parts, apply clamps to pull all joints up snugly but not overly tight. Make sure you cushion steel clamp jaws with plastic caps or softwood blocks to keep from damaging the chair's finish. Wipe off all excess glue using a wet or damp rag, and check all the joints to make sure they're pulled up tight.

4 *Test-fit all the joints after cleaning to make sure everything goes together properly.*

5 *Apply hide or polyvinyl wood glue to all joint parts, assembling the joints as you go.*

NOTE: If the wood surface is finished, you can allow the excess polyvinyl glue to set for about an hour or so, and then simply peel it off with the help of a razor blade or sharp wood chisel. Make sure you don't allow the glue to set completely, however, or you won't be able to remove it without damaging the finish.

6 *Once you've assembled all the joints, apply clamps where needed to snug up the joints.*

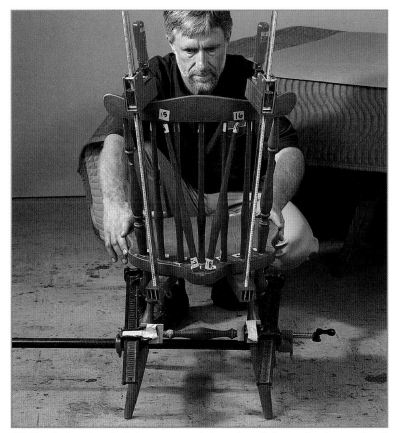

7 *Check that the chair is square and doesn't rock by setting it on a level surface.*

7 Square up the chair. Set the chair on a level surface, and make sure everything is square. Check that the chair doesn't rock and that any slip seats will fit back into the seat framework. Let the chair dry overnight.

Remove all clamps and labels, and do your final cleanup using mineral spirits and #0000 steel wool. After cleaning, you may have to use polish or wax to brighten the finish.

LOOSE JOINTS IN TABLES

There are many kinds of tables: dining, coffee, end, bedside, sofa, console, card-and-game, and lamp tables. Although these tables have a variety of styles, they all consist of a flat top supported by legs or a base. Generally, the construction of the legs or base follows one of two basic designs: pedestal-type tables or frame-type ones.

The pedestal table is usually made up of a single column supported by three or four legs. A block is mounted to the top of the column, which in turn is mounted to the underside of the table top. Tilt-top tables are pedestal tables made so that their tops can tilt up to a vertical position, allowing them to be placed in the corner of a room.

The frame table consists of a frame with legs at each corner. The legs may be joined to the frame with bolts, dowel joints, or—in the best tables— mortise-and-tenon joints. The top is then attached to this leg-supported frame.

Whether you're dealing with a pedestal or frame table, your primary concern will be the legs or table base when you reglue loose joints.

PEDESTAL-STYLE TABLES

Regluing pedestal-table legs can be challenging because of the odd angles you're likely to encounter when clamping some of the joints. With improvisation and special clamp blocks, however, you can overcome these difficulties. (See "Clamping Jigs for Pedestal Tables," page 79.)

Pedestal tables usually become loose in any of several areas: where the legs join the pedestal column, where the mounting block joins thetop of the pedestal column, and where the top attaches to the mounting block. Legs are joined to pedestals in a variety of ways including dowels, mortise-and-tenons, sliding dovetails, and even lag screws on some hollow-pedestal Victorian-style

Catch

Pivot

Mounting Block

Bearer

Turned Column

Metal Plate

Leg

Pedestal tables have several weak spots: at the leg-and-column joint, at the mounting-block-and-column joint, and at the table-top-and-mounting-block joint.

Repairing Dowel & Mortise-and-Tenon Leg Joints

If the pedestal column is solid and you can't see any evidence of the joint by looking at the bottom of the column, the legs are likely joined by either dowel or motise-and-tenon joints. You'd reglue both kinds of joints in the same way.

Difficulty Level:

Tools and Materials

Chisels	Mallet
Wedges (if necessary)	Clamps
Masking tape and marker	Rag
Clamping jig (if necessary)	
Glue solvent or rasp, chisel, or utility knife	
Wood glue and glue brush or palette knife	

1 Remove the legs. Turn the pedestal upside down, and insert a wood chisel downward into the bottom of the leg joint. Tap the chisel with a mallet to loosen the joint. As the joint loosens at the bottom of the column, tap the leg on top of the foot to loosen the top of the leg joint. Alternately tap the bottom and top of the leg until it can be removed. If the joint is stubborn, make narrow hardwood wedges and drive them into the joint to help separate it.

2 Clean the joints. Make sure all the matching joint parts are labeled with numbers; then clean off old glue from all the joint surfaces using solvent or a chisel, knife, or wood rasp. Test-fit the legs to ensure that the joints fit properly, and install any clamps you'll use to be sure they'll work to

tables. Some pedestals also have metal plates attached to their bottoms to lock the legs together at the column. If legs are loose and need to be reglued, remove the metal plate (also called a spider) first and reinstall it after the job is complete.

If the legs seem loose, turn the table upside down and inspect the various joints to see which ones have movement in them. Then follow the appropriate instructions for regluing or tightening.

1 Use a chisel and mallet to loosen the leg joints. A wedge can help in loosening a stubborn leg.

THE PROS KNOW

CLAMPING JIGS FOR PEDESTAL TABLES

As anyone who's worked in a furniture shop can tell you, clamping pedestal legs can be a challenging task. You may need to make a clamping jig to pull up the joints in certain pedestal-leg configurations. Here are two time-tested jigs, one using wood blocks and plywood and the other using ¾-inch plywood.

Make a block-and-plywood jig. Cut a solid piece of wood (about the same thickness as the leg) and a piece of ¼-inch plywood the same size. The length and width of these pieces will depend on the size of the pedestal legs to be glued. Make sure the block and plywood are large enough to fit the leg as illustrated. Trace the outline of the leg on the wood block as shown, and cut the block at the traced outlines.

Mount the two end pieces of the block onto the ¼-inch plywood as shown using glue and small nails. After the glue dries, the block is ready to use as illustrated. To protect the leg's finish you can glue felt to the inside edges of the block where it makes contact with the leg.

Make a plywood jig. Trace and cut out blocks of plywood to fit the legs so the plywood will hook over the toe as illustrated. Cut a notch at the top of the block as shown. You may want to line the block with felt or some other padding where it makes contact with the leg to prevent finish damage. You can also make the block thicker for large legs by gluing two pieces of plywood together. After fitting the legs to the pedestal column, pull them tight using a tourniquet clamp or a band clamp.

Wood Block

¼" Plywood

Cutout Pieces of Wood Block

¼" Plywood

Bar Clamp

Column

Leg

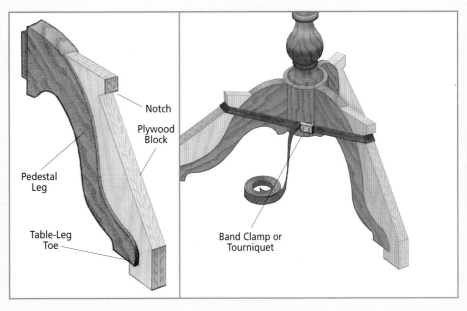

Notch

Plywood Block

Pedestal Leg

Table-Leg Toe

Band Clamp or Tourniquet

pull the joints tight. If the clamps are too awkward or won't mount properly to tighten the joints, consider making a clamping jig before regluing the legs. (See "Clamping Jigs for Pedestal Tables," page 79.)

3 Glue the joints. Once you're sure the legs fit properly and you have the proper clamping method to tighten the joints, remove the legs from

2 *Label the joints, clean off old glue, and test-fit them using clamps to make sure the clamps fit.*

3 *Apply hide or polyvinyl wood glue to all joint surfaces, and assemble the joints as you glue them.*

SLIDING-DOVETAIL JOINTS

Sliding-dovetail joints are excellent for joining legs to a pedestal column. This joint virtually locks the leg into the column with a flared tenon, almost guaranteeing that the joint won't come apart. To determine whether the legs are mounted to the column with sliding dovetails, check the pedestal bottom and look for dovetail-shaped tenons extending into the column of the table.

Sliding-Dovetail Joints.
Common on well-made pedestal tables, a sliding dovetail locks the legs into the column with flared tenons.

Dovetail (Flared Tenon)

Mortise Cut for Leg Tenon

Pedestal

Even though this kind of joint rarely if ever comes completely apart, it can loosen. Most often this is caused by the column itself splitting around the dovetail joints. If a split in the column is the problem, often you can work glue into the split and clamp it without having to remove the leg. (See "Repairing a Split in a Pedestal-Table Column," page 133.) If the dovetail itself is loose, you may need to remove the leg and repair the split in the column before remounting the leg.

To reglue sliding dovetails, hold the table base right side up and tilt it until the loose leg is off the floor or bench surface. Tap the top of the leg at the column with a rubber mallet to drive the dovetail down and out of the column. Carefully clean old glue from both joint surfaces using solvent or a chisel, rasp, or knife.

If there are splits in the column, repair them by working glue into them using a thin spatula and clamping until the glue is dry. Reassemble the dry leg joint to ensure a proper fit. If the dovetails fit too loosely, glue a thin strip of veneer to one or both sides of the dovetail. After the glue dries, trim the shimmed dovetail to fit the mortise. Apply glue to all joint surfaces, and install the legs as you apply glue. You won't need clamps as long as you keep the pedestal upside down while it's drying.

LAG-SCREW TABLE-LEG JOINTS

When the pedestal column is hollow, special fasteners with a screw thread on one side and bolt thread on the other (sometimes called rail bolts or hanger bolts) are used to attach the legs. The fastener extends from the leg through the wall of the pedestal column and is held by a nut and washer.

If the legs become loose, tighten them by turning the pedestal upside down and reaching into the bottom of the hollow column to tighten the nut on the end of the bolt with an open-end wrench. As you tighten the nut, the leg should pull up tight. If the nut doesn't tighten, the screw side of the fastener is probably stripped out of the table leg. (See "Repairing a Tilting Table Top," page 83, for instructions on how to fix a stripped screw hole.)

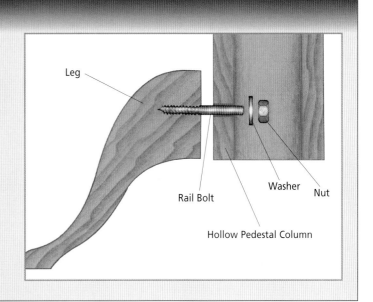

Leg

Rail Bolt

Washer

Nut

Hollow Pedestal Column

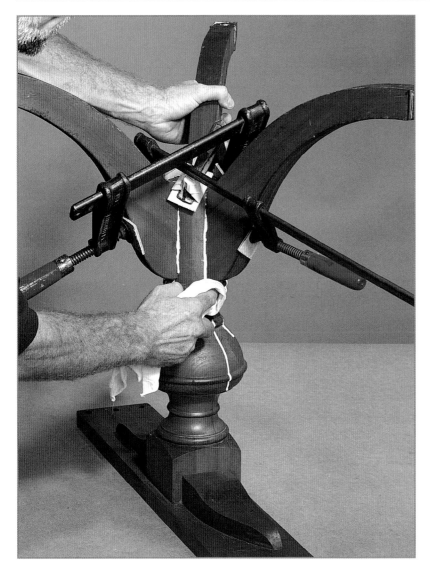

4 Apply clamps to tighten up the joints, and clean off glue squeeze-out using a damp rag.

the pedestal again and apply glue to all joint surfaces, spreading it to a thin film. Assemble the joints as you go.

4 Reassemble the piece. Install the clamps and tighten them to pull the joints up snug; do not overtighten. Clean excess glue from joints with a damp rag, and make sure they're tight. Be certain the legs are aligned properly with the pedestal and each other. After the piece dries, remove the clamps and clean up the finish with #0000 steel wool and mineral spirits. Use wax or polish to brighten the finish.

Repairing a Loose Pedestal Table Top

If the top of a pedestal table is wobbly or loose and the leg joints are tight, turn the table over and check where the mounting block joins the top of the pedestal or where the table top joins the mounting block. When you turn the table over, place it on a padded surface so you don't scratch the top.

The mounting block is usually attached to the pedestal with a mortise-and-tenon type joint. The top is usually attached to the mounting block with screws or bolts. Check these screws first to make sure they're tight. Sometimes a wobbly top can be stabilized simply by tightening the screws or bolts. If this doesn't help, the mounting block is probably loose where it joins the column, and you'll have to reglue it.

1 Back the screws out of the mounting block using a screwdriver, and remove the top.

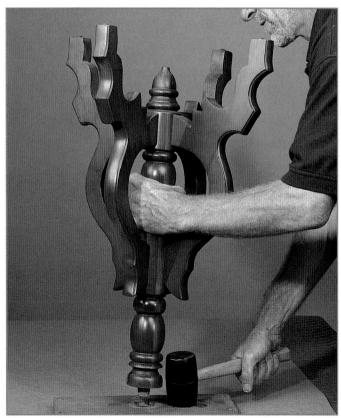

2 Tap on the mounting block using a rubber mallet to separate it from the pedestal column.

Difficulty Level: 🔨 🔨

Tools and Materials

Screwdrivers	Rubber mallet
Clamps	Rag
Solvent or rasp, chisel, or utility knife	
Wood glue and glue brush or palette knife	

1 Remove the top. With the table upside down on a padded surface, remove the screws that attach the table top to the mounting block, and remove the top.

2 Remove the mounting block. Check the top of the mounting block to see whether the tenon extends through the block. If so—and the joint is only slightly loose and hard to disassemble—drill a few small holes down the sides of the tenon and inject thinned glue (with 25 percent water) into the holes with a syringe or squeeze bottle, and work glue into any loose parts of the joint using a thin spatula. Clamp the joint, and let it dry. If the joint is loose enough to disassemble, tap on the bottom of the mounting block around the column to separate the two pieces. If the joint does not separate easily and the tenon is exposed on the top of the mounting block, turn the pedestal right side up and set the mounting block across an open vise or a pair of sawhorses. Use a wooden block and hammer to tap the tenon top, driving it out of the mounting block.

3 Clean the joint. Clean old glue from the joint using solvent or by gently scraping with a rasp, chisel, or knife. Test-fit the joint. If the tenon is wedged, you may want to remove the old wedge and make a new one from hardwood. Do not install the wedge until the final gluing.

3 Clean the old glue off all joint surfaces. Use solvent or carefully scrape with a rasp, chisel, or knife, and test-fit joint.

4 Apply glue to the joint parts, and clamp the joint. Clean off excess glue, and check the assembly for alignment.

4 Glue and clamp the assembly. Disassemble the joint, and apply glue to the joint surfaces. Reassemble the mounting block to the column, tapping it into place. Apply clamps, and reinstall the tenon wedge if necessary. Clean excess glue from the joint, and check for tightness and alignment. Remount the top to the mounting block when the glue is dry.

Repairing a Tilting Table Top

As mentioned previously, tilt-top tables have a pedestal base with a top that can swing up vertically. Although the legs and mounting block are usually joined to the column in a way similar to other pedestal tables, the top is attached to the mounting block differently.

In most cases, two long pieces of wood called bearers are mounted with wood screws to the underside of the top. The mounting block is generally situated between these two bearers, with two dowel pivots on one end of

the block extending into the bearers and allowing the top to tilt. The top usually latches down on the mounting block with a brass spring catch at the opposite end from the pivots.

If the top of the table wobbles, it's probably because the screws holding the bearers are stripped. To take the tilting top off the base, remove the screws from one of the bearers. Sometimes these screws are concealed by wooden plugs or putty, which must be removed to expose the screwheads. After you remove one bearer, the entire top will come loose from the block.

If one or more of the bearer mounting screws are stripped, install larger-gauge screws of the same length. If this doesn't work, remove the bearer and plug and redrill the appropriate screw holes as follows.

Difficulty Level: 🔨 🔨

Tools and Materials

Screwdrivers	¼-inch chisel
Drill and assorted bits	Masking tape
Appropriate-size dowels	Fine-tooth backsaw
Wood glue	Scratch awl

1 Remove the bearer. Turn the table upside down to remove the bearer from the table top. Be sure to use a padded surface so you don't mar the top. Remove any wooden buttons or dig out the putty concealing the mounting screws using a ¼-inch chisel. Back the screws out using a screwdriver.

1 Dig out the putty or buttons hiding the screwheads, and back out the screws using a screwdriver.

2 **Drill new holes.** Drill out the stripped screw holes in the table top. Use a ⅜-inch-diameter bit to install a same-diameter piece of dowel. Measure the depth of the table top, and mark a slightly shorter depth on the drill bit with tape so you don't drill the hole completely through the top.

3 **Mark, cut, and install the dowels.** After drilling the hole or holes, insert a section of dowel and mark it for cutting. Cut the dowel to size with a fine-toothed saw, and install it with glue into the hole.

4 **Drill new holes.** When the glue is dry, set the bearer back in its original spot. Extend a scratch awl through the bearer's screw holes and mark a center hole for drilling new pilot holes. Remove the bearer, and drill the holes for the bearer screws using the appropriate-size bit. Be sure to mark the depth on the drill bit to keep from drilling through the top.

5 **Replace the bearer.** Reinstall the bearer using the original screws. This time, however, they will tighten into the new holes you've made.

2 *Drill out the stripped holes using a ⅜-in.-dia. bit. Mark the bit for depth using tape.*

3 *Mark a ⅜-in.-dia. dowel, cut it to length using a backsaw, and glue it in place.*

4 *Put the bearer back in place, and use a scratch awl to mark a center point for new holes.*

5 *After drilling the new screw holes, reinstall the bearer using the original screws if possible.*

Top

End Rail

Side Rail

Mortise-and-Tenon Joints

Turned Leg

Rail

Leg

Rail

Wing Nut

Metal Corner Brace

Frame-Style Tables. The connection between the legs and the rails of frame tables may be through joinery (main drawing) or through corner braces and bolts (inset).

FRAME-STYLE TABLES

The legs of a frame table may be attached to the frame or apron through joinery or bolts. The majority of older frame-style tables have legs joined to apron rails with dowels or mortise-and-tenons.

Many modern tables, especially dining-room tables, use rail bolts (fasteners with a screw thread on one side and bolt thread on the other) to attach the legs to wooden corner blocks or metal corner braces on the table's underside. Though not a mark of high-quality construction, this kind of leg joint holds up fairly well and is easy to tighten unless the screw holes in the leg have been stripped.

To check for the kind of construction your table uses, turn the table over and look at each corner where the leg mounts. If you see a wooden corner block with no bolts or nuts visible, the legs are attached via joinery. If you see a corner block or metal brace with one or more bolts coming out of the leg and extending through the block or brace, the legs use rail bolts.

Regluing Table Legs

Because the joints in a frame table may take a large amount of stress over the years, especially if the table

is moved often, as when adding and removing extension leaves, even mortise-and-tenon joints may come loose. You'll have to disassemble the joints and reglue the table.

Difficulty Level: 🔨 🔨

Tools and Materials

Screwdrivers	Rag
Clamps	Scratch awl
¼-inch chisel	Wood glue
Chisels and mallet	
Masking tape and marker	
Solvent or rasp, chisel, or utility knife	

1 Remove the table top.
Turn the table upside down on a padded surface, and examine the underside to see how the top is attached to the base. Most table tops are attached using screws through metal clips or wooden blocks or directly through the apron or frame of the base. Remove the screws, and place them in a sealable, labeled plastic bag. Look for additional glue blocks that may be used to attach the top. If you find any blocks, break them loose using a wood chisel and mallet. These can also be saved and reinstalled when reattaching the top.

1 Turn the table upside down, and remove the screws holding the table top to the rails.

2 Label the joints. With the top removed, label all the leg joints using masking tape and a marking pen. Give each leg a number, and code the leg and adjoining joint part with the same number.

3 Separate the joints. Disassemble the labeled joints by striking the inside of each leg with a mallet and working the leg free by moving it back and forth gently but persuasively.

4 Clean the joint parts. Clean the mating parts of the joints with solvent or by gently scraping with a chisel, rasp, or knife edge. Make sure you remove all old glue, but be careful not to take off any wood in the scraping process, if you choose to go that route.

5 Reassemble the table. Apply glue to all the joints, and put the table frame back together again, using clamps. Make sure the table top fits properly and that the screw holes in the frame align with the holes in the top. It's a good idea to align these holes using a scratch awl and to reinsert the screws to hold the frame in the proper position before tightening down on the clamps, cleaning the glue, and allowing the joints to dry.

2 Using masking tape and a marker, label all the joints you'll take apart so you don't get them mixed up.

3 Knock the joints loose using a mallet, and work the legs free from the rails.

4 Use solvent or a rasp, chisel, or knife to remove all old glue from the joints.

5 Glue and clamp the joints tight. Make sure that the legs and the table frame are square before allowing the glue to dry.

Repairing Bolted Legs

If your table has bolted legs and any of them are loose, try tightening the nut. If the nut continues to turn without pulling up the leg, the screw is stripped out in the leg. You'll need to plug the screw hole.

1 Turn the table upside down, and free the leg by removing the nut using an adjustable or open-end wrench.

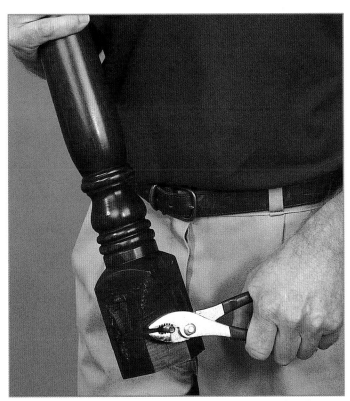

2 Remove a badly loosened bolt using pliers, and plug the stripped hole with a dowel.

Difficulty Level: 🔨

Tools and Materials

Adjustable or open-end wrench
Appropriate-size dowel (if necessary)
Pliers   Drill and assorted bits
Scratch awl   Masking tape

1 Remove the leg. Turn the table upside down on a padded surface. Back the nut off the bolt using an adjustable or open-end wrench, and take the leg off the table.

2 Remove the bolt. Using a pair of pliers to grip it, try to tighten the screw part of the rail bolt farther into the leg. If the screw tightens into the leg, reinstall the leg on the table, inserting the bolt through the corner brace. If the screw doesn't tighten, remove the rail bolt from the leg by unscrewing it or by pulling it out with the pliers. Drill and plug the screw hole in the leg with a slightly larger wood dowel. (See "Repairing a Tilting Table Top," page 84, for how to plug a hole)

3 Mark the new screw hole. Once you've plugged the leg, place it back into its original position on the table. Using a scratch awl extended through the hole in the corner block, mark the leg with a center hole where you'll install the rail bolt.

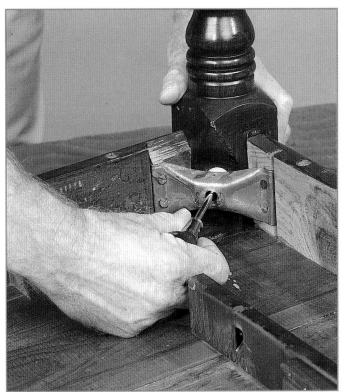

3 With the leg in proper position, use a scratch awl to center-point a new bolt hole.

4 Remove the leg, and drill a new hole for the bolt, marking the correct depth on the bit. Reinstall the rail bolt.

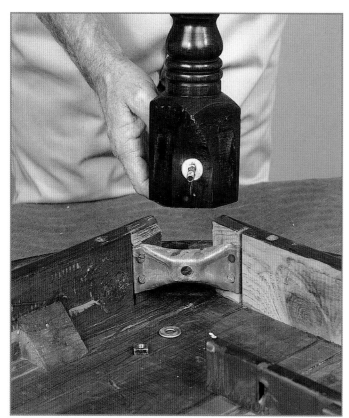

5 Reattach the leg, with the bolt through the corner brace, and tighten down on the nut.

4 Install the bolt. Remove the leg, and drill a hole using the center mark you just made to begin drilling. When drilling, make sure you drill the hole at the same angle as that of the original hole. Usually you can do this simply by eyeballing it. Use the correct-size bit, which should be the same diameter as the threaded portion of the screw minus the threads. Drill to the correct depth by marking the drill bit with masking tape. Once you've drilled the hole, insert the rail bolt and tighten it down with pliers.

5 Reinstall the leg. Place the leg back in its original position on the table, insert the bolt through the corner brace, and tighten down on the nut to finish the job.

LOOSE JOINTS IN CASEGOODS

Chests, dressers, and other cabinets fall into a category of boxlike structures that usually have drawers, sometimes in combination with doors or lids. These boxlike structures are also known as casegoods. They include such furniture items as chests of drawers, dressers (chests with mirrors), vanities, desks, highboys (high chests mounted on legs), lowboys (chests on legs with the top at about table height), armoires, blanket chests, china cabinets, sideboards, and hutches. Storage is usually their main function.

Casegood Construction. Casegoods can be made with or without a frame. Those constructed without a frame have solid wood tops, sides, and bottoms, and may be overlaid with veneer. Frame-type carcases are constructed with a framework that forms the basic structure with enclosed panels.

Cabinets containing drawers have drawer-divider rails at the front of the cabinet joining both cabinet sides. The back of casegood furniture is usually set into a rabbet or groove on the back edge of the cabinet sides and held in place with nails or screws. The insides of drawer-type casegoods contain drawer runners and guides to support and align each drawer. The bases of these cabinets may have bracket-type feet, turned or carved legs, or a simple frame-type base with no legs.

Casegood construction can include many different kinds of joints and should be examined carefully before attempting any disassembly. Because this type of furniture is customarily stationary, sitting against a wall in a room, the main structural joints are rarely subjected to much stress. Most problems occur in the moving parts, such as drawers, drawer runners, doors, hinges, or lids.

Side Panel

Frame

Top

Drawer

Dust Panel

Drawer Divider Rail

Drawer Runner

Casegood Construction.
Casegoods can be made using frame-and-panel construction (left) or solid-wood construction (right), with or without legs or feet.

boards, some of which were joined together with tongue-and-groove joints; other pieces used horizontal boards or a framework with panels. Most modern cabinets use ¼-inch plywood backs that are easily removable.

Regluing a Chest of Drawers

Often a chest of drawers may not require regluing all the joints. If only some joints are loose, you might be able to drill a few small holes around the loose tenons, dowels, or dovetails and inject glue into these

Top

Side Panel

Back Panel

Top Rail

When a piece of furniture is subjected to adverse conditions like excessive heat or moisture, however, the main structural joints may be affected. If a cabinet such as a chest of drawers, a bookcase, or an armoire is loose at the corners, making it unstable, the first place to look for problems is the back.

Key to Structural Integrity.
The back of a casegood can provide an amazing amount of stability and rigidity for the piece. If the cabinet joints are only slightly loose, sometimes you can solve the problem by simply reattaching the back securely to the cabinet with either screws or nails. Check the cabinet for squareness when reattaching the back. If the back is damaged or pieces of it are missing, you may have to repair or replace it. Many older pieces used vertical

Drawer Runner

Drawer Stop

Dust Panel

Drawer Divider Rail

Base

Drawer

*A **casegood back** adds stability and rigidity to the piece. When you reinstall the back, check that the piece is square.*

joints. You may also be able to force the joint apart somewhat to work glue into it before clamping. If most or all of the joints are loose, however, the case must be disassembled, cleaned, and reassembled.

Difficulty Level: 🔨🔨

Tools and Materials

Screwdrivers and/or a hammer	Clamps
Sealable bag	Long block
Chisel and mallet	Rag
Masking tape and marker	Square or measuring tape
Hide or polyvinyl wood glue	
Glue solvent or rasp, chisel, or utility knife	

1 Remove the back. Check to see how the back panel is mounted, and remove it. If you find nails or staples, remove the drawers and tap the back loose from inside the cabinet using a long wood block and mallet. Work along the perimeter of the panel until you're able to knock it loose. If the back is attached with screws, remove them with a screwdriver and put them in a labeled bag.

2 Remove the top. After removing the drawers and back, put the chest on its back across a set of sawhorses or on a bench. Locate and remove any screws that attach the top. Look for any glue blocks, and remove them by tapping them loose with a chisel and mallet.

3 Knock the joints apart. With the chest still on its back, check the underside to see whether it has a removable base. If so, remove the base. Examine the joints on the framework to determine their type. Check for pegs or pins through the joints. Check for any dove-

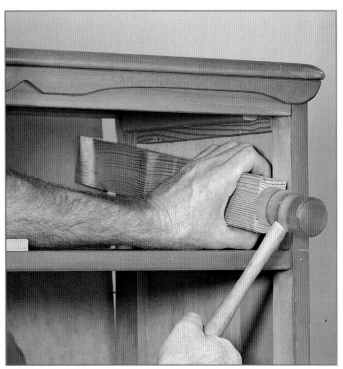

1 If the back is attached with nails or staples, knock it loose using a long block and a mallet.

2 Lay the chest on its back, and remove the top by removing any screws or glue blocks.

tail joints with flared tenons, being sure that these are removable before trying to force them apart. On some veneered pieces, sliding dovetails may be hidden under veneer surfaces, making them difficult to detect. It's usually advisable not to disassemble this type of joint because of the damage it will cause to the veneer surface when removing the dovetail. Instead, use the method for regluing a joint without taking it apart. (See "Regluing Joints without Disassembly," page 73.)

If you decide you can separate the joints, mark them all with masking tape and a marking pen and tap them apart using a mallet. Take care not to split or break the surrounding wood.

3 *Label all the joints, and tap them apart using a mallet. Make sure there are no pins or pegs in the joints.*

4 *Clean the joint parts with glue solvent or by gently scraping them with a rasp, chisel, or knife. Test-fit the joints.*

4 Clean the joints. Gently scrape all the joint parts clean of old glue using a rasp, knife edge, or chisel, or use solvents to remove the glue. (See page 43.) Test-fit all the joints, and then disassemble them again.

5 Rebuild and Clamp the Piece. Apply glue to all joint surfaces. If the chest contains solid-wood panels mounted inside frames, do not apply glue to the panels because they need to move freely in their framework to prevent cracking from expansion and contraction. Assemble the chest parts as you apply glue.

Install appropriate clamps to pull the joints up, cleaning off excess glue with a damp rag. Check the cabinet to make sure it's square and that drawers still fit properly.

There are several ways to check for squareness. One is to clamp up the box, and then use a square on several areas of the carcase and eyeball it for squareness. Another is to measure the diagonals of the carcase once you've clamped it up. When the measurements are exactly equal, the box is square. Yet another way is just to ensure that the drawers will fit. To do this, install the drawers in their places and clamp the carcase with the drawers in position. If you use this method, be sure there's no excess glue inside the cabinet that could glue the drawer in place on the runners. Also check to make sure the drawers can move freely enough to remove them from the casework after it's dry.

5 *Reassemble the chest using glue, clamp it up, and make sure it's square. (See text for several ways.) Clean up excess glue.*

CASEGOOD BASES, LEGS, AND FEET

Casegood carcases are supported by several methods. They have legs, feet, or enclosed frame- or box-type bases. Often the legs or feet may be extensions of the chest framework itself, in which case they don't need to be reglued separately.

Turned Feet. Other designs have detachable turned feet or bracket-type feet. Turned feet are round or otherwise-shaped feet that have been turned on a wood lathe, usually attached to the chest with a dowel pin. If this type of foot is loose, clean the joint, reglue it, and clamp it.

Bracket Feet. Bracket feet are created from two wood brackets mitered together to form a right angle. They may be screwed, glued, or both, to the bottom of the cabinet or to a separate underframe attached to the cabinet with screws. Bracket feet often have glue blocks attached to their backside to strengthen the foot and to help attach them securely to the chest. If bracket feet are loose, check for screws attaching them to the case. If the feet are only screw-mounted and not glued, you may be able to tighten the screws to secure the feet. If the feet were originally glued, remove and reglue them. After removing the screws, break the feet loose by tapping a wood chisel into the joint lines on the backside. Check for missing or damaged glue blocks and replace them. Clean the joint surface, apply glue, and reattach the feet with the original screws or clamps.

Bases. Frame- or box-type bases may consist of flat or molded boards set on edge to form a frame on which the casegood carcase sits. They may also be a frame with legs joined to the carcase frame at each corner, using dowels or mortise-and-tenon joints. The flat or molded board-type bases usually make ample use of glue blocks to strengthen the frame and attach it to the carcase. To remove these bases, check for and remove any screws, then knock the glue blocks loose to free the box frame from the carcase. If the frame has loose joints, knock them apart and then clean

and reglue them. Replace any missing glue blocks, and remount the base to the cabinet. Frame bases with legs are most likely mounted with screws and can be removed easily. If you find that the legs are loose after removing the frame, mark the joints, knock them apart, and then clean and reglue them.

Both varieties of base discussed here should be clamped until dry and checked for squareness. Check also to make sure the frame will line up with the casegood upon reinstallation and that it isn't twisted.

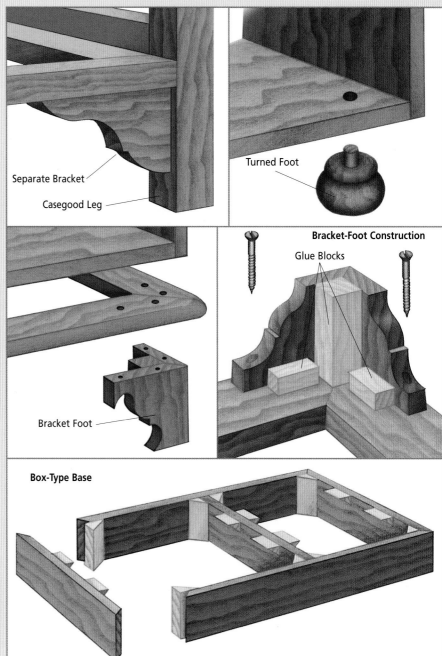

Separate Bracket

Casegood Leg

Turned Foot

Bracket Foot

Bracket-Foot Construction

Glue Blocks

Box-Type Base

Drawer Back

Drawer Side

Groove for
Drawer Bottom

Drawer Front

Loose Joints in Drawers. *Most drawers have four glued dovetail, dado, and/or rabbet joints. The bottom panel sits in grooves and is not glued in place.*

LOOSE JOINTS IN DRAWERS

Drawer corners usually use dovetail, dado, or rabbet joints to hold the main framework together. The drawer bottom then slides into the framework from the back, fitting into grooves in the sides and front. After sliding the bottom in, you then nail or screw it to the drawer back's bottom edge to hold it in place. Although corner joints of drawers are glued, drawer bottoms are not.

Regluing a Drawer

Difficulty Level: ⚒

Tools and Materials

Clamps	Rag
Wood glue	

Screwdrivers and hammer
Masking tape and marker
Square or measuring tape
Glue solvent or rasp, chisel, or utility knife

1 Remove the bottom. Turn the drawer upside down on your workbench, and remove the nails or screws holding the drawer bottom to the drawer back. If the drawer has a center guide mounted on the bottom to keep the drawer running straight in the chest, you may need to remove it first. Pull the bottom panel toward the back, removing it from the drawer frame.

2 Knock out the sides. Label the side joint parts, and knock the sides outward using a hammer and softwood block held against the inside corners. On most drawers, the sides should be knocked outward from the drawer front and back to keep from breaking the wood in the joint. Examine drawer joints carefully before knocking them loose.

1 Remove the nails or screws holding the drawer bottom, and then slide it out the back.

2 Knock the drawer sides outward from the drawer front and back after labeling the joints.

3 Clean all old glue from the joints, and test-fit the drawer parts.

4 Glue and clamp the drawer, and reinstall the drawer bottom, nailing it back in place.

3 Remove old glue from the joints. Clean the drawer joints of old glue using solvent or a chisel, wood rasp, or knife edge. Assemble the drawer joints without glue to be sure they fit properly, make any necessary adjustments, and then take them all apart again.

4 Glue and reassemble the drawer. Apply glue to all joint surfaces, assembling the joints as you go. Install clamps to pull the joints up snugly, but don't overtighten them. You might want to use large wood blocks to ensure that the full width of the drawer sides will pull up tight without using addi-tional clamps. Clean off excess glue with a damp rag, and check the drawer for squareness. Reinsert the drawer bottom, and drive nails or screws into the bottom edge of the drawer to hold the panel in place.

LOOSE JOINTS ON BEDS

Beds are similar to chairs in that they have to support weight, and they get daily use. In a bed, joint soundness helps to ensure soundness of sleep: Imagine having your bed collapse under you just as you're reaching your maximum REM level. Obviously, tight joints are a must.

Bed Construction

Most beds are a framework of joined parts supporting a box spring and mattress. The main parts of a bed are the headboard, head rail, footboard, foot rail, side rails, and four corner posts. A bed may have all or some of these parts; for example, a bed might have a foot rail but no footboard. Most headboards, foot-

boards, head rails, and foot rails are joined to corner posts via mortise-and-tenon or dowel joints. Beds usually have wooden slats that rest on ledgers attached to the side rails to support the box spring and mattress. Some beds use heavy metal angle brackets attached to the side rails to support the box spring. Beds are built to be disassembled for easy transfer; otherwise, most

Beds are a framework of parts that support a box spring and mattress. Some beds use heavy metal angle brackets attached to the side rails to support the box spring.

would not fit through doors or up staircases. Side rails connecting the head and foot of a bed, for example, are always removable. These rails can have any of several kinds of joints to connect them to the head and foot corner posts. Also, some antique beds or good reproductions have bolts holding the corner posts to the head and foot rails; these bolts can be removed and the posts dismantled from the headboard and footboard.

Bed Bolts. *Some beds use a bolt to reinforce the mortise-and-tenon joint between the side rails and bedposts.*

Bed Bolts. High-quality beds use bolt construction for side rail assembly, in which a bolt extends through the head and foot posts and into the end of the tenon at each end of the side rail. The bolt then threads into a nut that is mortised into the side rail. As the bolt tightens into the nut, it pulls the tenon on the side rail into the mortise in the bedpost and locks them together.

There are also some European beds that reverse the bolt and nut by setting the nut into the bedpost with the bolt inserted into a slotted area in the side of the rail. The threaded end of the bolt then extends out the rail's end and into the post to be threaded on the embedded nut. These bolts usually have a hole through the side of their heads into which you insert a scratch awl or narrow screwdriver to turn the bolt and tighten it down.

Simple Bed-Bolt Repair. If a bed bolt will not tighten, check the wood around the head of the bolt to be sure it's not damaged. If the bolt head is digging deeply into the wood, you can remove it and reinstall it with a metal washer or washers to correct the problem. If the bolt continues to spin, the problem is probably with the embedded nut. (See "Repairing Bolted Bed Joints," page 96.)

Steel-Plate Connectors. Another type of side-rail joint uses steel or iron plates with interlocking parts. A slotted plate is mounted into the post with another interlocking bracket mounted in or on the side rail. This side-rail plate has T-hooks that insert and, by forcing the side rail down, tighten into the slotted post plate.

Some bed bolts will not tighten because they've dug into the wood inside the bed post. Install a metal washer to fix the post.

Steel-Plate Connectors. *Interlocking steel plates on the side rails and bed posts form strong headboard and footboard joints.*

If an interlocking steel-plate joint is loose, it's likely that the mounting screws are loose or stripped from the wood. Remove the side rail, check all screws in the post and the side rail, and tighten them securely if possible. If the screws are stripped, try to install longer ones that will tighten. If that doesn't work, plug the stripped screw holes with dowels. (See "Repairing a Tilting Table Top," page 83, for steps on how plug stripped screw holes.)

Hook-and-Pin Connectors. One of the more common types of bed-rail construction uses two or more flat metal hooks extending from the end of the side rail. You insert the hooks into a narrow slot cut vertically into the bedpost, and mount the hooks on pins inside the slot. As you force the rail down, the hooks pull the rail joint up tight.

To fix loose hook-and-pin-type joints, first try to force the rail downward with a firm hard tap from a rubber mallet. If this doesn't tighten it, remove the rail by lift-ing or tapping it upward at each end. Check the metal pins in the side rails and corner posts to see whether they've become dislodged or the wood around them has cracked or been damaged. If so, you may have to replace the pins with longer ones or fix the damaged wood. (See "Replacing Side-Rail and Post Pins," page 100, and "Rebuilding a Hook-and-Pin Side-Rail Joint," page 117.) If the pins look secure, you may be able to tighten the joint by shimming it. (See "Shimming a Hook-and-Pin Joint with Metal," page 98, and "Shimming a Hook-and-Pin Joint with Wood," page 99.)

Bed Rail

Metal Pins to Secure Plate

Metal Hook Plate

Metal Pins to Receive Hooks

Bedpost

Hook-and-Pin Connectors. *A common bed joint uses a hook plate in the side rails and metal pins embedded in the bedposts.*

Repairing Bolted Bed Joints

If a bed bolt spins freely in the hole without tightening, the problem is probably a misaligned or stripped nut.

Difficulty Level: 🔨 🔨

Tools and Materials

Bed-bolt nut (if necessary)	¼-inch chisel
Stain and finish to match	Mallet
Wood for wedges and a plug	Wood glue
Block plane or sandpaper and block	

1 Cut out the nut plug. Remove the side rail, and lay it flat on a bench with the inside of the rail facing up. Look for a rectangular mortise near the end of the rail that has been filled with a wooden plug. Using a ¼-inch wood chisel and mallet, dig out the wooden plug to expose the embedded nut.

2 Thread the bolt onto the nut. If the nut is mis-aligned, fish it out of the hole and drop it in as straight as possible. Insert the bolt into the end of the rail, and thread it into the nut to make sure the threads

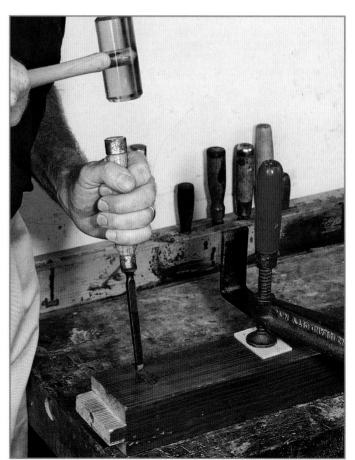

1 *To remove the bed-bolt nut, dig the wooden plug out of the rail using a narrow chisel.*

are not stripped and the nut is mounted securely in the rail and aligned properly with the bolt. If the nut or bolt has stripped threads, you'll have to replace one or both of them. Because bed bolts come in various lengths and with different thread sizes, take the hardware with you when searching for a replacement. Check good hardware stores, furniture repair shops, antique dealers, or woodworkers' websites for replacements.

3 Wedge the nut in place. Make some narrow hardwood wedges the same thickness as the mortise. After applying glue, drive the wedges down into the

mortise at the top and bottom of the nut to secure it in the proper position. Remove the bolt from the rail, and install the rail into the bedpost. Reinsert the bolt through the post into the side rail, and tighten it securely.

4 Fill the hole. If the joint appears tight, remove the side rail from the bedpost and place the rail back on the workbench. Using wood that matches that of the side rail, cut a small block the same size as the mortise. Using a mallet, drive the block into the mortise to plug it and conceal the set nut.

2 If the concealed nut is not aligned properly in the hole, remove the nut, drop it into the mortise as straight as possible (left), and thread the bolt into it (right).

3 Install wedges on the top and bottom of the nut by gluing them and tapping them in place.

4 Cut a small wood block to fit the mortise, and then tap it in place to conceal the nut.

5 Trim the wooden plug flush with the rail surface using a chisel or block plane, and touch it up to match the existing finish.

5 Trim the plug. Use a wood chisel, block plane, or sandpaper block to make the plug flush with the rail surface. Stain and touch up the plugged area to match the surrounding wood.

Shimming a Hook-and-Pin Joint with Metal

Over time, wear and tear can cause a bed's hook plates to loosen their holding pins just enough to make the side-rail joints loose but not enough to cause joint failure. If your bed's hook-and-pin joints seem a little loose but you can't find any structural problems, you may need just to shim them. You can buy thin, corrugated-metal shims from some furniture-repair supply companies.

Difficulty Level: 🔨

Tools and Materials

Metal hook-and-pin shims   Rubber mallet

1 Install the shims. Hook-and-pin shims are slotted in the center so they'll fit over the hooks and mount flat on the end of the side rail. Slide the shim onto the rail as shown. If one of these shims isn't enough, use two or more together.

2 Tighten the joint. When you install a side rail with shims, pound down on the joint with a rubber mallet. This action will snug the rail up to the bedpost, making the joint tighter.

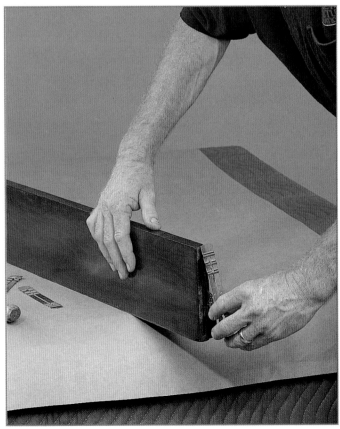

1 Install a corrugated metal hook-and-pin shim over the hooks on the end of the side rail.

2 When you put the bed together, pound on top of the shimmed side rail to tighten the joint.

Shimming a Hook-and-Pin Joint with Wood

Difficulty Level: 🔨

Tools and Materials

⅛-inch-thick wood shims	Pencil
Epoxy	Rubber mallet
Matching stain and finish	Backsaw

1 *Cut ⅛-in.-thick shims, leaving them long. Place the shims on each side of the hook plate, and mark them for width.*

2 *Glue the shims to the side rails using epoxy or CA glue (which dries faster), and install the rail, tapping it down with a mallet.*

Another way to shim a side-rail joint is to use wood strips; strips about ⅛ inch thick will usually do the job.

1 **Cut the shims.** Cut strips of ⅛-inch-thick wood wide enough to mark and fit on each side of the side-rail hooks. Place the strips on the end of the side rail, and mark them for width using a pencil. Leave them longer than side-rail height.

2 **Attach the shims.** Using a two-part epoxy or CA glue, apply the shims to the end of the side rail, and fit the rail into the bedpost slot. Tap the rail down with a rubber mallet until a little pressure is applied to the joint, tightening the shims in place. Make sure excess glue doesn't join the side rail to the post. Allow the glue to dry for the amount of time instructed on the label, and remove the side rail.

3 **Trim the shims.** Cut the shims even with the side-rail edge using a small backsaw or sharp chisel. Stain the edge of the shim to match the side rail (stain markers work well to hide shims or raw wood that has been exposed). Reinstall the rail in the post, and tap it down securely with a mallet. If you can't force the side rail all the way down to hook the pins, remove it and trim down the thickness of the shim using a sharp wood chisel. If the rail seats all the way down but won't form a tight joint, you may need an additional shim.

3 *When the adhesive is dry, trim the shims flush with the top and bottom of the side rail using a fine backsaw.*

Replacing Side-Rail and Post Pins

The small metal pins in a hook-and-pin assembly undergo a lot of stress and must be mounted securely in the posts and side rails for the joints to be strong. Most manufactured beds contain pins that are too short. Even minor damage or overeager bed assembly can knock the pins out of place, weakening them. Longer pins cover more area in the wood, enabling them to withstand more stress. You can remove short pins and replace them with longer ones for a stronger joint. The procedure is the same for both side rails and corner posts.

If the wood around the metal pins in the post is split, you may be able to reglue and clamp these splits before replacing the pins. If the damage is severe, you'll have to rebuild the joint. (See "Rebuilding a Hook-and-Pin Side-Rail Joint," page 117.)

Difficulty Level: 𝍖

Tools and Materials

New metal pins	Drill and bits
Hammer	4d finishing nail

1 Drive out the pin. Some rails have thin wooden blocks on the inside surface covering where the pins enter, so check this first and remove the block if necessary. Drill a small hole in the wood opposite the original pin hole to remove a pin. Using a 4d finishing nail inserted into the drilled hole, tap the pin out through the original hole.

2 Deepen the pin hole. Drill the original pin hole deeper to accommodate a new pin. If you can't locate a longer pin at a good hardware store, cut a new one from a bolt of the same diameter. Make sure the pin is at least ⅛ inch shorter than the thickness of the side rail. Use the pin to set the depth of the hole on the bit, marking the depth with masking tape.

3 Install the new pin. If the pin is used to secure a hook plate, be sure the plate is in place first. Using a hammer, drive the new pin into the hole. Reattach the pin cover using brads of the appropriate length.

1 Remove any pin cover, drill a small hole opposite the pin hole, and drive out the pin using a nail and hammer.

2 Drill the original pin hole deeper for the new pins. Mark the depth on the bit using tape.

3 Tap the new pin into the hole using a hammer, and reattach the pin cover using brads.

Repairing Loose Headboard and Footboard Joints

If headboard and footboard joints are loose, check to make sure they aren't bolted joints. If they are bolted, you may be able to tighten them simply by tightening the bolts. If the joints aren't bolted, you'll need to reglue them to tighten them.

Difficulty Level: 🔨🔨

Tools and Materials

Rubber mallet	Square
Masking tape and marking pen	Clamps
Diagonal pliers and wood block	
Wood glue and glue brush or palette knife	
Chisels and glue solvent, wood rasp, or utility knife	

1 Remove any pins or pegs. Disassemble the bed, and lay the headboard or footboard on a padded bench or across a set of sawhorses. Check for pins or pegs through the joints. If you find pegs, drill them out. (See "Removing Pegs from Joints," page 71.) If you find evidence of nails or pins, dig out the putty or wood buttons covering them with a ¼-inch chisel to expose the nailheads, and then pull them out with a pair of diagonal pliers. Place a small scrap of wood under the pliers to protect the furniture wood and to provide a fulcrum for the levering action of the pliers.

2 Separate the joints. Label the joints, and then tap the posts loose using a rubber mallet to separate them from the head or foot rails.

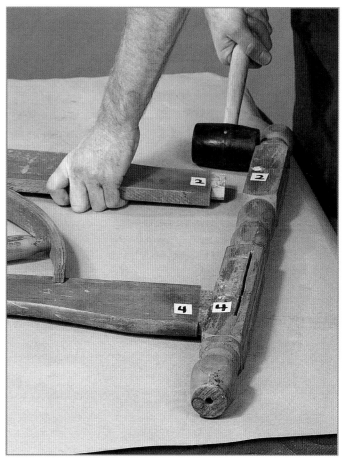

1 For a pinned joint, dig around the pins using a chisel (top) and pull them using diagonal pliers and a block.

2 Label all the joints using masking tape and a marker, and then knock them apart using a mallet.

3 Clean the joints using glue solvent or a rasp, chisel, or knife, and test-fit all the parts without glue.

4 Spread glue on the joints using a glue brush or palette knife, and assemble them as you apply the glue.

3 Remove glue from the joints. Clean all glue joints using solvent or a wood rasp, chisel, or knife edge. Assemble the joints to make sure they fit, and then disassemble them again.

4 Glue and assemble the joints. Apply wood glue to all joint surfaces, spreading the glue evenly with a brush or a palette knife. Reassemble each joint as you finish applying the glue.

5 Clamp the joints. Install clamps, and tighten them to pull the joints up. If you don't have long pipe or bar clamps, you can use inexpensive strap clamps or even make a tourniquet clamp. (See "Improvising Tools," page 29.) Clean off excess glue using a damp rag. Make sure the joints are tight and that everything is aligned and square. Allow the glue to dry for at least 1 hour, and then remove the clamps. Allow the glue to dry overnight before using the headboard or footboard.

5 Install the clamps, making sure the assembly is square, tighten them, and clean up excess glue.

LOOSE MIRROR AND PICTURE-FRAME JOINTS

Mitered corner joints, such as those used in mirror and picture frames, aren't strong in themselves and usually use some kind of reinforcement. Some frames have a back attached to them to give the joints strength; others may be reinforced with nails, dowel pins, or splines. If you find miter joints that are loose and coming apart, examine them to see what type of reinforcement was used—if any—before you take them apart and reglue them. Often, when you reglue a miter joint, you'll want to reinforce it with pins or splines.

Regluing a Mitered Mirror Frame

Difficulty Level: 🔨🔨

Tools and Materials

Hammer	Rubber mallet
Plywood	Clamps
Measuring tape	
Wood glue and glue brush or palette knife	
Diagonal pliers, screwdriver and nail puller	
Chisels and glue solvent, wood rasp, or utility knife	

1 Remove the backing. Most pictures and mirrors have a backing that's attached to the frame with small nails. Remove the back, along with any picture, glass, or mirror by prying and removing the nails with a small nail puller, diagonal pliers, or a screwdriver and hammer.

2 Disassemble the joints. Tap the joints apart with a mallet, removing any nails or other reinforcement.

3 Clean off old glue. Clean the joints with glue solvent or by scraping off the old glue with a wood rasp, chisel, or knife edge. Be careful not to chip the wood.

1 Remove the back from the frame, and then remove any picture, mirror, or glass and put it aside.

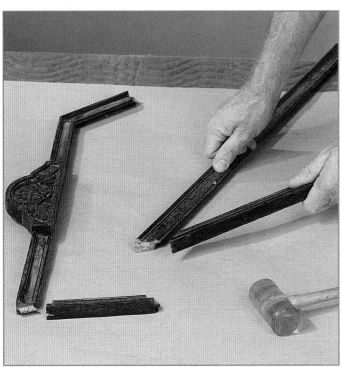

2 Using a mallet, gently knock the joints apart, and remove any splines or other reinforcement.

3 Remove all old glue from the joints using solvent or by gently scraping them clean with a rasp, chisel, or knife.

4 After test-fitting, clamp the frame, laying it flat on plywood, and make sure it's square.

4 Clamp the frame. After you've cleaned the joints, assemble the frame parts and clamp them without glue. Picture framing or miter clamps work well for frames.

If you don't have one of those clamps, use a strap clamp. Be sure the frame is laid flat, and clamp it to a flat bench or board so it doesn't get warped or twisted when you pull the joints tight. (See photo.) Remove the clamps, and apply glue to the joint surfaces. Assemble the frame pieces again, and reinstall the clamps, making sure the joints are aligned and tight. Also, make sure the frame is square by measuring diagonally from corner to corner. When the two diagonal measurements are the same, the frame is square. Clean off excess glue.

Reinforcing a Miter Joint

After you glue up a miter joint, you might want to reinforce it with finishing nails. To install the nails you'll need to drill pilot holes of the appropriate size so you don't split the wood. The pilot hole must be large enough so that the nail can pierce the wood without splitting it but can still tighten. Fill the holes with putty or colored wax sticks to conceal them. Another way to reinforce the miter is by installing a spline in the joint.

Difficulty Level:

Tools and Materials

Backsaw	Wood for splines
Chisels and utility knife	
Wood glue and glue brush or palette knife	

1 Cut a kerf. With the frame clamped vertically in a woodworking vise, use a backsaw to cut a slot into the frame's edge across the joint. With a thin frame, cut as far into the frame as you can without cutting through the corner. With wider frames (3 or more inches wide), cut about halfway into the corner.

1 Clamp the frame in a vise, and using a backsaw, cut a kerf across the miter joint.

2 Slice the spline. Next cut a wooden spline the same thickness as the kerf from a piece of scrap wood, with the grain direction running perpendicular to the joint. Test-fit the spline in the slot. You should end up with a snug fit, but not so tight that the spline binds as you slide it in.

3 Install the spline. Dribble wood glue into the slot, and spread it on the shim with a brush or palette

knife; then fit the shim into the slot, leaving it long. Let the glue dry for at least 1 hour.

4 Cut and Trim the Spline. After the glue dries, cut the spline flush with the frame's wood surface using a backsaw. Fine-tune the cut with a sharp block plane or chisel and sandpaper with sanding block to make the surface perfectly flush. Stain and touch up the wood to match the existing finish.

2 *Cut a spline the same exact thickness as the kerf from a small block of scrap wood. The spline should be snug, but not so tight that it can't be pushed into place by hand.*

3 *Spread glue onto the spline and into the slot. Push the spline into place.*

4 *Cut the spline flush with the frame, trim it using a sharp chisel, and touch it up with stain and finish to match the surrounding wood.*

6

STRUCTURAL REPAIRS II: BROKEN JOINTS

When you discover broken joints while repairing furniture, a simple regluing may appear to answer the problem. That quick fix is usually not enough, however. Because joints are designed to withstand stress, you must repair them back to their original strength if at all possible. In most cases, you'll have to reinforce the joint. Sometimes you'll find you need to rebuild the joint totally, depending on the kind of joint it is.

BROKEN CHAIR JOINTS

Joints frequently break in chair foot rails and stretchers (rungs) or in chair-back spindles and posts. These joints get a lot of stress, and when one breaks, it puts undue stress on the others and can cause them to crack or break as well. If a foot rail or spindle breaks at or near the joint, you should be able to repair rather than replace it.

Repairing a Broken Chair-Rung Joint

Difficulty Level: 🔨 🔨

Tools and Materials

Drill and assorted bits	Dowels
Backsaw	Clamps
Chisels or wood rasp	Rag
Wood glue and glue brush or palette knife	

1 **Examine the break.** Remove the rung or foot rail from the chair, and examine the broken piece left in the hole. If the piece is solid and glued tight, as in the photo, don't plug the hole. If the piece is loose, drill it out using a slightly smaller-size bit, and clean the hole using a narrow wood chisel. Next, plug the hole using the correctly sized wood dowel, gluing it in and cutting it flush with the surface.

2 **Drill a pilot hole.** Using a small-diameter bit ($\frac{1}{16}$ to $\frac{1}{8}$ inch) drill a pilot hole into the center of the plugged hole, making sure to follow the same angle as that of the original chair rung.

3 **Drill the chair rung.** Clamp the chair rung in a vise with the broken end up, and drill a pilot hole in the center of its end using a $\frac{1}{8}$- to $\frac{1}{4}$-inch bit. To ensure a straight hole, use another person to sight

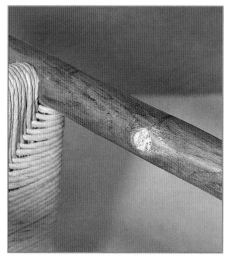

1 If the broken piece is lodged in the hole, as it is here, you don't have to plug the hole.

2 Drill a pilot hole into the plugged hole. Follow the same angle as the original part.

3 Clamp the rung and drill a pilot hole; then drill a larger hole for a dowel into the rung and the plugged leg hole.

4 After installing the correct-size dowel in the rung, glue the joint surfaces and install the rung.

5 Clamp the chair tight, and clean up any excess glue using a damp rag.

across the drill bit and chair rung as you drill. Following the pilot hole, drill a hole about half of the diameter of the chair rung into the damaged end of the rung and into the plugged hole in the leg. Drill the holes straight, and make sure you don't poke through the other side of the leg. Make the hole in the chair rung about twice as deep as the hole in the plug.

4 Dowel and reinstall the rung. Prepare a hardwood dowel of the correct diameter and cut it about $1/8$ inch shorter than the combined depths of both holes. With the dowel clamped lengthwise in a vise, use a backsaw to cut a groove along the length of the dowel

to allow glue and air to escape when it's forced into the hole. Chamfer or bevel the ends of the dowel pin. Apply glue to the dowel, and spread it into the holes with a palette knife or glue brush. Insert the dowel into the rung and the rung into the chair leg.

5 Clamp the chair. Apply clamps to the legs on each side of the rung or rungs. If you don't have padded clamps as in the photo, use small blocks of wood and masking tape on the clamp jaws to protect the furniture. Place the chair on a level surface, and make sure it doesn't rock. Clean excess glue from all joints, and keep the chair clamped until it's dry, about 2 hours.

Repairing a Broken Back-Spindle Joint

Sometimes one back spindle in a chair will break while the rest of the back remains tight and solid. In such cases, the back posts and rails can't be easily disassembled without breaking the wood. Because of this, you must repair the back spindle without taking apart the other joints.

If a back spindle is broken at both top and bottom joints, here's how to repair it without removing the back of the chair. (See the box "Repairing a Spindle Broken at the Bottom," page 110, if the spindle is not broken at the top joint.)

Difficulty Level: 🔨 🔨

Tools and Materials

Wood glue and glue brush or palette knife	
Clamps	Backsaw
Drill and assorted bits	Dowels
Chisels or wood rasp	Rag

1 Glue in the spindle. Place the chair on a padded workbench. If the breaks are not smooth but jagged, reinstall the spindle in the chair back, gluing and clamping it in place. If the breaks are smooth (straight across and at the ends of the spindle), go to Step 3.

2 Cut the spindle flush. After about 4 hours, when the glue is dry, cut the spindle out at the top and bottom using a backsaw to make clean flush cuts.

3 Drill pilot holes. Drill a ⅛-inch-diameter pilot hole down through the seat in the center of the spindle cutoff, following the spindle's angle. The pilot hole should come out at the bottom of the seat. Clamp the broken spindle in a vise with the top end facing up, and drill a pilot hole down into the top end of the spindle. Then drill a larger hole to insert a dowel. Make this hole about two-thirds the diameter of the spindle at the top, drilling deep enough to let the dowel extend well into the spindle. Use the same drill bit to drill a hole in the chair top rail at the center of the broken spindle, following the same angle as the spindle.

1 Glue and clamp in place a spindle that has a jagged break at the top and/or bottom joints.

2 After the glue dries, use a backsaw to cut the broken spindle out with clean crosscuts.

3 Drill a pilot hole all the way through the seat. Then drill the top end of the spindle and bottom of the top rail for a dowel.

4 Install a dowel in the top end of the spindle; then glue and install the spindle into the top rail.

4 Install the spindle. Cut the correct-diameter dowel to fit into the spindle top and the chair top rail. Make this dowel $\frac{1}{8}$ inch shorter than the combined depths of the spindle and top-rail holes. Chamfer the dowel ends, and cut a groove in the dowel using a back-saw. Put glue in the holes, on the dowel, and on the bottom end of the spindle. Install the spindle in the chair, clamping it in place.

5 Drill the bottom of the spindle. After the glue is dry, turn the chair upside down on the bench. Drill a hole following the pilot hole you drilled in Step 3 through the bottom of the chair seat and into the bottom end of the back spindle. Use a drill bit approximately two-thirds the diameter of the bottom end of the spindle you're drilling into, and drill well up into the spindle. To make sure the drill bit is aligned with the spindle while you're drilling the hole, get someone to sight across the angle of the bit and the spindle from one direction while you sight from another direction.

6 Insert and trim the bottom dowel. Turn the chair right side up to clear any wood shavings from the hole, and cut a dowel of the correct diameter, leaving it longer than the depth of the hole. Chamfer one

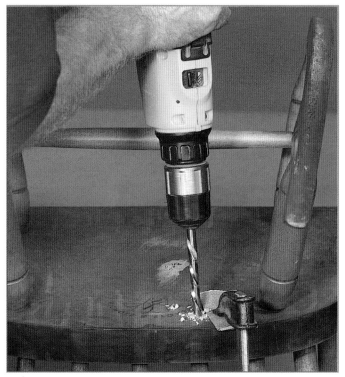

5 Follow the pilot hole to drill a hole one-third the diameter of the spindle into the spindle.

REPAIRING A SPINDLE BROKEN AT THE BOTTOM

Sometimes the back spindle of a chair is broken only at the bottom joint. If so, follow these directions:

Pull the bottom of the spindle out slightly to clear the bottom joint, and tap it loose at the top joint, separating the spindle from the chair. If the broken portion of the spindle that's left in the joint is loose, drill it out using a slightly smaller-size bit. Clean the hole using a narrow wood chisel to preserve the original shape of the hole.

Plug the hole with the appropriate-size dowel, gluing it into the hole and cutting it flush. Drill a small-diameter pilot hole ($\frac{1}{16}$ to $\frac{1}{8}$ inch) into the center of the plugged hole and the broken end of the spindle while it's clamped in a vise. Be sure your hole follows the spindle angle in the plug and is straight in the spindle. Following the pilot hole, drill a hole about half the diameter of the spindle in the plug and in the broken end of the spindle. Prepare a dowel pin $\frac{1}{8}$ inch shorter than the combined depth of the two holes, chamfer the ends, and cut a groove lengthwise in the dowel pin using a backsaw. Put glue on one end of the dowel and into the drilled-out hole in the spindle, and insert the dowel pin into the spindle.

Look at the opposite end of the spindle (the unbroken end) and the hole where it was joined to the chair's top rail. With the correct-size bit, drill this hole deeper. When you install the spindle, you'll be able to slide it up into this hole, allowing the other end to clear the chair surface and drop back down into the newly plugged hole.

Test-fit the spindle, sliding it up into the deepened hole as far as possible and making sure it clears the chair at the bottom joint. If it doesn't clear the chair seat, you may have to cut a little off the top of the spindle or the newly installed dowel at the bottom of the spindle. You may also have to deepen the hole or ream it out a little bigger at the top of the spindle.

After making sure you can get the spindle in place, apply glue to all joining surfaces and push the top of the spindle up into the top rail as far as it will go. Drop the spindle back down to insert the bottom into the chair-seat joint. If the reamed hole is too big, make some small hardwood wedges and insert them around the spindle at the joint. Cut the wedges flush using a chisel, and clean off any excess glue with a damp rag.

6 Glue a dowel into the hole, and cut it flush with the seat bottom using a backsaw or flush-cut saw.

end and cut a groove the length of the dowel. Make sure the dowel fits the hole; then apply glue to the hole and the dowel, and install the dowel in the hole, chamfered end first. Clean up excess glue, and use a backsaw to cut the dowel flush with the underside of the seat.

Repairing a Broken Back-Post Joint

Back posts often can be fixed by drilling through the bottom of the chair seat and installing a hardwood dowel to reinforce the joint. A key to this repair is that the broken end remains tight in the seat.

Difficulty Level: 🔨 🔨

Tools and Materials

Mallet	Drill and assorted bits
Dowels	Backsaw
Clamps	RagChisels or wood rasp
Wood glue and glue brush or palette knife	

1 Remove the back and drill a pilot hole.
Often, when a back post breaks, the top rail has experienced enough movement that the joints at

When a back post is broken, you can usually repair it by installing a dowel through the break.

1 *Remove the back post, and drill a pilot hole through the seat, following the post's angle. A sliding T-bevel helps alignment.*

the top of the spindles have become somewhat loose. Remove the top rail by tapping it with a mallet. Drill a pilot hole $\frac{1}{8}$ inch in diameter in the center of the broken-off portion of the post that's still in the chair. Drill through the seat's bottom, following the back post's angle. You can use the other back post or a sliding T-bevel as a guide, and have someone sight the bit for you if necessary.

2 Replace the back. Apply glue to the broken areas of the post and to the spindles and spindle holes in the top rail. Put the post and the top rail back together, clamping it in place as shown in the photo. Be sure to clamp the back of the chair at the correct angle. Wipe away any excess glue.

3 Drill the dowel hole. When the glue is dry, turn the chair upside down on a padded bench, allowing the back to overhang. If it's possible to leave the clamps on the chair, do so. Following the pilot hole, drill a hole at least one-half the diameter of the back post through

2 *Clean the joints, and reinstall the back using glue, clamping the top rail in position.*

3 Drill for a dowel through the bottom of the chair seat, following the pilot you drilled previously.

the seat and into the back post. Get someone to sight across the post and drill bit to be sure your angle is correct. Keep the bit aligned with the post. Drill this hole into the post about twice the distance of your hole in the seat. If the hole through the seat is 1½ inches deep, for example, drill into the back post about 3 inches if possible. It's important to get enough of the dowel pin into the back post to make the repair strong.

4 Fit the dowel. Turn the chair right side up, and allow the wood chips to fall out of the drilled hole. Prepare a wood dowel pin of the correct length and diameter, chamfering the end that will fit into the back post. Cut a groove lengthwise on the dowel to allow glue and air to escape when you drive it in. You can cut this dowel longer than needed and cut off the end flush with the chair bottom after you insert it. Turn the chair upside down again, and put glue on the dowel, spreading a thin layer inside the hole with a palette knife or glue brush. Put the chamfered end of the dowel pin into the hole, tapping it down into the back post while holding the back post firmly with one hand. Gradually tap it down until you can feel that it's all the way in.

5 Trim the dowel. Clean off excess glue with a damp rag, and cut the dowel flush with the underside of the chair seat using a backsaw or flush-cut saw.

4 Clean out the hole, then prepare and install the dowel, tapping it until it bottoms out.

5 Clean off any excess glue, and trim the dowel flush with the seat bottom using a backsaw.

MORTISE-AND-TENON AND DOWEL JOINTS

Although mortise-and-tenon and dowel joints are among the stronger wood joints, they can still break under certain conditions. Here are some ways to restore them to their original strength—or close to it—when they break. Examine your piece, and decide which method will work best for you before proceeding.

Rebuilding a Tenon

Perhaps the best way to repair a broken mortise-and-tenon joint is to rebuild the broken tenon. Here's one way to do that, using a chair rail as an example.

Difficulty Level: 🔨 🔨

Tools and Materials

Combination square	Marking scribe
Mortising chisel and mallet	Backsaw
Block plane or sander	Scrap hardwood
Touch-up finish to match	Clamps
Wood glue and palette knife	Rag

1 **Mark the rail.** Remove the tenoned rail from the chair, and clamp it in a vise with the damaged end facing up. Using the broken tenon's position as a guide, scribe lines lengthwise on the top and bottom of the rail to cut out a section of the rail that matches the thickness of the tenon. Make these lines the same length, about one to one-and-one-half times the length of the original tenon. Using a square positioned along the rail, draw a line across the top and bottom of the rail to join the long lines at their ends.

2 **Cut out the broken tenon.** Using a backsaw, cut lengthwise down the rail on each side of the broken tenon, following the scribe lines on the top and bottom of the rail. After making the cuts to the end of the scribed lines, use a sharp mortising chisel to make the final cut between the ending points of your two saw cuts. You'll have to reposition the rail in the vise to use the mortising chisel effectively. When making this cut, come in from both the top and bottom of the rail using the lines you've drawn as a guide.

3 **Cut the patch.** After removing this cutout section of wood from the rail, cut a piece of matching hardwood to fit the cutout area long enough to extend beyond the end of the rail at least the length of the original tenon. It's better to cut this piece

1 *To rebuild a tenon, clamp the rail in a vise and scribe lines lengthwise on its top and bottom.*

2 *Cut along the scribed lines using a fine backsaw (top), and chisel out the broken tenon (above).*

slightly thicker than the cutout area, and then use a block plane or belt sander to fit it precisely and snugly into the rail.

4 Glue in the patch. Glue the hardwood patch into the cutout area of the rail, and clamp it in position. Make sure the wood grain in the patch runs in the same direction as that in the rail. Clean excess glue with a damp rag, and allow the repair to dry for about 2 hours.

5 Trim the patch. After removing the clamps, mark and cut the top and bottom of the tenon to fit the

mortise, and cut it the right length if needed. Clean out the mortise in the matching joint part. Sand and smooth the top and bottom edge of the rail so that the new wood patch is even with the rail wood surface.

6 Assemble the joint. Test-fit the joint, and make any necessary adjustments. Disassemble the joint, and then apply a thin layer of glue to all joining surfaces. Install the tenon into the mortise, clamp the joint tight, and clean up any excess glue with a damp rag. Touch up the top and bottom edges of the patched rail to match the surrounding wood.

3 Cut a piece of matching wood to fit the cutout area in the rail so that it fits snugly in the slot.

4 After fitting the patch, glue it into the rail and clean off the excess glue using a damp rag.

5 After the glue dries, mark and cut the tenon patch to fit the mortise, and sand it smooth.

6 Install the patched tenon into the mortise using wood glue, and clamp the joint tight.

Repairing a Broken Dowel Joint

Dowel joints have been used for over a century and are among the most common of all furniture joints used today. They are strong but still can break when stressed. In a classic case of dowel-joint failure, two dowels in the gate-leg table in this project broke after years of the owners' pulling on the leg to open the table.

Difficulty Level: 🔨 🔨

Tools and Materials

Drill and assorted bits	Backsaw
Chisels and wood rasp	Dowels
Needle-nose pliers	Clamps
Wood glue and glue brush or palette knife	Rag

THE PROS KNOW

USING DOWELS TO FIX A BROKEN MORTISE-AND-TENON JOINT

If you feel you can't or don't want to rebuild a mortise-and-tenon joint, an easier way to repair one is to convert it to a dowel joint.

Cut off the broken tenon flush with the wood surface, using a backsaw. Clean out the mortise using a chisel to remove old glue and broken tenon pieces; then cut a wooden plug to fit the mortise, and glue the plug into the mortise, allowing it to dry. Now you've essentially created a butt joint, which you can dowel.

Put the piece from which you cut the broken tenon in a vise, damaged end facing up, and mark two lines across the damaged end where you want to install two dowel pins. Place these lines about one-quarter of the way down from the top and bottom edges of the original tenon. If the original tenon was 2 inches high, for example, mark your lines about ½ inch from the top and ½ inch from the bottom.

Center a doweling jig over the line, and drill a hole into the end of the piece. (See "Clean Out the Holes," page 116, for how to use a doweling jig.) The hole diameter should be approximately one-half the thickness of the wood into which you're drilling, and the depth should be about three or four times the diameter. Insert the correct-size dowel centers (see photo) into the holes and remove the piece from the vise, aligning it into its original position. Tap the joint together so that the dowel centers mark the plugged mortise, providing center marks to drill your next holes. Drill these holes at the proper angle to align with the tenoned piece. Drill at least as deep as the plugged mortise.

Cut two dowel pins of the right diameter and ⅛ inch shorter than the combined depth of the two holes they must enter. Chamfer both ends of each of the dowel pins, and cut a groove lengthwise. Apply a thin layer of glue to all the joint surfaces. Install the dowel pins, and then clamp the joints to pull it tight. Clean off any excess glue with a damp rag.

Broken Tenon

Rail

Dowel Centers

Plug

Mortise

Post

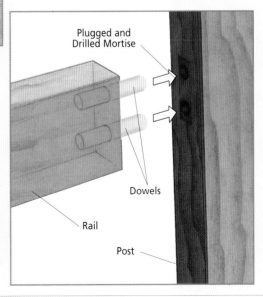

Plugged and Drilled Mortise

Dowels

Rail

Post

1 Clean out the holes. Remove any loose pieces of dowel from the holes using needle-nose pliers. If a broken end of a dowel is tight, use a slightly smaller bit to drill out the hole following the original angle of the dowel. Using a doweling jig will enable you to drill accurately in the center of the joint (and in the original dowel hole) with confidence. To use the jig, turn the dial until you get the correct-size hole on the right side of the tool. Clamp the jig in place over the joint, centering

1 Drill out the broken dowel using a doweling jig to ensure alignment with the hole.

the dowel hole in the jig over the joint's dowel (or aligning the tool's gauge mark with a center mark if you were drilling a new hole). Now just drill the hole.

Note: If you were making a new dowel joint in same-thickness wood, you'd line up the jig with marks that match those in the first piece. If you were using different-thickness wood for the joint, you'd insert dowel centers in the holes you just drilled, and tap the joint together to make center marks on the mating joint piece. You'd then use those marks as centers for the holes in that mating piece.

After drilling out the hole, work any remaining dowel pieces around the edge of the hole loose with a narrow chisel, and pick them out using needle-nose pliers, thus cleaning out the original dowel hole.

2 Prepare the dowels. Cut each dowel pin ⅛ inch shorter than the combined depth of the two holes it will enter, chamfer the ends using a wood rasp or file, and cut a groove lengthwise with a backsaw to allow glue and air to escape the hole.

3 Assemble the joint. Apply a thin layer of wood glue to the dowels, the holes, and all joint surfaces, spreading the glue with a palette knife or glue brush. Install the dowels, and assemble the parts, clamping them tight. Clean up excess glue using a damp rag. Keep the joint clamped for at least 2 hours.

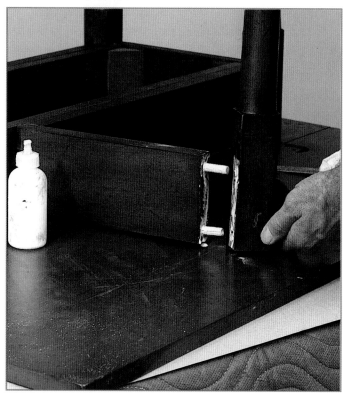

2 Prepare the dowel by cutting it 1/8 in. short, cutting a groove, and chamfering the ends with a rasp or knife.

3 Apply glue to all joint parts, install the dowels, assemble the joint, and clamp it tight.

BED JOINTS

Joints in beds can be stressed and broken, especially when the bed must be moved often to be made up. Broken joints usually occur in one of two spots: where the slat ledger joins the side rail and where a side rail joins a bed post. Hook-and-pin assemblies are especially vulnerable to breakage because the wood members have slots cut in them, which can easily break. When the wood around the pins in either the post or side rail is split, cracked, or otherwise severely damaged, you'll have to rebuild that section of the post or rail, recutting the slot and remounting the hardware in the new wood. The procedure is the same for either member.

Rebuilding a Hook-and-Pin Side-Rail Joint

Difficulty Level:

Tools and Materials

Combination square	Scratch awl
Router or mortise chisel	Mallet and hammer
Wood to make a patch	Screwdriver
Backsaw and circular saw	Block plane
Clamps	Drill and bits
Wood glue and glue brush or palette knife	

1 Mark the damaged area. Using a combination square and a scratch awl to scribe straight lines, mark off the area you need to remove. If you're working on a side rail as opposed to a bed post, remove the side-rail slat ledger. Avoid cutting out wood surfaces in highly visible areas such as the front of the side rail, if possible, as this will make your repairs more visible and harder to hide with touch-up finishing.

2 Cut out the damage. Remove all the hardware and rout or chisel out the damaged area. If you use a router, use guides such as a router fence or straight blocks clamped to the post or rail to allow you to get straight cuts. Remember that the simpler you make your cuts and angles, the easier it will be to fit the new wood into the post or rail, so keep your angles at 90 or 45 degrees.

3 Fit the patch. After routing and chiseling out the area, cut a piece of wood to fit. Make sure the wood grain runs in the same direction as that of the rest of the rail or post. It's crucial that you fit all the joint surfaces tightly when fitting the new wood to the cutout; this requires patience and fine-tuning

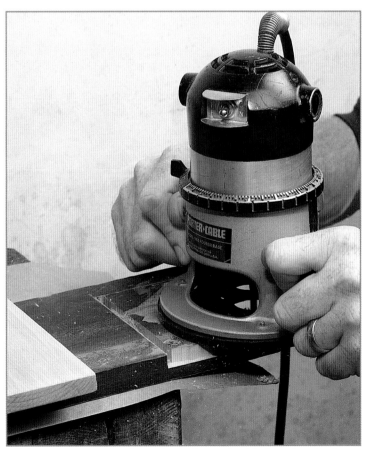

1 *Mark the damaged area to be cut out using a square and scratch awl. Note that the ledger (at bottom of rail) has been removed.*

2 *Use a router with a fence (or a clamped guide board, as in the photo) to cut out the damage.*

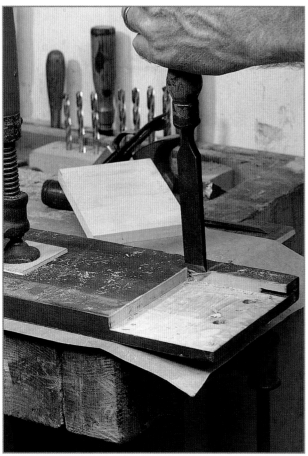

3 Prepare a patch for the cutout, and use a chisel and block plane to create a tight fit for the patch.

4 Apply glue to the joining surfaces, and install the patch, clamping it firmly in place.

with a block plane and chisel. When cutting the new block, make it slightly thicker than the cutout area and allow the outside edges of the block to extend beyond the surface of the post or rail. You'll plane and sand all these areas flush after you install the block.

4 Install the patch. After fitting the patch, apply wood glue to all joining surfaces. Spread the glue with a palette knife. Install clamps as shown, and clean up any excess glue with a damp rag. Check the joint areas to make sure they're tight.

5 Trim the patch. After about 3 hours, when the glue is dry, remove the clamps. Plane, chisel, and sand the new wood flush with the surface of the post or rail. If you have a lot of wood to remove, use a belt sander or large plane, followed by a sanding block and sandpaper.

6 Mark the hook-plate slot. Measure and mark the lines for slots and center points for the pin holes by using the measurements from an undamaged side-rail joint. For the slot depth, hold the hook plate in the appropriate position on the

5 After the glue is dry, trim the patch perfectly flush using a plane, chisel, and sandpaper.

6 *Use the hook plate as a pattern to determine the depth and pin locations, and mark the plate's slot.*

7 *Cut the hook-plate slot using a circular saw as shown, or use a drill and narrow chisel.*

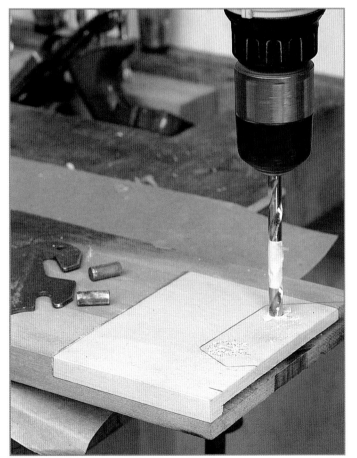

8 *Mark the drill bit for the proper depth, and drill the holes for the hook-plate mounting pins.*

side of the rail or post, mark an outline, and measure. Make your slot depth slightly deeper (about ⅛ to ¼ inch) to provide easy joint assembly.

7 **Cut the slot.** Cut the slot for the hook plate using a circular saw or by drilling a series of holes into the wood and chiseling out the slot with a narrow mortising chisel. To drill the holes in a straight line, clamp a straight block along the slot line to use as a sight guide for aligning the drill bit. You must drill the holes straight so that the slot is straight. Mark the drill bit with masking tape to determine hole depth.

If you use a circular saw to cut the slot, clamp two short pieces of two-by lumber on each side of the rail end to provide a surface on which to rest the saw's base plate. Clamp the rail so it sits vertical and stationary, as in the photograph. Make sure you're using a conventional circular-saw blade and not a thin-kerf type. Set the proper depth on the blade before plugging in the saw. Position the saw as shown, align the blade over the slot line, and start the saw. Holding the saw firmly in position, gradually plunge the blade into the slot line, moving slowly until you reach the full blade depth. Release the power trigger, and remove the saw. The kerf left by the blade will be thick enough to accommodate a hook plate.

8 **Drill the pin holes.** To install the metal pins, drill straight into the wood where you've marked the holes. These holes must be straight or the pin position may not

9 *Slip the hook plate into the slot, and tap the pins into position using a hammer.*

10 *Using stain and finish to match the rest of the bed, touch up the patch area.*

be right in the slot. If you feel it's necessary, have someone help you sight across the bit, making sure it's perpendicular with the wood to ensure a straight hole. Better yet, use a drill press or drill guide if you have one. Mark the depth of your hole on the bit with masking tape. Check the size of your drill bit to guarantee a snug fit of the metal pin by drilling into a scrap piece of wood first and trying the pin to see how it fits.

9 **Install the hook plate.** Slide the hook plate into the side-rail slot, and tap the metal pins into the holes until they lock the plate in position. To hold the metal pins in place, install a thin piece of luaun plywood over the holes.

10 **Finish the patch.** Touch up all sanded surfaces—both new and existing wood—with stain, and finish to match the rest of the side rail.

Repairing Side-Rail Ledger Joints

Box springs and mattresses can be supported in various ways. Some beds are equipped with angle irons that mount to side rails to support platforms or box springs on which the mattress rests. Most beds have wooden strips, called ledger boards, attached to the inside of the side rails with glue and screws. Wooden slats rest on these ledgers, spanning the width of the bed and supporting the box spring and mattress. If these support strips or slat ledgers are loose or split, the mattress and box spring may collapse.

Loose Slat Ledgers. If the slat ledger is loose, remove the mounting screws and clean off the old glue. After applying glue, remount the ledger by installing and tightening the screws. If any screw is stripped, drill a new screw hole beside the old one, and then reinstall the screws to mount the ledger.

Split Slat Ledgers. If the ledger has a minor split, work glue into the split and apply clamps. Install additional wood screws in any weak areas for extra strength after the glue is dry and you've removed the clamps.

Replacing a Side-Rail Ledger

If the side-rail slat ledger cannot be repaired to its original strength, you'll have to replace it.

Difficulty Level: 🔨🔨

Tools and Materials

Chisels, wood rasp, or utility knife	Screwdriver
Wood for ledger	Masking tape
Wood glue and palette knife	Clamps
Drill and assorted bits	Rag

1 **Remove the damaged ledger.** Back the mounting screws out of the old ledger to remove it. Pry off any ledger parts that don't come off the rail easily, and clean the old glue from the rail using solvent or by gently scraping with a chisel, wood rasp, or the edge of a knife.

2 **Make a new ledger strip.** Make a new ledger from a hardwood strip to match the original ledger. Drill and countersink screw holes in the strip, spacing them to miss the holes in the rail from the original ledger.

3 **Drill pilot holes.** Apply glue to the joining surfaces of the new ledger and side rail, and then clamp the

ledger in place. Drill pilot holes in the rail for the new screws. Mark the hole depth on the drill bit with masking tape so you don't drill through the front of the rail.

4 **Mount the new ledger.** Install the screws in the new ledger, remove the clamps, and clean off any excess glue with a damp rag.

1 *Back out the screws on a badly damaged side-rail slat ledger, and pry the ledger loose for replacement.*

2 *Cut a new slat ledger to size, using the old one as reference, and drill it for mounting holes.*

3 *Glue and clamp the ledger, and drill pilot holes into the rail for the mounting screws.*

4 *Install the mounting screws using the appropriate screwdriver, and then remove the clamps.*

7

OTHER REPAIRS

Furniture repair can involve a variety of problems. Although loose and broken joints are basic, structural problems, many other areas can be damaged through normal wear and tear, not to mention abuse or neglect.

Drawers, for example, may be pushed in and pulled out of casegoods thousands of times over a period of years. This movement can wear wooden runners down and break the drawer stops loose. Changing temperatures and humidity can affect solid wood, causing drawers to swell and stick, veneer to pop loose, or panels and tops to split or warp. Old rocking chairs may have split or broken rocker runners because of stress caused by age and constant use. Some furniture may be damaged in transit, or it may sustain damage by being accidentally knocked over by children or pets. This chapter addresses common repair problems you may encounter in furniture restoration.

DRAWERS

Few things are more aggravating than trying to open and shut drawers that don't work properly. If a drawer isn't working smoothly, make sure it's not overloaded; if it is, lessen the load and you'll likely solve your problem. Next, check the runners on the drawer and in the cabinet. If they're badly worn or damaged, they may need to be rebuilt.

Determining Whether Runners Need Rebuilding

To determine how badly drawer runners are worn, remove the drawer and turn it upside down. Use a carpenter's framing square to line up the drawer front and drawer bottom. Fit the square tightly against the drawer front, allowing it to extend down the length of the runner on the drawer bottom. Look at the distance between the drawer runner and the edge of the square as it extends toward the back of the drawer. The spacing should give you an indication of the extent of wear on the runner.

Extent of Drawer-Runner Wear

Square

Determining Whether Runners Need Rebuilding. *Set a large square against the bottom of the drawer, and check the space between the square and the drawer runner along the drawer's length.*

Next, sight down the runner on the inside of the cabinet. This will allow you to see whether the inside runner is straight and flat or dished out and grooved from wear. Most older pieces of furniture will show some wear on runners. If the wear appears minimal, either on the drawers or on the runners inside the carcase, and there appears to be no other serious damage, there are some quick solutions you can try.

Easy Solutions for Problem Drawer Runners

Try rubbing paraffin or candle wax on the runners at the bottom of the drawers to make them work more smoothly. Sometimes strategically placing a thumb-tack or small furniture glide at the front of the runner inside the carcase will help drawers work better, but only temporarily.

Some drawers have runners that are mounted under the middle of the drawer, centered inside the cabinet. If these centered runners are loose, drawers can become crooked, causing the drawer to bind in the cabinet. Try remounting the runners in their proper position to correct your problem.

Another Easy Drawer-Runner Solution

Yet another easy way to make runners work better is by using shellac and wax.

Difficulty Level:

Tools and Materials

Shellac	Paste wax
Brush	Rag
Fine sandpaper (280- to 320-grit)	

1 Apply a coat of shellac. Brush a coat of shellac on the bottom and sides of the drawer runner. Allow it to dry for several hours.

2 Sand the drawer bottom. After the shellac finish is dry, lightly sand the bottom of the drawer with fine sandpaper (280- to 320-grit).

3 Apply paste wax. Using a rag, apply a coat of paste wax to the sanded runner. Wait about 10 to 20 minutes until the wax dries, and then buff the runner with a clean rag.

Rubbing paraffin on drawer runners will sometimes make them work more smoothly.

2 When the shellac is dry, sand the runner using 280- to 320-grit sandpaper.

1 Brush a coat of shellac on the drawer side and runners to make them run smoothly.

3 Apply paste wax to the drawer sides and runners, and buff them after about 20 minutes.

Replacing Worn, Damaged, or Missing Runners

If runners on the bottom of a drawer are severely damaged, worn, or missing, the solutions mentioned on page 119 may not work. Damaged or worn runners need to be rebuilt and missing runners replaced.

Difficulty Level: 🔨 🔨 🔨

Tools and Materials

Framing square or other large square	Scratch awl
Block plane and sandpaper	Chisel
Wood for a new runner	Clamps
Wood glue and palette knife	Handsaw
Touch-up stain, finish, and wax	Damp rag

1 Mark the drawer. Place the drawer on a padded workbench with its side facing up. Using a large square and a scratch awl, scribe a straight line the length of the drawer directly above the damaged area.

2 Cut out the damage. Cut the damaged area off the drawer side using a handsaw; if necessary, remove the drawer side to do this.

3 Plane the drawer. Turn the drawer or the drawer side upside down, and smooth the cut edge of the wood with a finely tuned block plane. If the side remains on the drawer and you can't plane all the way to the drawer front, use a wood chisel to smooth this area. Keep the edge as straight as possible.

4 Glue up a new runner. Measure the cut, and fit a new piece of wood for the runner. If you make the patch slightly larger, you can plane or sand it after

1 To repair a damaged drawer runner, first scribe a straight line above the damaged area.

2 Using a handsaw, cut away the damaged area. Remove the drawer side if necessary.

3 Plane the bottom of the runner cut to smooth it. Use a chisel to smooth hard-to-get-at areas (inset).

4 *Cut a new strip of wood for the runner. Glue and clamp the new runner in position on the drawer.*

5 *Plane the runner edge until the drawer fits and works smoothly in the cabinet.*

attaching it. Plane the joint edge of the patch, making it dead straight for a good fit with the drawer-side edge. Glue and clamp the new runner in position. Remove any excess glue with a damp rag, and then let the glue dry for two hours.

5 **Plane the patch.** If you removed the drawer side (Step 2), reinstall it. Smooth the runner with a block plane, and trim it at the back if necessary. Fit the drawer to the casegood carcase by planing and sanding the new runner until it runs smoothly. Stain, finish, and touch up the patch where necessary. As a last step, apply wax to the runner.

Switching Interior Drawer Runners

If the runners inside the cabinet are worn or damaged, you can sometimes remove them, switch them to the other side of the cabinet, and turn them upside down. This gives the drawer a new surface to run on while still using the original runners.

If this won't work because of the runners' design—or if a runner is missing—you may need to make new ones to match. Remove the old runner to get the exact measurements you need for the new one. Try to duplicate the original type of wood if you're working with old collectible or antique cabinets, as this will help to preserve their character. On newer cabinets this is not as important, and any hardwood will work fine. If runners are mounted using screws or nails, drill pilot holes for these fasteners to keep them from splitting the wood.

Freeing Stuck Drawers

If you can't open or close a drawer or if it gets stuck in one position, the wood in the drawer sides may have swollen, making the drawer too large for its opening. To be sure, check the following items:

• If the drawer is lockable, check to make sure it's not locked; if it is and the key is lost, try other drawer keys to see whether they'll work. If that doesn't work, remove the drawer's back panel or reach through an upper drawer opening and try to remove the lock. As a last resort, try to pry the drawer rail up to clear the lock bolt. If you're afraid this will damage the piece, call a locksmith.

Sometimes you can remove worn runners *(inset) inside a casegood and switch them to the other side of the carcase by turning them upside down. Use a mallet and chisel for removal.*

• Drawers are sometimes made to fit only their particular opening; if they get exchanged with another drawer, they won't work well. Move the drawers around to different openings to see whether this solves the problem.

• Remove the drawer above the stuck one, and investigate to make sure nothing inside is preventing the drawer from opening. You can remove the back of the piece of furniture to look inside if necessary. You may find that a dust panel above the drawer has warped or fallen down in front of the back of the drawer or below it, preventing it from opening.

• If you've checked all these things and still not found your problem, the drawer is most likely swollen. Remove the drawer; if it's badly stuck and you can't free

Some areas of a drawer side may need to be planed or sanded to allow the drawer to work smoothly.

METAL DRAWER RUNNERS

Most kitchen-cabinet drawers and many manufactured desk drawers use metal drawer runners, which allow the drawers to open and close smoothly. The runners are usually made of two main parts: Metal guides mount inside the cabinet with screws, and a track, or slide, mounts to the drawer side. The drawer track then slides in or on the cabinet guide.

Drawer Slide

Drawer Guide

To remove a drawer with metal runners, pull it out as far as possible from the cabinet or desk, and look for any kind of clips, buttons, or levers on the slide to release it. Some hardware has an additional setscrew that you must also remove. If the drawer runner doesn't work smoothly, make sure the drawer slide is seated properly in the metal guide mounted in the cabinet. You may also need to lubricate the runner's moving parts, such as rollers or ball bearings, with a silicone spray or light machine oil. Make sure all mounting screws inside the cabinet and on the drawer side are tight.

If the drawer is out of line with the opening, adjust the drawer by loosening the mounting screws on the slide or the guide and repositioning it. Most drawer hardware is equipped with slotted screw holes to allow for this kind of adjustment. If you find that the runner's sliding mechanism is damaged or broken, take it out and look for a replacement on woodworker- or furniture-supply websites. When ordering a new one, pay attention to the size you need and the amount of clearance required on each side of the drawer.

Oil Here

it, try removing the cabinet back and tapping along the back edge of the drawer with a hammer to free it. After removing the drawer, try to determine where the drawer is sticking by looking for shiny areas on the wood. Use a belt sander or a sharp block plane to sand or plane these areas down enough for the drawer to move freely. This procedure is often a matter of trial and error; just continue to plane or sand until the drawer works well. Lastly, shellac and wax the runners to keep them working smoothly. (See "Another Easy Drawer-Runner Solution," page 123.)

Repairing Warped Drawer Bottoms

Often drawer bottoms made from solid wood can warp or split. To correct a warp, you can usually remove the bottom, flip it over, and reinstall it. Repair splits and cracks by gluing and clamping them. (See "Repairing a Split Drawer Bottom," page 132.) If a drawer bottom is warped or damaged beyond repair, you'll have to replace it. The easiest way to do this job is by using a piece of ¼-inch-thick plywood. Luaun plywood, available at home centers or lumberyards, works well for this. Remove the old bottom, cut the new panel to size from the plywood, slide the new panel in place, and attach it.

Missing Drawer Stops

When you close a drawer, in most cases it should stop flush with the front edge of the furniture. If the drawer seems to go too far into the opening when you close it, you're probably missing the drawer stops.

Most wooden casegoods use small blocks of wood to stop the drawer at the proper position when you push it closed. Stops are mounted inside the carcase and may be back- or front-mounted. These stops can break loose and get lost or damaged. Remove the drawer, and look inside the cabinet to see where the old stop blocks were mounted. You'll find that most stops are mounted on the rearmost rail at the back of the carcase. Sometimes you'll find stops installed on the front rail, just behind the face of the drawer front. Clean old glue from these areas to prepare for the new blocks.

Replacing Back Drawer Stops

Difficulty Level: 🔨

Tools and Materials

Block plane
Measuring tape
Saw to cut blocks
Wood glue and glue brush or palette knife
Scrap plywood or one-by blocks and shims as necessary

1 Measure for the stops. Push the drawer all the way into the cabinet until it hits the back. While the drawer is pushed all the way back, measure from the front edge of the cabinet to the front edge of the drawer. Use this measurement to determine the size blocks you'll need to act as drawer stops.

2 Install the stops. Cut the appropriate-size blocks from scrap ¾-inch plywood or one-by lumber. Remove the drawer, and place the blocks at the back of the cabinet. Gently reinstall the drawer until it makes contact with the new drawer stops. Check to see whether the drawer front is flush with the carcase front. For

1 To determine the width of the drawer stops, push the drawer in and measure from the front.

2 Cut the block, test-fit it, and then apply glue to the block and install it in the back of the carcase.

fine-tuning, trim the block with a block plane to bring the drawer farther into the carcase, or glue veneer shims to the front of the block to move the drawer out. Attach the block.

1 When installing front drawer stops, measure the thickness of the drawer front.

2 Scribe a line on the drawer rail using a combination square set to the drawer-front thickness.

Replacing Front Drawer Stops

Difficulty Level:

Tools and Materials

Measuring tape	Brads
Combination square	Hammer
Scratch awl	Nail set
Saw to cut blocks	
Wood glue and palette knife	
Scrap ¼-inch plywood or solid wood	

1 Measure the drawer front. Measure the thickness of the drawer front at the bottom edge. You'll use this measurement to determine how far back from the cabinet front to mount drawer stops on the drawer rail.

2 Scribe a reference line. Set a combination square to the measurement you obtained in Step 1, and scribe a reference line on the drawer rail where you want to install a stop as shown in the photo.

3 Install the stops. Cut the stop or stops from ¼-inch solid wood or plywood, and align them on the reference line you marked on the drawer rail. Mount the blocks using glue and small brads. Countersink the brads using a nail set. Install the drawer to double-check the drawer stop position.

3 Glue and nail stops cut from ¼-in.-thick stock, aligning them with the reference line.

SPLITS AND FRACTURES

Breaks in wood are caused by too much stress or pressure being applied to wood, sometimes from misuse or abuse and other times as a result of natural expansion and contraction of solid wood. There are two general kinds of breaks: splits and fractures. A split occurs with the grain; a fracture occurs across the grain.

Legs and stretchers on tables not only get loose but sometimes break or split. Delicately turned finials can snap off easily, and solid-wood panels can crack and split as the wood ages. These splits and breaks can generally be repaired satisfactorily, restoring the structural integrity of the piece and improving its appearance.

Splits. Breaks that occur in the direction of the grain will usually make strong joints that do not need reinforcement, as long as they're free from old glue and will pull up tight when clamped. For this reason, you can usually fix a split by working glue well into the opening, clamping it tight, and allowing it to dry. If the split has been glued previously, clean the joint before gluing.

Splits in solid-wood panels, like chest tops and sides, table tops, chair seats, and framed panels, are common. The panels are not necessarily all repaired in the same way, however. Some wood panels, for example, can be reglued by clamping (chest tops, table tops), while others need to be repaired by shimming (chest sides).

If a wood panel is free from other wood crosspieces like aprons, drawer runners, or interior framework, the split can probably be reglued like any other. But if the panel is attached to crosspieces of wood, it must be detached before regluing. Check the panel to see whether it's independent or attached to another wood piece. Table tops are usually attached to aprons or frames that may need to be taken off before you try to reglue splits in the top. Chest sides often have drawer runners attached to the inside, making cracks impossible to pull up without first removing the runners. Because it's usually impractical to remove drawer runners, this problem is most often solved by shimming the split with thin strips of wood or veneer (page 131).

Fractures. If wood is broken across the grain (that is, with the break running perpendicular to the direction of the grain in the wood), reinforcement is usually needed. Fractures often occur at the weakest, most vulnerable points in a piece of furniture and need to be repaired correctly. Common sites for fractures include turned pieces like legs or stretchers, which get too much stress, and delicate, decorative pieces, like finials. Turned objects, also called turnings, are pieces of wood that have been "turned," or fashioned on a lathe. As the wood revolves in the lathe, chisels are used to shape it into things like legs, stretchers, spindles, posts, and finials. When you repair broken turnings, you usually need to use wood or metal screw dowels as reinforcement.

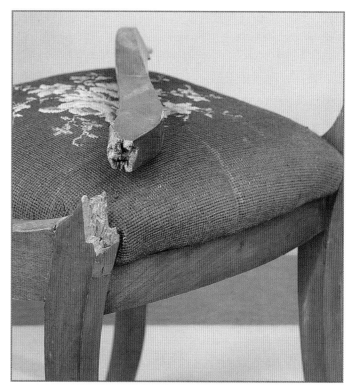

Splits, even in chair legs, will usually be strong once fixed if they're glued and clamped properly.

With fractures, where wood is broken across the grain, the repair will be weak unless you provide additional reinforcement.

There are other places where wood has a tendency to break. One such area is where curved cuts are made to produce a curved pedestal or chair leg. This design leaves short wood grain, which is weak, in certain key areas, like the bottom part of a leg. If too much stress is applied, the short grain will fracture.

Another area susceptible to fractures is where multiple joints are cut into a relatively thin piece of wood in one place, weakening the wood. For this reason, some chair back posts break where the seat rails join them.

The following section looks at these and other fractures, as well as various kinds of splits, and shows how to fix them step by step.

Regluing a Split in a Solid-Wood Panel

If you can detach the panel and pull up the crack by applying slight pressure to it with clamps, the regluing job is easy. In this project, the solid-wood-panel top to a gentleman's shaving drawer (which traditionally is mounted on a dresser) was glued in place, which probably helped cause the split in the first place: Because the panel was glued, eliminating any possibility of movement, the natural expansion and contraction of the wood built up stress in the panel and caused the split. Whenever you attach a solid-wood top and the wood grain does not run in the same direction as the grain in the piece to which you attach it, you should screw the top in place without glue.

Difficulty Level: 🔨

Tools and Materials

Screwdriver	Mallet
Wood glue and palette knife	Clamps
Hacksaw blade if necessary	Rag
Glue solvent or chisels, wood rasp, and utility knife	

1 Remove the top. Remove any screws holding the top to the piece of furniture; also, remove any framework, such as aprons, from the top. If the top is glued in place, tap it with a mallet to free it.

2 Clean the joint. If the joint was previously glued, clean it using glue solvent or by gently scraping it with a chisel, wood rasp, or the edge of a knife. If the split won't open up completely and it has old glue in it, use a hacksaw blade to clean it.

3 Glue and clamp the panel. Install clamps on the panel to pull the split up; if the clamps work and the split closes up, remove them. Apply glue, making sure it gets well into the split. If the split won't open up, rub

1 To reglue a split wood panel, you must first remove it from frames, aprons, or bases.

2 If the split contains old glue, clean it off using glue solvent or by scraping with a knife-blade edge, chisel, or rasp.

3 Test-fit the panel parts, disassemble them, and then glue and reclamp them for several hours.

4 Reattach the panel to the framework using screws, not wood glue and clamps.

back and forth across it with your fingertips, forcing the glue down into the split. Reinstall the clamps as before, and apply pressure, pulling the split tight. In some cases you may need to clamp across the split as shown in the photo. If so, wooden hand screws work best. Protect them with wax paper. Clean up any excess glue with a damp rag, and allow the joint to dry for several hours.

4 Reattach the panel. Remove the clamps, and reattach any aprons or other framework or pieces. Do not glue these pieces to the solid-wood panel if the wood grain runs in a direction different from that in the panel; doing so could cause the panel to split again later. Use screws or some other means to attach these pieces.

Shimming a Split in a Solid-Wood Panel

Some solid-wood panels have attached framework or other wood pieces that either can't be removed or are

impractical to remove. For this reason you can't glue up a crack in the panel in the normal way. An example of this is a solid-wood side in a chest of drawers that has drawer runners mounted on the interior running across the grain of the panel. As the chest begins to shrink, the drawer runners don't shrink with it, and the side eventually splits from top to bottom. To repair the cracks, use thin strips of wood or veneer to shim them.

Often this kind of split or season crack is small and won't affect the piece's structural integrity. If this is the case, make a decision about repairs based on appearance. If the appearance bothers you, make repairs; if not, leave it and let the split be part of the natural character of the piece. On some older pieces, season cracks aren't that objectionable, but you'll likely want to make repairs on newer pieces.

Difficulty Level: 🔨 🔨

Tools and Materials

Hacksaw blade	Veneer shims
Chisel or block plane	120-grit sandpaper
Wood glue and palette knife	Rag
Touch-up stain and finish to match	Utility knife

1 Clean the split. If the split is not open enough to fit veneer shims into it, insert a fine hacksaw blade into the crack and cut it open so the shims will fit.

2 Prepare the shims. Cut veneer shims or a thin wood strip from the same type of wood to fit the split. If the split is open enough for a thicker wood strip, cut the strip, tapering it on one edge so it will fit the crack easily, and wedge it tightly into the split. Put glue in the crack and on the shims. Install the shims into the crack, forcing them into place. If you're using a wood

1 Use a hacksaw blade to open up or clean out the split so that veneer shims will fit.

2 Apply glue to the veneer shims and the split, and push the shims into the split openings.

3 After the glue dries, trim the shims flush with the panel surface using a chisel or plane.

4 Touch up the repaired area using an artist's brush and stain, followed by finish.

strip, force it down into the crack with a hammer and a wood block. Clean up the excess glue with a damp rag, and allow the repair to dry for several hours.

3 Trim the shims. Trim the shim or shims flush with the surface of the panel using a sharp chisel or a block plane. Do final smoothing using 120-grit sandpaper.

4 Touch up the repair. If you're not refinishing the piece, touch up the repaired area using an artist's paintbrush, stain, and finish to match the surrounding wood. Use the back of a piece of sandpaper or a small paper plate as a palette on which to mix the stain colors.

Repairing a Split Drawer Bottom

Drawer bottoms made from solid wood often warp or split. This is one reason why bottoms are now almost always made from thin plywood or other panel material. To correct a warp, you can sometimes remove the bottom, flip it over, and reinstall it. You can usually repair splits by gluing and clamping. Sometimes you can do the repair by detaching the mounting nails or screws as well as any small glue blocks on the bottom of the panel between the split and the drawer back, thus enabling the wood to move freely so that the split can be pulled together. In this way, you can glue and clamp the split with the drawer bottom still in the drawer. After the glue dries and you've removed the clamps, make sure the panel is in the proper position, and reinstall the nails, screws, and/or glue blocks to secure it.

If it's not possible to fix the bottom panel while it's in the drawer, remove it and follow the steps below.

Difficulty Level: 🔨 🔨

Tools and Materials

Hammer, screwdriver, nail puller	Chisel and mallet
Wood glue and palette knife	Rag
Wax paper or clear plastic wrap	Wood battens
Drill and assorted bitsClamps	Dowels
Backsaw	Wood rasp (or chisels)

1 Remove the bottom and apply glue. Using a hammer and screwdriver or nail puller, pry loose the nails holding the drawer bottom in place. Remove any glue blocks that may be attached using a wood chisel and mallet. Slide the bottom free of the drawer, and apply wood glue to the split edges.

1 Remove all nails, screws, or glue blocks, slide out the panel, and apply glue to the split edges.

2 Clamp battens across the split to keep the panel rigid, and then clamp the panel using bar clamps.

3 After the glue dries, remove all clamps, and slide the drawer bottom back into place.

2 Clamp the drawer bottom. Put the pieces of the drawer bottom together, wiping off any excess glue with a damp rag. Cover the glued crack with clear plastic or wax paper on both sides of the panel. Apply two rigid wood battens across the split on one side of the panel and two battens on the other side, running from front to back of the drawer bottom panel. Clamp these battens together with the drawer bottom sandwiched between them. Clamp the drawer bottom from front to back with bar clamps, pulling the split up tight. If needed, loosen battens slightly to pull the split tight. Clean any excess glue with a damp rag, and make sure drawer bottom parts are aligned.

3 Reinstall the panel. Wait until the glue is dry, about 2 hours. Remove the clamps, and reinstall the drawer bottom using brads and a hammer.

Repairing a Split in a Pedestal-Table Column

If you find a split in the column of a pedestal table, it's likely to be around a sliding-dovetail joint holding a leg to the column. (See "Sliding-Dovetail Joints," page 80.) Because sliding dovetails are such strong joints, you should avoid taking them apart if the joints themselves aren't loose. Often you can work glue into the split and clamp it without removing the leg.

Difficulty Level: 🔨

Tools and Materials

Scratch awl and mallet	Hand screw or clamps
Wood glue and palette knife	Rag

1 Glue the break. Squeeze wood glue into the split, forcing it in with a palette knife. If the split isn't wide enough to work glue into it, widen it a bit by inserting a scratch awl at the top of the break and striking it lightly with a mallet until the split widens.

A split in a pedestal column is most likely to occur at a joint. Try to fix the damage without taking the joint apart.

1 Widen the split with a scratch awl, and force glue into the crack using a palette knife.

2 Attach a clamp to pull the crack tight, and clean off excess glue with a damp rag.

2 Clamp the break. Apply a clamp to the break, cleaning up any excess glue with a damp rag. Keep the leg clamped until the glue dries—about 2 hours. Wooden hand screws work best for this kind of clamping job because you can adjust them to fit odd angles and configurations.

Reinforcing a Split Using Dowels

Some split repairs require reinforcing. If the wood will undergo stress, as in a chair seat or table top, you can reinforce it by installing dowels into the wood across the split, as shown in this project, or by installing wooden battens on the back or underside of the split wood (next project). If you have a long crack, you can use dowels on both ends of the crack.

Difficulty Level: 🔨 🔨

Tools and Materials

Wood rasp or utility knife	Backsaw
Wood glue and palette knife	Rag
Sandpaper and sanding block	Drill and assorted bits
Touch-up stain and finish to match	Dowels

1 Drill the hole. After you've glued the crack and it's dry, choose a dowel with a diameter not more than one-half the thickness of the wood. Drill a hole into the edge of the panel, drilling diagonally across the crack or split area. Get a helper to sight across the drill bit as it enters the wood, keeping it aligned with the panel's edge. Start the hole close enough to the crack so that when you sink the drill bit all the way into the wood, it can pass through the cracked area.

2 Install the dowel. Clean shavings from the hole, and cut a dowel to size. Cut a groove lengthwise in the dowel using a backsaw, and chamfer the tip using a wood rasp. Make sure the dowel will fit the hole properly before applying glue. If the dowel is too tight, shave it down with a wood rasp or the edge of a sharp knife until it's snug but not overly tight. Put a thin layer of wood glue in the hole and on the dowel. Install the dowel into the hole, tapping it all the way in. Clean up any excess glue with a damp rag, and allow it to dry.

1 To reinforce a split, drill a hole so that the dowel runs diagonally through the split.

2 Prepare the reinforcing dowel, apply glue to it, and tap it into the hole using a mallet.

3 Trim the dowel flush. Cut the end of the dowel sticking out from the chair flush with the wood's edge, using a backsaw.

4 Touch up the repair. Block-sand the repair until it's smooth using 120-grit sandpaper, and touch up the repaired area to match the surrounding wood using stain and an artist's brush. Mix the stain color on the back of a piece of sandpaper. Apply finish after the stain dries.

3 Using a fine-toothed saw, cut the dowel end flush with the edge of the chair seat.

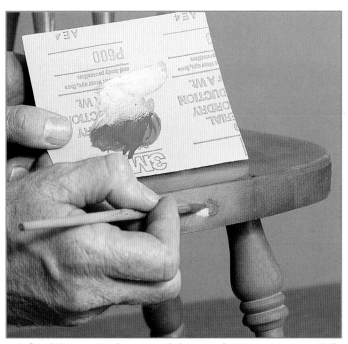

4 Sand the repaired area, and then touch it up using an artist's brush and matching stain and finish.

Reinforcing a Split Using Battens

In certain situations, especially with chair seats and some table tops, you can use wooden battens to strengthen the cracked area. A wooden batten is a rigid strip of wood mounted across the panel's split to reinforce it.

Difficulty Level: 🔨 🔨

Tools and Materials

Measuring tape and pencil	Wood for battens
Plane or belt sander	Drill and assorted bits
Wood screws and screwdriver	

1 Measure the panel. After you've repaired the split, turn the panel upside down and measure it to determine what size to make the battens and how many to use. A chair seat may need only a couple of battens, for example, while a table top may require more. Judge for yourself what it will take to strengthen the split sufficiently.

2 Cut and mark the battens. Cut lengths of wood to be used for the battens, making sure they're flat on the bottom edge. You can bevel the top edges to provide a finished look using a large plane or belt sander.

1 Measure the length and width of the panel to determine the size and number of battens required.

2 *Cut the battens to size, and mark where you'll install the mounting screws—one in each wood section.*

3 *Drill and counterbore the battens, drill pilot holes in the panel, and install the wood screws.*

Because you'll attach the batten with wood screws, determine where the screws will be, and mark the holes in the battens. Try to place one screw in each section of wood that makes up the panel.

3 **Install the battens.** Drill and countersink slightly oversize holes for the wood screws to allow for wood movement in the panel. Generally speaking, use screws that are long enough to sink about two-thirds of the way into the panel. For most jobs #8 or #10 screws will be appropriate. Lay the battens across the split on the backside of the panel, and mark a center point for each screw. Remove the battens, and drill pilot holes. To avoid poking through the other side of the panel, use a piece of tape to mark the drill bit for proper depth. Using the wood screws, install the battens without glue to the wood panel.

Repairing a Broken Turning through One End

If a turned piece such as a chair leg or stretcher is broken close to one end and a hole can be drilled deep enough into the end of the piece to go through the broken area, then you can make a dowel repair from the outside.

Difficulty Level: 🔨🔨

Tools and Materials

Wood glue and palette knife	Clamps
Drill and assorted bits	Rag
Dowels	Backsaw
Wood rasp	

You can reinforce a turned piece *that's broken near the end by drilling from the outside and inserting a dowel.*

1 Glue and clamp the break. Reassemble the two pieces of the turning, and glue and clamp them together, making sure they're straight and aligned with each other. Clean up the excess with a damp rag, and allow the glue to dry for about 2 hours.

2 Drill from the end. Remove the clamp from the workpiece, and put the piece in a vise with the shortest broken end pointing up. Mark a center point in the end of the turned piece, and drill a small pilot hole straight down into it beyond the broken area. Keep the hole straight and centered while drilling. Use a helper to sight across the drill and the turned piece to keep them aligned. Following the pilot hole, drill a hole for the size dowel you'll use for reinforcement. The dowel should be about ¼ inch smaller in diameter than the narrowest part of the turned section you're repairing. Be sure to

drill the hole straight so you don't drill out the side of the piece as the hole goes deeper.

3 Insert the dowel. Remove the turned piece from the vise, and turn it upside down. Tap the piece lightly to remove wood shavings from the hole. Reinstall the piece in the vise, and cut a dowel to fit the hole, shaving or rasping it for a snug fit. Leave the dowel a little longer than the depth of the hole. Cut a groove lengthwise in the dowel with a backsaw, and chamfer the dowel tip. Spread a thin layer of wood glue on the dowel and in the hole. Insert the dowel in the hole, chamfered end first, and tap it all the way down.

4 Trim the dowel. After about 2 hours, when the glue is dry, cut the dowel end flush with the end of the turned piece using a backsaw to complete the repair.

1 To fix a wood turning that's broken near the end, first glue and clamp the break.

2 Drill a pilot hole in the end closest to the break (left), followed by a larger hole (right) for the dowel.

3 Clean out the hole in the turning, prepare the dowel, and then tap it fully into the hole.

4 Using a backsaw, cut the end of the dowel flush with the end of the wooden turning.

Repairing a Broken Turning in the Middle

If a turning is broken and you can't drill a hole into the end of the turned piece deep enough to go through the break, you'll have to reinforce the break by installing a dowel from within.

Difficulty Level:

Tools and Materials

Drill and assorted bits
Backsaw or dovetail saw
Clamps
Rag
Dowels
Chisels or wood rasp
Wood glue and palette
Knife or stick

1 **Drill into the break.** Examine the turned piece for any spot near the break where you can make an inconspicuous cut—usually any decorative turned area will have a groove or shoulder where you can make this cut. Put this section of the piece in a vise, and drill a pilot hole into the center of the broken end and straight through and beyond the spot where you've chosen to make your cut. Following the pilot hole, drill a larger hole for the reinforcement dowel, again drilling as far as possible beyond the spot chosen to make your cut. Make the reinforcement dowel about one-half as thick as the section where you'll make the cut.

2 **Cut the piece.** Using a fine-toothed backsaw or dovetail saw, cut across the turned piece at the spot you've chosen, and remove this piece.

3 **Glue the repair section to the break.** Glue and clamp the cut-off repair section to the other turned section at the break. After about 2 hours, when the glue is dry, remove the clamp.

4 **Drill into the break.** Secure the glued part of the turned piece in a vise, and drill deeper into the piece, following the hole you've already drilled and going as far as possible beyond the

1 *Drill through an area where you can make an inconspicuous cut, first with a pilot bit, and then with a larger one.*

2 *Saw through the turned piece where you drilled the dowel hole.*

3 *Glue and clamp the short piece you just cut off back to the turning at the original break.*

original break. Prepare the correct-size dowel, making it at least $\frac{1}{8}$ inch shorter than the combined depths of the holes in both sections of the turned piece. You may have to shave the dowel with the edge of a utility knife blade or with a wood rasp to get a proper fit. Chamfer both ends of the dowel and, using a backsaw, cut a groove lengthwise in the dowel.

5 Assemble the piece. Insert the dowel into the glued-up piece without using glue on the dowel, and test-fit the two sections of the turned piece together

4 After the glue dries, drill into the predrilled hole, going as deep as possible beyond the original break.

5 Prepare the proper-size dowel, and then glue and clamp the turning around the dowel.

with the dowel. Once you're sure everything fits together properly, apply a thin layer of wood glue to the dowel and in the holes, using a long, thin stick to spread the glue. Insert the dowel, and clamp the turned piece together. Check for straightness and alignment, clean off any excess glue with a damp rag, and allow the repair to dry.

Repairing a Turning with a Metal Screw Dowel

A metal screw dowel is a metal rod threaded like a wood screw with a tip at both ends. When you install a metal screw dowel in a broken turning, it will tighten into both pieces, pulling them together tightly.

Difficulty Level:

Tools and Materials

Wood glue and palette knife	Clamps
Measuring tape and pencil	Backsaw
Drill and assorted bits	Adjustable pliers
Metal screw dowel	Rag

1 Glue the break. Glue and clamp the two pieces of the broken turned piece together at the break, making sure they're straight and aligned. Let the assembly dry for about 2 hours.

1 Glue (top) and clamp (above) the broken turning, making sure the pieces are straight and aligned.

2 Cut the piece. Remove the clamp, and look for a shoulder in the turning as close as possible to the original break to make a crosscut. Using a fine-toothed backsaw, crosscut the turning at this spot.

3 Drill centered holes. Find the center point at the cut end of both sections, and mark it. Drill a small pilot hole straight into the center of each section. Following the pilot hole, drill a larger hole to accommodate the screw dowel in each section. Drill the hole as straight as possible. The diameter of this hole should be the same as the screw-dowel shank minus the threads. The depth should be about ⅛ inch deeper than half the length of the screw dowel. Because the metal screw dowel is strong, it's not necessary to use a large diameter; however, its length is important to make the repair

strong. Use as long a screw dowel as possible without increasing its diameter to more than two-thirds the diameter of the repair area.

4 Insert the screw dowel. Test-fit the screw dowel into the holes to be sure of the fit. Apply a thin layer of wood glue to the screw dowel and the turned piece's cut ends, and in the holes. Insert one end of the screw dowel into one of the holes, and holding it at the unthreaded middle section, thread it into the wood.

5 Screw the sections together. Insert the other end of the screw dowel into the hole of the other section. Turn and tighten the two sections together. Stop turning when the pieces are pulled up snug and are aligned with each other. Clean any excess wood glue.

2 After the glue dries, remove the clamp, and cut the piece in an inconspicuous spot near the original break.

3 Find the center point of each cut section, and drill straight holes for the screw dowel.

4 After test-fitting, apply glue to all joint surfaces, and screw the dowel into one of the sections.

5 With the metal dowel installed in one section, screw the other section onto the free end of the dowel.

Reinforcing Short Wood-Grain Breaks

This type of break generally occurs in the direction of the wood grain. Often the grain is short, and if the part will undergo much stress, the repair will require reinforcement. For this reason it's included with the section on breaks in the wood rather than splits.

Difficulty Level:

Tools and Materials

Clamps	Rag
Wood glue and palette knife	Mallet
Drill and assorted bits	Dowels
Backsaw	Wood rasp
Touch-up stain and finish to match	

1 Glue and clamp the short break. Test-fit the parts before gluing to determine the correct clamp setup.

2 Leave as many clamps attached as possible, and drill a straight dowel hole through the break.

1 Glue up the break. Test-fit the break, clamping it in place. Clamping some pieces, such as a bent leg, where this kind of break is likely to occur, can be tricky and may take some trial and error. You may have to clamp along the length of the leg, as well as across the break itself, to keep all the pieces in line. After deciding how to clamp the break and which clamps to use, remove the clamps and apply wood glue to both broken pieces. Reapply the clamps to pull the parts together. Clean any excess glue with a damp rag, and make sure that the parts are aligned and the break is tight. Let the assembly dry overnight.

2 Drill the dowel hole. If possible, leave the clamps in place for this step. At the least visible area, drill a pilot hole into the broken pieces, passing through the break. If you're drilling into the bottom of a chair or table leg, remove the caster or glide before drilling. Using the pilot hole as a guide, drill a hole for a dowel with a diameter about one-half the thickness of the wood being repaired. Drill as deeply as possible through the first piece of wood and into the second. To make sure you drill straight, have someone sight your bit for you.

3 Install the dowel. Cut a dowel to fit the hole, leaving it a little long. Cut a groove lengthwise in the dowel, and chamfer one end with a wood rasp. After cleaning wood dust and shavings from the hole, test-fit the dowel without glue. If necessary, shave or rasp the dowel to fit. Apply a thin layer of wood glue to the dowel and into the dowel hole with a long, thin stick. Insert the chamfered end of the dowel into the hole, and tap it all the way in using a mallet.

3 Fit the dowel, leaving it a little long. Then prepare it, and tap it in place using a mallet.

4 Trim the dowel flush using a fine-toothed saw, sand it smooth, and touch up the area if necessary.

4 Trim the dowel. Cut the dowel end flush with the wood surface using a backsaw. Block-sand it smooth, and touch up the area to match the surrounding wood. Replace any caster, glide, or other hardware you removed.

Reinforcing Broken Wood with a Mortised Splint

Certain breaks can't be adequately reinforced with wood dowels and must be repaired using another type of reinforcement. A round chair back, for example, may have a particularly bad break—say, a piece of wood broken out of a joint—that requires strong reinforcement

Some breaks, *such as the one on this chair back, need strong reinforcement but have no place to insert a dowel. In this case you'll need to use a mortised splint.*

but has no place to put a dowel. In such cases, a mortised splint can provide the needed strength.

Difficulty Level: 🔨 🔨 🔨

Tools and Materials

Wood glue and palette knife	Rag
Scribe or scratch awl	Clamps
Touch-up stain and finish	Backsaw
Combination square	Chisels and mallet
Matching wood block as a patch	Block plane
Sandpaper, sanding block, and dowels	Measuring tape

1 Clamp up the piece. Assemble all the pieces of the break and put them back together, clamping them without glue. Clamping a round-back chair can be quite tricky and may require trial-and-error fitting before you come up with the best configuration of clamps. Make sure all parts of the break are secured. Once you're satisfied with the clamping setup, disassemble it, work wood glue into all surfaces of the break using a palette knife, and attach the clamps. Clean up any excess glue using a damp rag, and allow the glue to dry overnight.

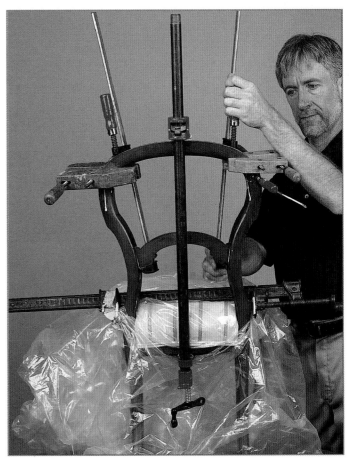

1 Test-fit the joint using clamps, and then apply glue to all joint surfaces and reinstall the clamps.

2 **Mark the mortise area.** Remove the clamps, and mark an area of the wood that you'll cut out for the wooden splint or patch. Use a marking gauge, as in the photo, or a scratch awl and a straightedge. The wood you remove should be about one-third the thickness of the wood in the area of the broken joint, running at least

2 *After the glue dries, scribe an area overlapping the break by several inches on each side.*

3 *Use a saw to make multiple cuts in the patch area (top), and then chisel out the wood (above).*

several inches on each side of the break to be strong. Cut both ends of the mortise area at about a 45-degree angle to provide a better glue surface for the patch.

3 **Cut the mortise.** Use a backsaw to cut into the wood to the depth you marked for the patch. Follow the angled lines at each end of the cutout area. Make additional 90-degree saw cuts every ⅜ to ½ inch until you cover the entire area with kerfs. Cut only as deep as the lines you made for the mortised area. Next, use a sharp wood chisel and mallet to remove the kerfed wood from within the scribed area. Work down to the scribed lines, smoothing the surface as much as possible.

4 **Cut and install the mortise block.** Cut a rectangular block from the same kind of wood as the chair and leave it about ½ inch thicker than the mortised area. Mark and cut the 45-degree cuts at each end of the block about ⅛ inch shorter than the mortise so that when you drop the block into place, there is a slight gap at the joint ends. To

4 *Cut a patch of matching wood to fit the mortise. Then glue and clamp the wood in place.*

close the gap and achieve a tight fit, turn the wood patch upside down in a vise, and use a sharp block plane to shave a little at a time from the bottom of the patch. Keep trying the block in the mortised area until it drops down sufficiently to close up the 45-degree joints at each end. When you have a good fit, apply wood glue to all joint surfaces, and clamp the patch in place. Clean up the excess glue with a damp rag, and let the joint dry overnight.

5 **Plane and sand the patch.** Remove the clamps, and use a block plane, wood chisel, and 120-grit sandpaper (using a sanding block on flat areas) to make all surfaces of the patch flush with the chair surface. To sand curved areas smooth, wrap a dowel of the correct diameter with sandpaper as a fitted sanding block.

6 **Touch up the patch.** Touch up the patched area with stain and finish to match the surrounding wood. Mix the stain colors on the back of a piece of sandpaper, and apply it with an artist's paintbrush.

5 *When the glue is dry, remove the clamps. Then plane, chisel, and sand the patch smooth.*

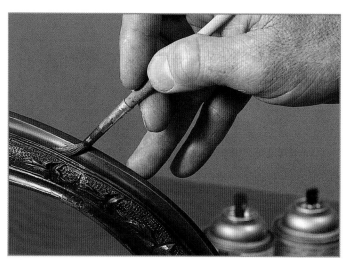

6 *Use stain, finish, and an artist's brush to touch up the patched area, matching the surrounding wood.*

VENEER REPAIR

Whether antique or modern, much furniture available today uses veneer, mostly for large flat areas. Veneer can be used to produce beautifully figured furniture surfaces that hold up well as long as the furniture is well cared for and the environmental conditions are favorable. But veneer can easily develop problems such as loose edges, bubbles, and chips. Because even minor veneer problems can develop into major problems if they're neglected, it's important to take care of them. Sometimes veneer difficulties aren't evident unless you look closely. (See "Loose Veneer," page 17.)

Repairing a Loose Veneer Edge

The most common veneer problem—and the easiest to repair—is the loose edge. Loose veneer edges can often be repaired without having to cut the veneered surface. In this case you'd work from the open edge.

Difficulty Level: 🔨 🔨

Tools and Materials

Utility or razor knife	Veneer roller
Wood glue and palette knife	Rag
Wax paper or plastic wrap	Clamping blocks
Clamps	

1 **Clean out old glue.** Use a thin blade, such as that in a utility or razor knife, to clean the area under the loose veneer. Thoroughly scrape out all old glue with the knife blade.

1 *Before repairing loose veneer, clean out as much old glue as possible using a thin blade.*

2 Work wood glue under the loose veneer using a palette knife or other thin-blade tool.

3 Clean up excess glue, and then clamp the veneer tight using a firm flat block over wax paper.

2 Reglue the edge. Spread wood glue under the loose veneer, using a palette knife to work the glue well into the loose areas. Using a veneer roller, roll the glued area lightly at first, and then increase pressure, forcing excess glue out to the edge.

3 Clamp the veneer. Clean up the excess glue with a damp rag. Lay wax paper or plastic wrap and a flat block that spans the repair area on the finish surface. Either 1/2- or 3/4-inch plywood makes a good block. Place a similar block beneath the repair area, and apply three or more clamps, one at each end and one or more across the middle. Leave the clamps in place until the repair is dry, at least 2 hours.

Fixing a Veneer Bubble Using Heat

Sometimes, especially on older pieces on which hide glue was probably used, you can fix a bubble by press-ing it back into place and reactivating the old glue with heat. If the bubble doesn't adhere after using this heating technique, you'll have to reglue it. (See "Regluing a Veneer Bubble," page 146.)

Difficulty Level: 🔨

Tools and Materials

Cotton cloth	Household iron

1 Cover the bubble. Place a clean cotton cloth over the bubble. You can dampen the cloth, but be sure to wring it mostly dry so you won't damage the furniture's finish if you leave it in place for too long.

2 Lay an iron on the cloth. Gradually press the veneer back into place using an electric household iron set on medium heat. Leave the iron in place for no

1 To reactivate the glue under a veneer bubble, begin by laying a damp cloth over the bubble.

2 Apply a hot iron to the cloth, and press the veneer flat, removing the iron after a few seconds.

3 After the bubble is flat, remove the cloth and apply the iron to the spot for a few more seconds.

1 To reglue a veneer bubble, apply a damp rag to the bubble to make the veneer more pliable.

more than 2 or 3 seconds at a time to avoid damaging the finish.

3 Lay the iron on the bare wood. After the bubble is flat, remove the cloth and briefly apply the iron to the wood surface to press the bubbled area. Don't leave the iron down for more than 1 or 2 seconds.

Regluing a Veneer Bubble

Difficulty Level: 🔨

Tools and Materials

Damp cloth	Veneer roller
Clamps	Rag
Wax paper or plastic wrap	Clamping blocks
Wood glue and palette knife	

1 Soften the veneer. Apply a damp cloth to the bubbled area to soften the veneer. Keep the cloth in place for about 30 seconds, or until you can see that the veneer is flexible.

2 Apply glue to the bubble. Cut a slit in the bubble, following the grain's direction, if it's not already split. Work wood glue into all parts of the bubble through the slit or split with a palette knife. Make sure the glue reaches all loose areas.

3 Roll the area. Use a veneer roller to roll the repair area flat, forcing extra glue out the bubble. Apply light pressure at first, and then increase the pressure, rolling toward the slit or split to allow excess glue to escape. Clean the glue seepage with a damp rag.

2 If the veneer is not split, cut it with the grain. Then work wood glue under the bubble.

3 Use a veneer roller to roll the bubble flat and force any excess glue out from under the veneer.

4 Clamp the bubble flat using a sturdy flat block over wax paper until the glue dries.

4 Clamp the bubble. Lay a sheet of wax paper or plastic wrap over the blister, and clamp the area with flat blocks under the jaws of the clamp. Make the blocks just slightly bigger than the repair area. If you can't reach the area with a clamp, use a heavy weight, such as large books, a concrete block, a bucket of water, or anything that can provide the necessary pressure to press the veneer flat. Allow the glue to dry for about 4 hours.

Repairing Veneer Edges

When veneer becomes loose and isn't repaired, often it breaks or chips, and pieces get lost. This happens frequently on edges that get hit or scraped. If veneer is missing on an edge, you can patch it.

Difficulty Level: 🔨 🔨

Tools and Materials

Utility knife	Chisel
Clamps	Rag
Wax paper or plastic wrap	Clamping blocks
Sandpaper and sanding block	Masking tape
Wood glue and palette knife	Straightedge
Touch-up stain and finish to match	
Piece of veneer to match the existing furniture	

1 Tape veneer over the damaged area. Decide on the type of veneer and the size of the patch you'll need to cover the damaged area. (See "Wood Identification," page 19, for tips on matching wood.) Cut a piece of veneer to match as closely as possible, making it a little bigger than the damaged area. Line up the grain in the patch with the wood to be patched, and tape the cut piece of veneer firmly over the damaged area.

2 Cut the patch. Using a utility knife and a straightedge, make a V-shaped cut in the patch, fanning out to the outer edge of the patch. Cut through the patch and into the old veneer underneath.

3 Cut out the damaged area. Remove the patch, and cut the old veneer following the V-shaped knife cut that should be visible. Use a sharp wood chisel to clean out the damaged area. Scrape the surface with the

1 Cut a similar piece of veneer, and tape it over the damaged area, lining up the grain.

2 Make a V-shape cut over the damaged area. Make several passes to scribe the surface below.

3 Remove the new veneer, and then cut out and remove the V-shaped area in the old veneer surface.

THE PROS KNOW

CENTER-PATCHING VENEER

Sometimes veneer gets damaged in the center part of a veneered surface. You'll make the repair in the same way as for a veneer edge, with the following alterations:

• Don't make a V-shape cut in the veneer patch. Instead, cut the patch shape as much with the wood grain as possible, and never straight across the grain. A diamond-shaped patch is often used to make the patch as invisible as possible.

• If you find that a clamp won't reach the patch, cover the patch with wax paper and a wood block, and then put a heavy object on top of the block and allow the glue to dry.

4 Glue the new patch in place, and then clamp it using a strong flat block over wax paper.

edge of a chisel or razor blade, cleaning old glue from the surface.

4 Glue and clamp the patch. Apply wood glue to the cut-out area, and tape the veneer patch in place, making sure it fits tight. Cover the patch with wax paper or plastic wrap, and clamp it in place using flat blocks under the clamp's jaws. Make the blocks slightly larger than the patched area. Let the glue dry for about 2 hours.

5 Sand the patch. When the glue is thoroughly dry, block-sand the patch flush with the surrounding wood. Use 120-grit sandpaper.

6 Trim the patch. After you've sanded the patch well, trim the edge to match that of the rest of the top, using a utility knife. Touch up the sanded and trimmed patch using stain and finish to match the surrounding wood.

Removing Veneer

If a veneered surface has extensive damage or most of the surface is loose or bubbled, you'll have to remove the old veneer and prepare the substrate for new veneer.

Difficulty Level: 🔨🔨

Tools and Materials

Household iron	120-grit sand paper
Scraper, knife blade	Wet towel
Power sander or sanding block	Rag

5 When the glue is dry, remove the clamp and sand the patched area flush with the surrounding surface.

6 Trim the patched area using a utility knife, and then touch it up to match the surrounding wood.

1 Soak the veneer with a wet towel. Strip all finish from the veneer surface. (See "Using a Chemical Remover," page 192.) Place a wet towel over the surface, and allow it to soak, checking it every few hours to see whether the old veneer has loosened. Allow the veneer to soak overnight if necessary.

2 Soften the glue with heat. Once the veneer is well soaked, use a hot household iron on the same damp towel to soften the glue and further loosen the veneer. At the same time, work a wide spatula or putty knife under the veneer, lifting it. You can also use a heat gun to apply heat under the veneer surface as you peel the veneer up.

3 Clean off the old glue. After removing the old veneer, prepare the subsurface by cleaning off the old glue. Use a damp rag or glue solvent to con-tinue to soften the glue, and scrape the surface clean with the edge of a sharp chisel or a utility-knife blade.

4 Repair and sand the subsurface. When the surface is clean, check it for defects like small chips and cracks, and repair them using wood putty. Repair-ing defects in the surface to be veneered is important because they can show up through the veneer, particularly after you apply the finish. Sand the surface well using a power sander or a sanding block with 120-grit sandpaper until the surface is even and smooth.

1 Strip the finish from the veneer surface, and then thoroughly soak the veneer using a wet towel.

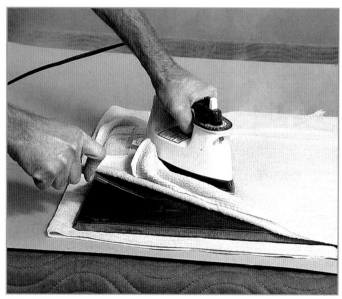

2 When the veneer begins to loosen, use a hot iron and wide spatula or scraper to remove it.

3 Use a utility knife blade or chisel edge to scrape any remaining old glue from the surface.

4 Sand the surface well using 120-grit and a power sander to prepare it for new veneer.

Applying Veneer

There are a number of ways to apply veneer, but the easiest is to use pressure-sensitive-type veneer. Pressure-sensitive veneer is thin, flexible veneer with a factory-applied adhesive on one side. To use the veneer, cut it to size, peel off the backing, position it on the work, and then press and smooth it onto the surface. When cutting the veneer to size, you can leave a slight overhang and trim it after application. You need to be extremely precise in positioning the veneer because once it sticks, you can't reposition it. Pressure-sensitive veneer needs an extremely smooth subsurface, and some veneer suppliers recommend

THE PROS KNOW

USING A VENEER PRESS

You can use standard polyvinyl woodworking glue to laminate veneer, but you must apply pressure to the veneer surface until the glue dries. To do this, make a veneer press from two flat panels slightly larger than the surface to be veneered. These flat panels, or cauls, will sandwich the veneered surface between them.

You can make cauls from smooth ¾-inch plywood, ¾-inch high-density-overlay (HDO) fiberboard, ¾-inch medium-density-overlay (MDO) fiberboard , or medium-density fiberboard (MDF) panels. You'll also need to make battens: strong, rigid pieces of wood that will span the cauls and squeeze them together as you apply clamp pressure. Be sure to make the battens thick enough to be rigid when pressure is applied, and they should be a little longer than the cauls they'll span. Make enough battens to apply even pressure over the entire caul surface. At each end of the battens, plane the edges that will make contact with the cauls so that they are slightly convex, with about a ⅛-inch crown, or rise, at the center. This allows the batten to apply pressure to the caul's center before tightening around the edges, forcing glue from the center of the veneered surface outward toward the edges. Forcing the glue in this way prevents surplus glue from being trapped under the surface, causing ripples in the veneer.

To use the press, cut the veneer larger than the surface to be veneered, with about a ½-inch overhang all around (a good rule for any veneering project). Lay the battens you'll use for the bottom of the press in position, convex side up, and put the flat caul on top of them. Lay these bottom battens across several

2x4s to raise them off the bench, allowing room to fit the clamp jaws under them when clamping. Lay the piece to be veneered on top of the bottom caul, applying wood glue to its top surface. Use a small short-nap paint roller to roll the glue into an even coat. Cover the whole surface evenly. Apply the veneer sheet to the surface, and put a piece of newspaper or wax paper over the veneer. Put the other caul on top of the paper, and position the other battens across the top of the caul directly over the battens below.

Clamp the center batten together on both sides, and then apply clamps to the other battens. Use a helper if necessary to clamp one side while you're clamping the other. Gradually increase pressure evenly all around by tightening the clamps alternately. Let the glue dry overnight before removing the veneered piece from the press.

coating the subsurface with a couple of coats of finish before applying the veneer. Shellac or lacquer works well for this application.

Another way to apply veneer is with contact cement. After preparing the substrate, brush the cement onto it and onto the underside of the veneer. Allow the glue to dry for about 1 hour, or until the surfaces are no longer tacky. Carefully position the veneer in place, starting at one end and gradually working across the surface, smoothing as you go with a veneer roller and veneer hammer or other smoothing tool. Because the veneer will bond immediately upon contact, be careful not to lay it on the surface before it's properly positioned. To make proper alignment easier, put a piece of wax paper or a few dowels between the veneer and the substrate surface until the veneer is in position. Gradually pull the paper or dowels out, and smooth the veneer as it makes contact with the surface. Then roll the surface well with a veneer roller to make sure no bubbles remain.

Iron-on glue sheets are still another helpful product developed for veneer application. These glue sheets are heat-sensitive, with a paper backing for easy application. They work best when using thin, flexible veneer available through most veneer suppliers.

Difficulty Level: 🔨

Tools and Materials

Glue sheet	Veneer roller
Veneer	Utility knife
Household iron	

1 Position the glue sheet. Veneer glue sheets come with paper on one side. After you've prepared the substrate surface, position the glue sheet on it, paper side up. Use an iron set on "cotton" setting to press the glue sheet onto the surface. After the glue sheet adheres, use a veneer roller to go over it, applying pressure as it cools. After the sheet cools, remove the paper backing.

2 Iron the veneer in place. Cut the veneer to fit the surface, with a fraction left over on all sides. Place the veneer in position on top of the cooled glue sheet, and place the glue sheet's paper backing on top of the veneer. Use the iron again to work over the surface of the veneer. Continue ironing the veneer until it seems firmly attached.

3 Roll the veneer. When you've finished ironing the veneer, firmly press it in place and smooth it with a veneer roller.

1 Position the glue sheet, paper side up, press it with an iron (top), and remove the paper (above).

2 Cut the veneer to fit, place the glue-sheet paper on top, and press the veneer with a hot iron.

3 After ironing, remove the paper, and firmly roll over the veneer using a veneer roller.

Trimming the Veneer

Difficulty Level: 🔨 🔨

Tools and Materials

Utility knife or veneer saw
120-, 180-, and 220-grit sandpaper
Sanding block

1 *Turn the panel veneer-side down on a flat surface, and trim the overhang using a utility knife.*

2 *Turn the panel upright, and sand the edges and top using 120-grit, and then 180- to 220-grit, sandpaper. Don't sand the top too much; the veneer is thin, and you don't want to sand through it.*

1 Cut from underneath. Turn the veneered panel upside down on a flat surface. Be sure the surface is smooth so you don't damage the veneer. While firmly holding the panel, use a veneer saw or sharp utility knife to trim away any overhang at the edges.

2 Sand with a sanding block. Turn the panel right side up, and use a sanding block and sandpaper to smooth the edges. To prepare the veneer for finishing, block-sand it with 120-grit sandpaper followed by 180- and 220-grit paper. If you use a machine sander, such as a random-orbit sander, be careful not to round off or cut through the edges of the panel. Finish the surface as you would any solid-wood surface.

ROCKING-CHAIR RUNNERS

Rocker runners receive more stress than any other part of the chair, so it's not surprising that they have a tendency to crack or break. Breaks often occur at the point where the rear leg intersects with the runner or toward the back of the runner, where the grain is short.

If the break is long and split along the grain of the wood rather than across the grain, you may be able to make successful repairs. If the break is a short cross-grain fracture, you'll probably have to replace the runner.

Repairing a Rocker Runner

Difficulty Level: 🔨 🔨

Tools and Materials

Masking tape	Finishing nail
Drill and assorted bits	Hammer
Clamps	Rag
Wood glue and palette knife	

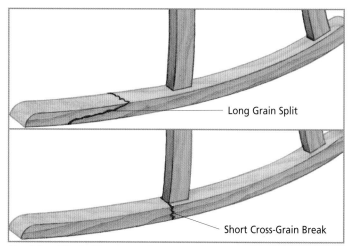

Long Grain Split

Short Cross-Grain Break

Rocking-Chair Runners. *Runners often break at the back end (top) or where they intersect the leg (above). Long splits can be repaired; cross-grain fractures usually have to be replaced.*

1 Wrap the joint with masking tape. Fit the broken runner pieces together properly, and wrap the joint with masking tape to hold it together.

2 Drill for a nail. Choose a finishing nail long enough to pin the joint pieces in place. Drill a hole for the nail through the runner at a right angle with the break. Drill through the joint into the other runner piece, but do not insert the nail.

3 Apply glue to the break. Remove the masking tape, take apart the joint, and apply wood glue to both pieces of the break. Spread the glue using a palette knife.

4 Tap the nail into the taped joint. Fit the runner pieces back together, and tape them firmly as before. Tap the finishing nail into the hole you drilled in Step 2 and through the break into the other runner piece. Leave the nailhead protruding so you can pull it out later.

1 Fit the split pieces together without glue, and firmly tape them using masking tape.

2 Drill a small hole to insert a finishing nail as a pin so that the nail intersects the break.

3 Remove the tape, take the joint apart, and apply glue, spreading it over the mating surfaces.

4 Assemble the split parts, and tape them up again. Then tap the finishing nail into the hole.

5 Remove the tape, and clamp the break. When the glue is dry, remove the clamps and nail.

5 Clamp the joint. Remove the masking tape, and clamp the joint tight, cleaning off excess glue with a damp rag. Allow the joint to dry for about 3 hours before removing clamps and the nail.

If the joint still seems weak, needing additional support, use a dowel to reinforce it through the bottom of the runner. (See "Reinforcing Short Wood-Grain Breaks," page 141.)

Replacing a Rocker Runner

If a rocker runner is broken beyond repair, replace it with a new one. You can make a new runner from a solid piece of wood, as in this project, or from three laminated pieces of wood. (See "Making a Laminated Rocker Runner," below.) The laminated method produces stronger runners, but many old rocking chairs have runners made from one solid piece that have held up well under normal use. If you use a solid-wood piece, be sure to allow the long wood grain to follow the length of the runner as much as possible so it will be strong.

Difficulty Level: 🔨 🔨

Tools and Materials

Belt sander or block plane	Clamps
Drill and assorted bits	Saber saw
Wood glue and palette knife	Pencil

1 Trace the pattern. Use an existing rocker runner to trace its outline on a board the same thickness as that of the existing runner.

2 Cut out the runner. Clamp the board to a bench, allowing it to overhang, or across two sawhorses, and cut out the runner using a saber saw.

1 Use an existing runner to trace a pattern on a piece of wood the same thickness as the runner.

THE PROS KNOW

MAKING A LAMINATED ROCKER RUNNER

To make a three-piece vertically laminated rocker runner, use an existing rocker runner as a pattern to trace outlines on three boards, each one-third the width of the runner. When you trace the outlines, position the template runner on the boards so that one board has the grain running in a different direction from the other two, as this will add strength to the runner when it's glued together. Clamp the boards across two sawhorses, and cut out each runner with a saber saw. Apply polyvinyl wood glue to both sides of the center runner (the one with the grain running opposite to that of the other boards) and to the inside edge of the two outer runners, and clamp the three pieces together between two wood blocks. Make sure the runners are in line and flush with each other before bearing down on the clamps, and clean up excess glue with a damp rag. Let the clamped-up assembly dry overnight.

Remove the clamps from the runner, and then finish and attach it as in Steps 3, 4, and 5 of "Replacing a Rocker Runner," page 155.

2 Clamp the board to sawhorses or a workbench, and use a saber saw to cut out the runner.

3 Using a belt sander with an 80-grit belt, smooth the top and bottom of the runner.

4 After marking the new runner for the leg-joint locations, drill it for the leg dowels.

5 After test-fitting the joints, attach the runner to the rocker legs using glue and clamps.

3 Sand the runner. Smooth the top and bottom of the new runner using a belt sander with an 80-grit belt, a block plane, or a spoke shave. Use a block with 120-grit sandpaper to do the final smoothing.

4 Drill for the leg joints. Mark the leg-joint locations by placing the new runner beside the existing one and aligning them. Drill for leg dowels or cut mortises (whichever is appropriate) for the leg joints.

5 Glue and clamp the leg. Test-fit the runner to the legs. If all's well, apply glue to each leg-joint hole and each leg. Clamp the runner to the rocking chair. Protect the furniture from the clamp jaws with small blocks of wood if you don't have padded clamps. Finish the runner to match the chair.

WARPED WOOD PANELS

Solid-wood panels can sometimes develop their own unique look by warping and twisting. This can happen especially to table drop leaves or cabinet doors that are not secured to a frame or that are unfinished on one side.

Warping is caused by unequal moisture content in the wood. When one side of a solid-wood panel absorbs more moisture than the other side, it swells, causing wood to bow and cupping the other side.

Because an unfinished surface will absorb more moisture than a finished surface, panels finished on only one side are prime candidates for warping.

Some warped wood can be difficult to straighten, especially if it's been that way for years. Even if you're able to remove the warp, the wood may want to return to its warped shape. So if the piece is old and the warp doesn't interfere with its function, consider living with it. If you find the warp objectionable, you'll have to take steps to remove it and stabilize the wood so it doesn't return.

Removing a Warp with Heat, Moisture & Pressure

Removing a warp while causing the least damage involves applying heat, water, and pressure. You'll have to remove the finish from the panel to do this. Remove the panel from the piece; remove any hardware; then strip the finish. (See "Using a Chemical Remover," page 192.)

After you strip the panel, cut stiff battens to span the warped surface about every 10 inches on the top and bottom. Make the battens long enough to extend a little beyond the panel's edge. Lay the bottom battens across a set of sawhorses, and put the warped panel on the battens with the cupped (concave) side up. Dampen the cupped side, and put the top battens in place, spanning the warp and aligning them over the bottom battens.

Keep the Warp from Coming Back. *One way to keep a panel straight is to install battens on the side that's out of view.*

Attach clamps to pull the battens together, using a helper if necessary. Don't try to remove the warp yet; just tighten the clamps enough to apply firm, even pressure all around. Place wet towels across the panel's cupped side, and clamp a heat lamp to a sawhorse leg under the panel. If you don't have a heat lamp, a regular clip-on lamp with an aluminum reflector shade will produce enough heat to dry the moisture on the convex side of the panel. Mount the lamp close enough to the panel so it heats the bottom side but doesn't burn it.

Let the panel stay clamped for three or four days, tightening the clamps a bit each day to remove the warp. Once the panel is flat, remove the wet towel and heat lamp, and keep the panel clamped for another day.

Keep the warp from coming back.
Remove the clamps and do one or more of the following to keep the warp from coming back:

• Install rigid battens or cleats prepared beforehand across the panel bottom. Use wood screws in slotted holes to secure the battens to the panel. Slotted holes allow for expansion and contraction of the panel, preventing splits.

• If the panel was originally mounted on a frame such as a table apron, remount it immediately using wood screws.

Removing a Warp with Heat, Moisture and Pressure. *Use sawhorses, wet towels, battens, and a heat lamp to remove a warp from a panel.*

• Sand and finish both sides of the panel with an equal amount of finish to prevent unequal moisture absorption, which could cause the warp to return.

Kerfing Wood to Remove a Warp

A more radical way to remove warps is to cut grooves on the back or underside of the solid-wood panel, making the panel flexible enough to clamp flat. After the panel is flat, you can fit and glue strips of wood into the grooves to stabilize the panel.

Cut grooves in the panel. Turn the panel bottom (convex) side up on a flat bench or set of sawhorses, and clamp it down. Measure and mark where you'll cut the grooves. End the grooves about 1 inch from the panel ends, spacing them ¾ inch to 2 inches apart, depending on the severity of the warp (closer spacing for severe warps; wider spacing for slight warps). Set a ¼-inch straight-cutting router bit at two-thirds the thickness of the panel, and then make the cuts, using a clamped, straight one-by board or piece of ¾-inch plywood with a factory edge as a guide. If you don't have a router, make two passes using a circular saw so you end up with a ¼-inch wide kerf. Set the saw to the same depth of two-thirds the panel thickness.

Cut Grooves in the Panel. *Using a router, cut ¼-in.-wide grooves about ¾ to 2 in. apart in the convex side of the panel.*

Panel (Convex Side Up)

Stabilize the panel. Make sure the panel is clamped flat. Attach rigid battens with wood screws to the back or underside of the panel. If you don't want to or can't use battens, cut strips of wood to fit the width of the grooves, using a table saw or a circular saw and a straightedge as a guide. You may also need to cut the wood strips to the depth of the grooves. Glue the strips into the grooves, and let them dry overnight. Use a hand plane to plane the strips flush with the panel surface.

Stabilize the Panel. *Flatten out the panel, and use sturdy battens or wood strips glued into the grooves to keep the panel flat.*

Sawhorse

Batten

CASTERS AND GLIDES

You'll find casters or glides on almost all types of furniture. Casters are small wheels, rollers, or balls mounted under the feet or base of furniture so it can roll. Casters are mounted to furniture by a plate attached to the wood with screws or through a shaft that gets inserted into a metal sleeve in the wood. Plate-mounted casters are the most sturdy but require a large flat area on the bottom of the furniture piece. Casters with a shaft, called stem casters, are used primarily on narrow wood, like chair legs, and they can often develop problems. Glides are flat metal or plastic buttons attached to the feet that enable the furniture to slide easily on a hard floor.

Casters and glides *make furniture easier to move, and they protect the floor. Casters may be the stem-type or plate-type; glides may simply fit over the feet of furniture or be attached by nailing or screwing them into the furniture leg.*

Replacing Glides

Glides usually have pointed tabs or a pointed shaft, like a nail, that you drive into the wood to attach them. You can pry off worn or missing glides and replace them with new ones. To get the right replacement glide, consider the floor the piece rests on: Carpet may not require glides but plastic glides work well on floors that are tile or wood. Metal glides with a fabric tab attached are also available to keep them from scratching floor surfaces.

Difficulty Level:

Tools and Materials

Flat-bladed screwdriver	Needle-nose pliers
Hammer	Replacement glide

1 Remove the glide. Turn the furniture on its back or upside down, and use a thin flat-bladed screwdriver to work under the button and pry it up. Then use needle-nose pliers to grasp the shaft, tapping it out with a small hammer.

2 Install the new glide. Hold the glide's shaft in position with a pair of needle-nose pliers, and tap the glide into the wood using a hammer.

1 You can usually remove a glide by prying it off with a thin, flat-bladed screwdriver.

2 Hold the new glide in place with needle-nose pliers, and then tap it into place using a hammer.

Caster wheels that have been worn flat like this one will have to be replaced. To get a match, it's sometimes necessary to replace the set.

Solving Simple Step-Caster Problems

Caster problems may result when caster wheels break or become worn flat on one side. If this is the case, replace the caster. You can sometimes find replacement casters to match your original, but more likely you'll have to replace all of them. Another option for some pieces is to remove casters altogether and replace them with furniture glides. If doing so won't change the height of the piece enough to matter and the function isn't affected, the piece may be fine without casters. If the piece is old, save the original casters in case you decided to reinstall them at a later date.

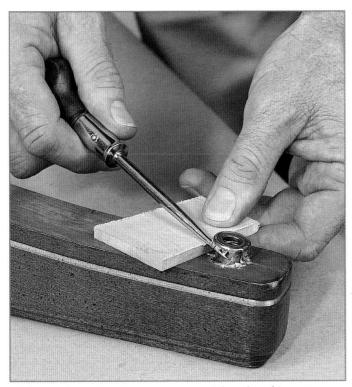

1 Pry up the caster sleeve using a scratch awl or thin screwdriver and a wood block.

Tightening a Stem Caster

A common problem with stem casters is that they continually fall out because they don't stay inserted in their metal sleeves. When this happens, you need to tighten the assembly.

Difficulty Level: 🔨

Tools and Materials

Scratch awl or flat-bladed screwdriver	Mallet
Small wood block	Adjustable pliers

1 Pry out the caster sleeve. Pull the caster and stem from the metal sleeve, and remove the sleeve using a scratch awl or flat-bladed screwdriver. Fit the tool under the teeth of the serrated flange, and pry up the sleeve, using a small wood block as a fulcrum. You may need to use pliers and a mallet to tap the sleeve out of the hole.

2 Tighten the sleeve. Using adjustable pliers, squeeze the bottom end of the metal sleeve together so the tabs snap over the stem end of the caster when it's inserted.

2 To tighten the sleeve so that the caster stem will stay in place, squeeze the bottom end using pliers.

3 *Reinstall the metal sleeve, and insert the caster, tapping it down until it snaps into place.*

3 Replace the sleeve and caster.
Put the metal sleeve back into the hole, and tap it down using a mallet until it's tight. Reinstall the stem caster, tapping it down into position until it snaps in place in the metal sleeve.

Shimming a Stem Caster

Stem casters can also get loose and fall out because the metal sleeve in which they're inserted becomes loose when the wood around it wears or splits. If the wood isn't split but the hole is just worn, you can shim the caster.

Difficulty Level: 🔨

Tools and Materials

Slender shims	Needle-nose pliers
Wood glue and palette knife	Hammer

1 Insert the shim.
Remove the loose metal sleeve and stem caster from the worn hole. Cut one or two slender hardwood shims, and apply wood glue to one side and inside the hole. Hold the shim or shims with needle-nose pliers, and insert them, gluing them to the side of the hole.

2 Reinstall the sleeve and caster.
Insert the metal sleeve in the hole to see whether it's tight. If so, drive the sleeve into the hole using a hammer, and then reinstall the stem caster.

1 *Remove the loose caster sleeve, and insert glued shims so they stick in the hole.*

2 *Tap the caster sleeve back into the hole using a hammer, and then replace the caster stem.*

Repairing Splits around a Stem Caster

Difficulty Level: 🔨 🔨

Tools and Materials

Rag	Clamps
Mallet	Dowels
Backsaw	Masking tape
Drill and assorted bits	Palette knife
Wood glue	

1 Glue up the split. When the wood around the hole is split, remove the metal sleeve, and then glue and clamp the split tight. Clean up any glue seepage. If the split or splits are minor, you can tap the metal sleeve back into the hole while the wood is still clamped and let the glue dry thoroughly overnight before removing the clamps. If the splits are major, go on to the next step.

2 Plug the old caster hole. After gluing and clamping the splits, plug the caster hole with the correct-size dowel. Prepare the dowel by chamfering the ends and cutting a groove in it; then apply glue to the dowel and caster hole. Drive the dowel into the hole using a mallet. Allow the glue to dry overnight, and then cut the dowel flush using a backsaw.

3 Drill a bigger hole. With the caster hole plugged, drill a hole about $\frac{1}{8}$ to $\frac{1}{4}$ inch larger in diameter and $\frac{1}{8}$ to $\frac{1}{4}$ inch longer than the original caster hole. Be sure to center this new hole on the plugged hole.

4 Plug the bigger hole. Choose a dowel the same diameter as and a little longer than the hole you drilled in Step 3. Prepare the dowel (with a chamfer and groove), and then glue and install it. Allow the glue to dry overnight; then cut the dowel flush using a backsaw.

1 Put the split pieces back together, and then glue and clamp them without the caster in place.

2 Prepare the correct-size dowel, and plug the old caster hole. Allow the glue to dry.

3 After cutting the dowel flush, drill for a larger-diameter dowel centered on the original hole.

4 Prepare the larger-diameter dowel, and plug the new hole. Allow the glue to dry overnight.

5 *After cutting the new, larger dowel flush, drill a hole sized for the original caster sleeve.*

6 *Drive the caster sleeve into the new hole using a hammer, and then install the caster.*

5 **Drill for the caster sleeve.** With the larger hole plugged, center and drill the proper size hole for the metal caster sleeve. The sleeve should fit snugly. Measure the caster stem for correct depth, mark the drill bit with masking tape, and drill the hole straight.

6 **Install the caster.** Reinstall the metal caster sleeve, seating it in the new hole with a few taps from a hammer, and drive the caster back in place using a mallet.

Tightening a Plate Caster

Plate casters rarely develop problems, but if they do, it's usually because the screws holding the caster plate are stripped from the wood. If this is the problem, you may be able to move or turn the plate slightly to provide new wood into which you can drive the screws. If you can't turn the plate, you'll have to plug the screw holes.

Difficulty Level: 🔨

Tools and Materials

Screwdriver	Small dowels
Hammer	Backsaw
Drill and assorted bits	Wood glue

1 **Remove the caster.** Take the plate caster off the leg by backing out the screws with an appropriate screwdriver.

2 **Insert the dowels.** Fill the screw holes by simply driving a small dowel, along with a little wood glue, into each hole. Be sure the dowels fit snugly, and cut them flush using a backsaw.

3 **Reattach the caster plate.** Put the caster plate back in position, and then drill pilot holes for the screws and remount the caster.

1 *Remove the plate caster by backing out the mounting screws using the correct-size screwdriver.*

2 *Plug the screw holes with small-diameter dowels and glue, and then cut the dowels flush.*

3 *With the holes plugged, position the caster and drill pilot holes before installing the screws.*

PART III
PRESERVING AN ORIGINAL FINISH

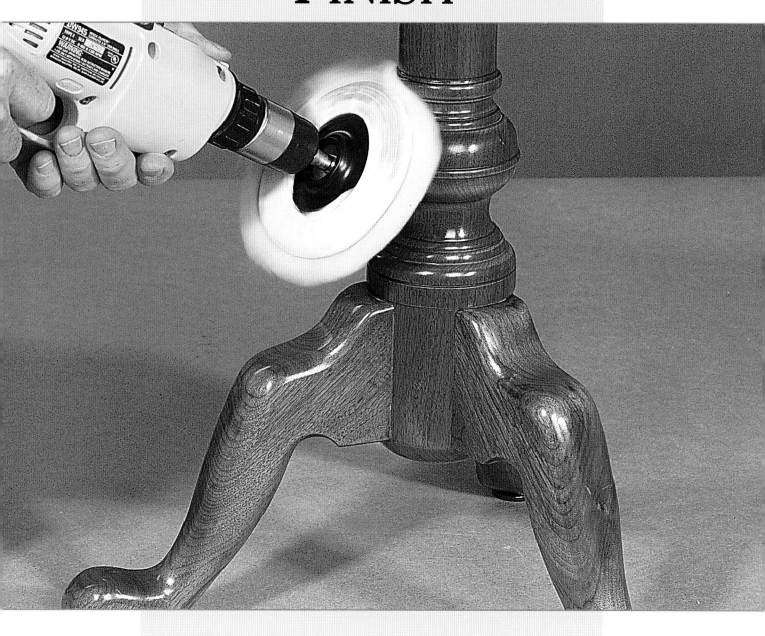

8

CLEANING AND REVIVING OLD FINISHES

For many things, new is better. But that's not necessarily true for furniture finshes. If an old piece of furniture has been maintained well enough that it still has its original finish, most professional restorers would say that the finish should be saved. An original finish is considered an intrinsic part of the furniture, and removing it may devalue the piece and detract from its beauty. Of course, there are times when stripping and refinishing is not detrimental and may even be necessary. Poorly refinished furniture and furniture with severe water, heat, or smoke damage are good candidates for refinishing. This chapter describes how to inspect the finish on your piece and decide on the best approach with these criteria in mind. If there's some question about which approach to take—reviving or refinishing—try cleaning and renewing the old finish first. You can always strip and refinish it later.

IS THE FINISH ORIGINAL?

Years of use and the natural aging of a finish can result in a pleasing effect called patina, which is the combination of a naturally distressed finish and deep wood color. To attempt to duplicate patina with a new finish is extremely difficult at best and usually results in an artificial look. That's a good reason for reviving an original finish. In addition, saving the old finish usually means less work, mess, time, and money. Stripping an old finish requires the use of strong chemicals with hazardous fumes—you'll need protective clothing and good ventilation. But how do you know whether you have a finish that should be saved?

To determine whether your piece's finish is original, you must become a detective and search for clues.

A refinished piece often looks new, without normal wear signs such as stains, scratches, or dents; if there are scratches or dents, they have been finished over and are in the wood rather than the finish. Sanding marks can also show up on a refinished piece. Coarse sandpaper may have left scratches, or a power sander may have scarred the surface with small vibrator marks or orbital sander markings. Traces of old finish can also be left in corners, crevices, and carvings, usually appearing darker than the new finish.

Look for runs in the finish, usually indicating it's not original. Inspect backs, undersides, and inside furniture for telltale

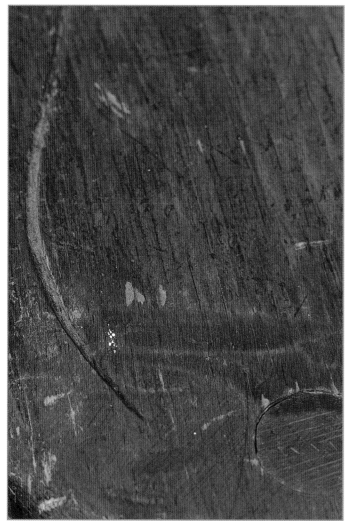

Although this finish has a few new scratches and dents, the piece also shows scratches and dents in the wood itself that have been finished over, indicating that the finish is not original.

Traces of old paint on the underside of the piece at the top show that it has been refinished. The finish runs on the edge of the middle piece indicate that a finish has been applied since the piece was made. Light-colored run marks on the inside back edge of the bottom piece show that it has been stripped before.

signs of refinishing; many refinishers don't clean up these areas well, and you'll be able to find traces of old finish or residue left by the stripping process and light-colored streaks where solvent ran across the area, removing color. Also look under hardware for signs of an older, darker finish.

There are good indications of a fine old finish that you can look for, as well. If the finish looks rich and mellow, with normal age and wear signs, it could be old. Some old finishes are also cracked, crazed, or "alligatored," a term used to describe a finish surface resembling alligator hide. Old finishes may be sun bleached in one or more areas from exposure to sunlight through a window. If an older finish has been waxed or oiled regularly, it can appear dark, dirty, and dingy because of dirt and dust accumulation. You can usually remedy this with a good cleaning, which will return the piece to its original color.

Some old finishes like this one have become "alligatored," a term used to describe a cracked or crazed finish that resembles an alligator hide.

Identifying the Type of Finish

If you decide to preserve the original finish after doing a cleaning and touch up, you may need to apply a top coat of finish over the old one to protect and renew it. If you do, it's always good to use the same type of finish as the original, which means you must first identify the original one.

Most furniture finishes are either shellac, lacquer, or varnish. Occasionally you'll find oil, wax, or painted finishes. Early furniture—dating from or before the eighteenth century—was usually finished with linseed oil and beeswax. This continued into the 1800s, when shellac finishing became popular, beginning with the French polish technique (1810 to 1820). In the early 1900s, lacquer began to be used; by the 1950s, most manufactured furniture had a lacquer finish. Varnishes have also been used for many years, particularly among custom cabinetmakers.

Penetrating Finishes. You can usually identify oil finishes by their appearance. Because they are a penetrating, rather than a film-building, finish, oil finishes give wood a natural look with very little if any finish film on the wood surface. Look across the wood, allowing the light to reflect off the surface; if the wood grain appears open, reflecting the light, and the sheen is dull rather than glossy, it may very well be an oil finish.

Film Finishes. To check for shellac, lacquer, or varnish, use the solvent test. Using mineral spirits on a rag, clean a spot in an inconspicuous area. Then apply denatured alcohol on a white cotton rag to the same inconspicuous spot, let the alcohol soak in for a few minutes, and rub the spot with the rag. If the finish begins to dissolve and the white rag picks up brown stains, you probably have a shellac finish. If not, go to the next solvent, lacquer thinner, and repeat the process to see whether the finish dissolves; if so, the finish is lacquer. If the finish still doesn't dissolve, or if it crinkles and lifts, you can assume it's some type of varnish.

Some recently developed cross-linked varnishes, however, are next to impossible to dissolve or remove, and they can't be recoated. If you encounter this type of finish, you'll soon know it. The best approach is to leave it alone. After all, it was designed to last indefinitely.

CLEANING AN ORIGINAL FINISH

Once you've handled any major repairs and decided to preserve the existing finish, the next step is cleaning the finish. You can do any necessary finish repairs after cleaning. (See "Repairing Minor Surface Damage," starting on page 174.)

Cleaning the finish involves removing anything on top of it, such as dirt, grime, fingerprints, oils, polishes, and waxes. Ideally, after you've completed this step, only the clean intact finish will remain.

One method of cleaning a finish uses warm, not hot, water and mild dishwashing detergent (the kind used for

A solution of warm water and dishwashing detergent may be used to clean an old finish. Note the dirt on the rag.

hand dishwashing, not dishwasher machines). Test in inconspicuous areas to be sure of no adverse effects on the finish. Water-based degreaser solutions can be found at home improvement or hardware stores. These can work well without chemical fumes. Another method uses mineral spirits, or paint thinner. Whichever method you choose, always try the cleaner in an inconspicuous area before you apply it to the entire piece. That way you won't damage the finish or the wood.

Using Detergent

A water-and-detergent solution works best on painted finishes but can be used on clear finishes, too. Mix detergent in water as you would to wash dishes, using a rag to wash down the furniture starting at the top and working down. An old washcloth or a piece of cheesecloth works well for this. Don't saturate the surface, or the water may damage the wood. Wring the cloth out till it's almost dry, and work one section at a time, rinsing the cloth often to remove dirt. Be careful not to snag any loose wood or veneer with the rag. Next, rinse the furniture surfaces using a clean cloth dipped in clear water. Finish using a clean, dry rag to rub down all wet surfaces.

Using Mineral Spirits

Use the same type of rag as you would for detergent, and wash the piece down, starting at the top and working down. Rinse the rag often in the mineral spirits,

Mineral spirits (paint thinner) also works well to remove any oil, polish, wax, or dirt from an old finish surface.

wringing it out each time. Clean one area at a time, and wipe it dry with a clean rag. If the clean rag still picks up dirt, wash the piece down again with clean mineral spirits and a clean rag. Dry the finish as much as possible with a dry rag, allowing it to air-dry for an hour or two before doing any additional work on it. Good ventilation is necessary when using mineral spirits.

With both the detergent and the mineral spirits methods, you can substitute #0000 steel wool for the cleaning rag when you have excessive dirt or wax buildup. Make sure you rub in the direction of the wood grain when using steel wool, as it will leave subtle rub marks on the finish surface.

A thorough cleaning job should take no more than about ½ hour for all but the largest pieces of furniture. Also, you don't have to start and finish in one day. You can begin a cleaning job, and then stop and pick it up the next day.

Is Cleaning Enough?

Examine the finish closely after cleaning to determine its condition. If the finish seems to be in good shape with the exception of being a little dull, a good waxing or polishing will probably bring it back to life. You may find that it needs more than a good coat of polish or wax to revive it, however. If the finish itself appears sound but has dents, nicks, scratches, or water stains, you can fix these problems fairly easily before waxing. (See "Water Rings, Stains & Candle Wax" and "Nicks, Dents & Scratches," pages 174 and 178.) If you find that the finish is alligatored, crazed, or cracked, these problems are more severe and you'll have to address them before you can wax or polish the finish. (See "Reviving an Alligatored, Cracked, or Crazed Finish," page 169.)

A finish can also appear hazy or foggy and may need special attention to revive it. (See "Reviving a Hazy or Foggy Finish," page 170.) Some pieces of furniture have a finish that is fine in one area yet breaking down and dissolving in another; an example of this is an armchair with soiled or worn finish on the arms. The finish may be so weak in these areas that a good cleaning removes it completely, exposing the wood underneath. In this case you'll have to strip and refinish the whole piece rather than just revive the finish.

WAXING AND POLISHING

In the same way that finishes are meant to protect and beautify wood, waxes and polishes are meant to protect and beautify finishes. Although neither wax nor polish offers a high degree of protection, wax is the better of the two; it's a little harder to apply but offers more protection and needs to be applied only about once a year. Polish offers a quick, easy way to liven up a relatively dull-looking finish. Don't use polishes that contain silicones, as they're incompatible with most finishes and will eventually harm them; instead, choose a good cream polish.

Applying Cream Polishes

To apply cream polish, dip a clean, soft rag into the polish or pour some onto the rag. Apply the polish to the finish using overlapping tight circles, and continue to apply polish until you cover the entire surface with a thin coat. Let the polish harden for 30 to 45 minutes, and then use a clean, soft cloth to buff the surface vigorously until it shines. You might want to use a lamb's-wool electric drill attachment for the buffing process.

Applying Paste Wax

A good furniture paste wax provides a thin, hard, protective coating that can't be beat for the final touch to a good finish. For waxing a dark finish, dark or amber paste wax works best; for waxing a light or bleached wood finish, use clear paste wax.

Difficulty Level: 🔨

Tools and Materials

Furniture paste wax	#0000 steel wool
Electric drill with lamb's-wool pad	Soft rag

1 Apply the wax. Wipe a soft rag or #0000 steel-wool pad in the wax, and apply a light, even coat to the finish surface. If you're using steel wool, rub the wax onto the surface in the direction of the wood grain. An exception to this rule is when you're waxing turnings, or small shaped or carved parts of furniture. You can use steel wool in any direction when applying the wax to these areas. Apply the wax on one section of the furniture at a time, and be sure to cover the surface with a thin, even coat.

2 Rub down the surface. Buff the waxed area with a clean, soft rag, rubbing in a circular motion. Allow the waxed surface to sit undisturbed for about 15 minutes.

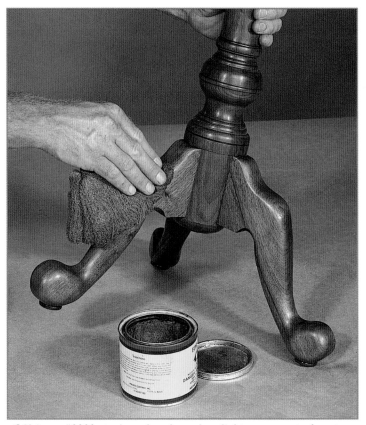

1 *Using a #0000 steel-wool pad, apply a light, even coat of paste wax to the finish surface.*

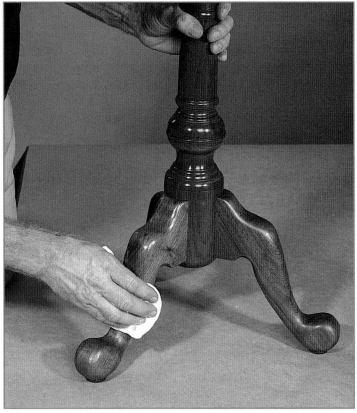

2 *Rub the waxed surface down using a clean, soft rag, and buff in a circular pattern.*

3 *After the wax dries, use a lamb's-wool buffing attachment in an electric drill to polish the surface to a high luster.*

3 **Buff the wax.** Using a clean soft rag, buff the surface with the grain until it produces a shine. If you want to polish to a higher luster, let the wax harden longer, then buff the surface again using a lamb's-wool buffing attachment in an electric drill.

REVIVING THE OLD FINISH

When a finish is alligatored, cracked, or crazed, it generally appears lifeless and tends to hide the natural beauty of the wood underneath.

An alligatored finish has intersecting cracks or ridges that give it a rough, textured look similar to alligator hide. Cracked or crazed finishes have small, irregular cracks that randomly crisscross the finish surface. These cracks are usually caused by overexposure to heat or sunlight, which causes the finish to dry out and shrink.

Other finishes can appear hazy or foggy. A painted or oil finish may simply need brightening up. There are ways to deal with all these problems, and in most cases the finish can be improved without stripping and refinishing.

Reviving an Alligatored, Cracked, or Crazed Finish

To restore an alligatored, cracked, or crazed finish to its original beauty, you must eliminate the tiny cracks or ridges in the finish. Even though these cracks are small, they can be deep, often going all the way down to the wood surface. Sanding them would remove so much of the finish that you would essentially be refinishing it. A better approach is to reamalgamate the finish, or redissolve and redistribute it, allowing it to flow together, thus eliminating cracks or ridges. This process will work on shellac and most lacquer finishes as long as the finish is free of wax and dirt. Varnish will not reamalgamate and must be treated differently. (See "Reviving Varnish," page 171.)

Difficulty Level:

Tools and Materials

Denatured alcohol or lacquer thinner	
2- or 2½-inch China bristle brush	
#0000 steel wool	Furniture paste wax
Tack cloth	Soft rag
3-lb. shellac or aerosol lacquer	Open-mouthed jar

1 **Apply solvent.** Using denatured alcohol for shellac and lacquer thinner for a lacquer finish, pour the cor-

1 *Apply the appropriate solvent to the surface using a pure bristle brush with light strokes in the direction of the wood grain.*

2 After the finish surface has completely dried, rub the piece down in the direction of the grain using #0000 steel wool.

3 After tacking the surface to remove any steel-wool residue, recoat the piece using the appropriate finish.

rect solvent into an open-mouthed jar large enough to accept a 2- or 2½-inch paint brush. Set the surface to be renewed facing upward on a horizontal plane so that the solvent doesn't run when you apply it. Apply the solvent to the finish with a pure bristle brush, using light strokes in the direction of the grain. Don't be in a hurry; do one horizontal section at a time, allowing the solvent a few minutes to work. You may have to apply several coats of solvent before the finish softens enough to begin to flow out, so watch it closely. After the solvent begins to work and the small cracks and ridges in the finish begin to disappear, move on to the next section until you finish the entire piece.

2 Rub with steel wool. Allow the finish to dry completely (about 4 hours), and then inspect it. You can repeat the amalgamation process if necessary. If the surface seems smooth, you can do one of two things: Rub the piece down in the same direction as the grain using #0000 steel wool dipped in paste wax, followed by buffing to complete the job, or rub the surface down well with dry #000 or #0000 steel wool.

3 Apply a top coat of new finish. If you did not wax the piece, recoat it with shellac or lacquer. Be sure to rub the surface well with a tack cloth to remove all steel-wool residue before applying the finish. If you use shellac, apply a 3-pound cut of commercially prepared shellac with a pure bristle brush. If you want to apply lacquer, use an aerosol can of finishing lacquer to apply a light coat. Be sure to have adequate ventilation when spraying. After the finish is dry (either shellac or lacquer), rub the surface down with #0000 steel wool and paste wax, and follow with a vigorous buffing.

Reviving a Hazy or Foggy Finish

Some finishes have a hazy or foggy appearance that remains after cleaning. This problem doesn't always cover the whole piece; sometimes it's limited to certain areas. The fact that the haze doesn't go away with cleaning indicates that the problem is in the finish, rather than on the surface, and it usually requires more than just a coat of wax to correct.

To determine the best solution, wet the hazy surface with mineral spirits to see whether the haze disappears. If it does, you can probably eliminate it entirely by applying a coat of finish. If the haze remains when the surface is wet, try the reamalgamation process described above.

If you decide to deal with hazy areas by applying finish, rub the surface down well with #000 or #0000 steel wool; then use a tack rag to remove any dust and steel-wool residue. Be sure to use the appropriate finish for the piece, applying shellac with a pure bristle brush and applying lacquer from an aerosol can. Follow either application with a #0000 steel wool rub-down using paste wax and a final buffing using a clean soft rag.

Reviving Varnish

Varnish is a tough, enduring finish, but when problems develop they are difficult to fix without refinishing. Alligatored or crazed finishes will not dissolve and flow back together as reamalgamated lacquer and shellac will, but you still may be able to improve the look of the overall finish by applying a coat of Danish oil. Danish oil works much like a scratch-cover polish except that it will dry rather than stay tacky and dull looking. Because it will penetrate any cracks or scratches in the damaged finish or wood, you can use a colored Danish oil finish to restore color to these areas.

Danish oil finish is available in a variety of colors. When choosing a color, remember that the match doesn't have to be exact. For example, a dark walnut oil will work fine for most dark finishes, and a natural or clear oil will do a good job on light or natural finishes. If all you can find is a clear or natural oil, you can first apply an appropriate color of wiping stain or oil stain, and then apply a coat of clear Danish oil. Use a soft, absorbent rag to apply oil to the finish, being sure to wipe it into any scratches, cracks, or crevices.

Allow the oil to penetrate these areas for about 15 minutes, and then wipe off all excess oil with a clean soft rag. Allow the finish to dry overnight; then apply a coat of paste wax. Buff the surface to finish the process.

Reviving a Painted Finish

Painted finishes, like transparent film finishes, are not necessarily all the same. Opaque coatings for furniture can be pigmented shellac, pigmented lacquer, pigmented oil varnish (oil-based paint), or pigmented water-based finish (latex paint). Also, some old pieces of furniture were painted with milk paint, developed during colonial times, using milk or buttermilk as a base.

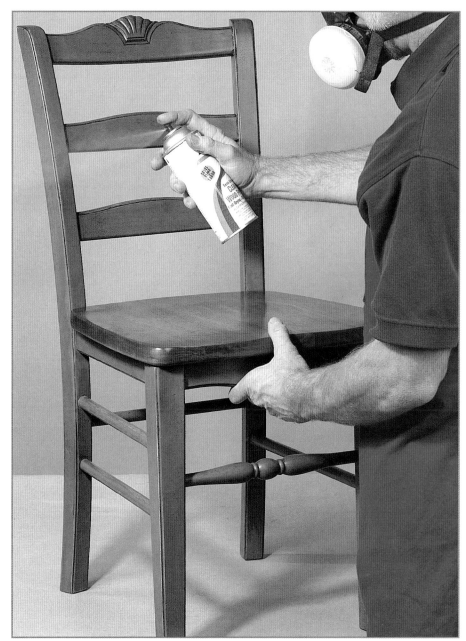

You can sometimes renew painted surfaces by coating them with a clear coat of the finish corresponding to the paint type.

If you have a painted antique piece with its original finish, it's better to consider imperfections a part of the furniture's history and charm and just treat the piece with careful cleaning and waxing. Other painted pieces can sometimes be rejuvenated by top coating them with a clear coat of finish corresponding to the paint type. Before applying the finish, be sure to remove all dirt, polish, and wax, and rub down the surface using #000 or #0000 steel wool or scuff-sand the surface using extra-fine sandpaper (280- to 320-grit). After the finish dries, apply a coat of clear paste wax using #0000 steel wool, and buff the surface to a shiny luster.

Renewing an Oil Finish

An oil finish is probably the easiest finish of all to renew because it's a penetrating finish rather than a film finish. Oil continues to penetrate the wood over time, and more finish can always be added.

Because oil finishes are interchangeable, there should be no problem of compatibility between the finish already on the piece and the oil finish you use to recoat it. Either a tung oil or a penetrating resin oil such as Danish oil should work fine.

Difficulty Level: 🔨

Tools and Materials

Mineral spirits, paint thinner, or turpentine
Soft rags   Oil finish
#0000 steel wool

1 **Clean the surface.** Use mineral spirits, or paint thinner, and a rag to clean the surface of the furniture.

2 **Apply thinned finish.** Thin the oil finish by adding 25 to 50 percent turpentine or mineral spirits, and then freely apply it to the surface with a soft, absorbent rag. Allow the oil to penetrate for about 15 minutes.

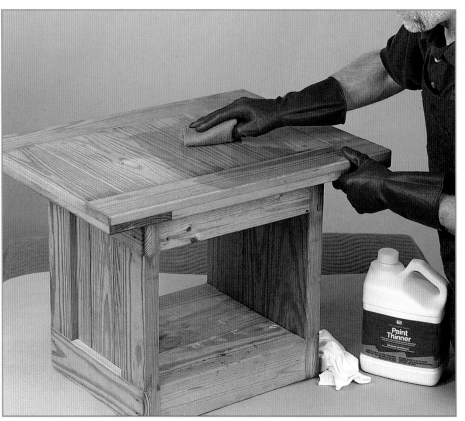

1 *To renew an old oil finish, first use paint thinner to clean the surface.*

2 *Apply a thinned coat of oil to the surface, and allow it to penetrate.*

3 Wipe the excess. Wipe off the oil that hasn't penetrated with a soft clean rag. Allow the surface to dry for about 3 hours.

4 Apply straight oil. Using unthinned oil finish, liberally apply the oil using the same type of rag as in Step 2. Let the oil penetrate for about 15 minutes, and then wipe off the excess. Let the piece dry overnight, and dispose of the rag. (See "Dispose of Used Rags Properly," page 27.)

5 Rub with steel wool. The next day, rub down the oiled finish using #0000 steel wool to give it a hand-rubbed look. Buff the surface lightly using a soft cloth.

3 Wipe off the excess oil, and allow the surface to dry for about 3 hours.

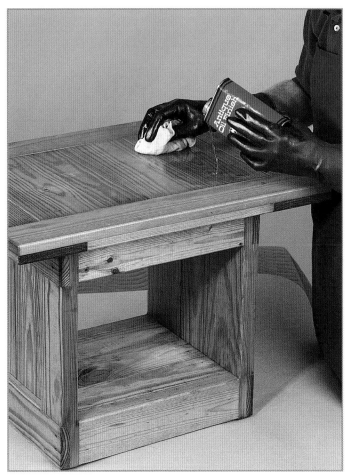

4 Apply a coat of the unthinned oil finish, and allow it to penetrate before wiping off the excess.

5 After the finish is dry (overnight), rub it down using #0000 steel wool in the direction of the wood grain, then buff it.

9

REPAIRING MINOR SURFACE DAMAGE

An important aspect of preserving and renewing a finish is repairing and touching up minor—and sometimes not so minor—damage to the finish surface. All the repairs in this chapter can be done without having to refinish the piece of furniture.

Of course, you'll want to remove water rings and stains from the finish. Many times an otherwise beautiful finish is ruined by scratches or a deep gouge. Cigarette burns and candle-wax drippings are other common surface problems. Even crushed corners and wood chewed by pets can be repaired without refinishing.

WATER RINGS, STAINS, AND CANDLE WAX

Water and other kinds of liquid can cause rings or stains in finish and wood. Shellac finishes are more susceptible to this problem than other types. Stains that are in the finish are usually white, while stains that have gone through the finish and into the wood will appear dark or black.

Dark moisture stains can't be removed without refinishing, and even then they are difficult to get out. You may be able to remove the finish, bleach the stain, and refinish the surface.

White stains, or those still in the finish, can often be removed without stripping the finish. The longer the stain is in the finish, the deeper it will penetrate into the surface. The deeper moisture penetrates into the surface, the harder the stain is to remove, so it's important to remove stains as soon as possible.

Finish discoloration that's caused by moisture is a result of moisture being trapped in or under the finish. To get rid of the discoloration, you must get rid of the trapped moisture. This can be done in one of two ways: Use a chemical called an amalgamator to soften the finish long enough for moisture to evaporate before the finish rehardens, or use an abrasive to cut into the finish to the depth of the moisture, allowing moisture to escape and causing the stain to disappear.

Removing a Moisture Stain Using Amalgamator

Amalgamator is an alcohol-based mixture sold by finish and touch-up supply stores to soften an area of the finish and cause the moisture stain to dissipate. The technique for applying the amalgamator to the finish surface is similar to that used for French polishing. (See "French Polishing," page 213.) If you can't get amalgamator, try using denatured alcohol instead, but be careful not to cut too deeply into the finish.

Note: Despite packaging promises to the contrary, there is no spray-on blushing agent that will work to remove moisture stains.

1 Make an applicator pad for the amalgamator by balling up a soft cotton rag.

Difficulty Level:

Tools and Materials

Soft cotton rag	Amalgamator
#0000 steel wool	Furniture paste wax

1 Apply amalgamator to a pad. Use a soft cotton rag to make an applicator pad. Ball or roll up the rag in a comfortable size to hold in one hand (about the size of a large egg). Smooth out the part of the rag that will make contact with the finish surface. There should be no wrinkles or creases. Apply amalgamator to the pad, allowing it to soak into the rag.

2 Disperse the amalgamator. Tap the padding rag into the palm of your other hand, causing the amalgamator to spread into the rag until the surface of the rag is damp, but not wet.

3 Pad the stain. Pad over the surface of the finish on top of the stain with a pendulum-like stroke in the direction of the wood grain. Briefly touch the padding rag to the stain surface, and then lift it off, keeping the pad in motion when it's in contact with the finish surface. The water stain may not immediately disappear, so continue to pad the area, adding more amalgamator to the rag if necessary. The trick is to keep your padding rag damp enough to soften the finish but not wet enough to cut through the finish to the wood surface.

4 Blend-in the repair area. When the stain is gone, allow the area to dry. Next, rub the finish down with #0000 steel wool to blend the sheen. Paste-wax the finish if necessary.

2 After applying the amalgamator solvent to the applicator, tap the rag into the palm of your hand.

3 Pad the stained finish with the rag using pendulum-like strokes in the direction of the wood grain.

4 After rubbing the surface down with #0000 steel wool, apply paste wax and buff the area with a dry soft rag.

Removing a Moisture Stain Using Abrasives

You can use any of a number of fine abrasives to remove a water stain from the finish, including #0000 steel wool, rottenstone, pumice, and 600-grit wet-or-dry sandpaper. Adventuresome refinishers have even used toothpaste, mayonnaise, or cigar ashes as abrasives. The depth of the stain will determine which one will work for you.

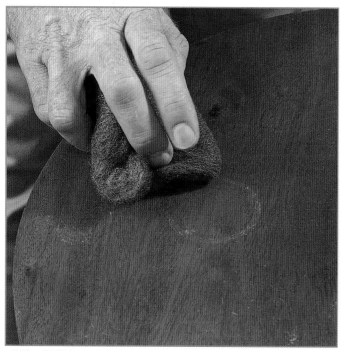

1 Use #0000 steel wool to rub over the stained area. Apply firm pressure in the direction of the wood grain.

Start with a mild abrasive. If that doesn't work, go to sandpaper. The less cutting into the finish you have to do to get rid of the stain, however, the better.

Difficulty Level: 🔨

Tools and Materials

#0000 steel wool	Furniture paste wax
600-grit sandpaper (plus 500- or 400-grit if necessary)	

1 Rub the stain area using steel wool. Rub #0000 steel wool over the stained area of the finish, rubbing with the grain and using firm pressure. If the stain is shallow, this may remove it. If not, go to Step 2.

2 Rub the area using sandpaper. Use 600-grit wet-or-dry sandpaper and a felt block to sand the stained area if steel wool doesn't get the stain out. A little soapy water or mineral spirits will work as a lubricant for the sandpaper. Use firm pressure and sand the area well, rubbing in the direction of the grain. If the stain doesn't disappear, go to a coarser wet-or-dry paper (500- or 400-grit), but remember that coarser papers may dull the sheen in the repair area and can even cut through the finish to the wood, so be careful. If you use a coarser paper, follow it by sanding with 600-grit paper to try to bring back the sheen.

3 Rub the area, again using steel wool. Rub out the finish using #0000 steel wool and paste wax, if it's needed to blend the repair area with the rest of the finish.

2 Use 600-, 500-, or 400-grit wet-or-dry sandpaper to sand the area. Use mineral spirits or soapy water as a lubricant.

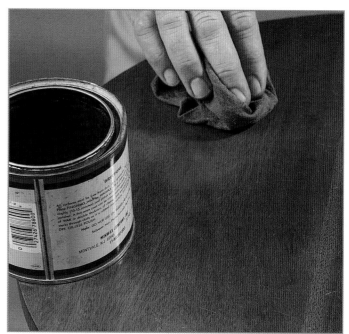

3 Rub in the grain direction using #0000 steel wool with paste wax. Follow by buffing with a soft rag.

Removing Candle Wax from a Finish

A common problem on table-top finishes is candle-wax drippings. When the hot wax drips onto the finish and hardens, it can be difficult to remove without damaging the finish. But not if you follow this procedure.

Difficulty Level: 🔨

Tools and Materials

Ice cube	Soft cotton rag
Credit card or plastic scraper	
Cream polish and #0000 steel wool	

1 **Freeze the wax.** Use an ice cube to harden the wax drippings, making them brittle.

2 **Scrape the area.** Use a plastic paint scraper or the edge of a credit card to scrape all the wax from the finish surface as gently as possible.

3 **Rub out the affected area.** Apply a cream polish to the surface using #0000 steel wool. Rub with the grain of the wood; this will remove any remaining wax residue.

4 **Polish the area.** Buff the repair area to a luster similar to that of the surrounding finish using a soft cotton cloth.

1 To remove candle wax from a finish, use an ice cube to freeze—or at least stiffen—the wax.

2 Use the edge of a plastic card or a nonmarring plastic scraper to scrape the wax free.

3 Apply cream polish to the area with #0000 steel wool, rubbing in the direction of the wood grain.

4 Rub the area with a clean soft cloth to restore the sheen.

NICKS, DENTS, AND SCRATCHES

You can touch up nicks, dents, and scratches in a number of ways. If the piece you're restoring is old and has a lot of nicks and scratches in it, use pigmented oil stain to touch them up. Use this technique when you don't want to render scratched areas invisible, but instead are willing to allow the furniture to have an old, distressed look. If the finish is free from wax, dirt, and polish, use a pigmented oil stain of the appropriate color. Apply the stain to damaged areas with an artist's touch-up brush. Wipe off any excess with a dry rag, and then apply finish over the damaged areas as described in Step 3 on page 179. (For larger damaged areas, see "Covering Scratches over a Large Area," below.)

Another quick, easy method to touch up nicks, dents, or scratches is to use a furniture touch-up marker in the appropriate color. These are usually available at paint and hardware stores or from home centers. If you can't find them there, try woodworkers' or furniture-supply websites. Touch-up markers look—and work— basically the same as permanent marking pens, except they contain a stain/polish mixture that colors defects to match or blend in with the surrounding finish. Matching the finish exactly is usually not crucial. A marker close to the same color will work fine.

Note: The sheen of touch-up markers is glossy, but your furniture might not be. If that's the case, wipe the repaired area just after maker application to remove the sheen, and to blend the repair into the surrounding area.

Wax sticks, like touch-up markers, are available in a variety of wood and finish colors for filling in surface defects. Although a wax stick will not always make a scratch, dent, or nick invisible, it's a quick way to help disguise these marks, making them much less objectionable. There are two ways to fill a defect with a wax stick, and either of them will work fine, so use the one you find easier. (See "Filling Defects Using a Wax Stick," page 179.)

Covering Scratches over a Large Area

Difficulty Level:

Tools and Materials

Pigmented oil stain	Soft cotton rag
Aerosol lacquer, polyurethane, or shellac finish	

1 Apply stain to the top. Clean the surface you want to renew using either mineral spirits or detergent and water. (See "Cleaning an Original Finish," page 166.) Using a rag, wipe matching pigmented oil stain over large damaged areas, such as a table top, then go immediately to the next step.

An easy way to touch up nicks and scratches is to use a furniture touch-up marker of the appropriate color.

1 *After cleaning the finish surface, apply matching pigmented oil stain over the damaged area.*

2 *Use a clean soft rag to wipe off as much excess oil stain as you can.*

3 After the stain dries, spray a coat of finish over the stained area.

2 Wipe off excess. Using a clean soft cotton rag, wipe any excess stain off the finish surface. Allow the stain to dry for the time prescribed on the can.

3 Apply new finish. Apply a coat of finish over the affected areas or over the entire piece if needed. For lacquer finishes, an aerosol lacquer works well. Spray one section at a time using long, overlapping strokes in the same direction as the grain. Apply a second coat if needed.

Other types of finishes, such as polyurethane and shellac, also come in aerosol cans but the finish works a little different than lacquer. Polyurethane is slower-drying and tends to run if you're not careful; shellac dries quickly, sometimes blushing (turning white) as a result of moisture getting trapped under the finish. If you use an aerosol finish, it can be quick and easy, but experiment first to familiarize yourself with how the finish goes on the surface. Be sure the can is warm so the finish sprays smoothly. If the can is too cold, set it in a pan of warm water for about a minute before spraying.

Fixing Defects Using a Wax Stick

Difficulty Level:

Tools and Materials

Colored wax stick	Burn-in knife (optional)
Soft cotton rag	Sanding block

1 Fill the defect. Rub the wax stick across the surface defect, forcing the wax into the recessed area

until it's full. You can also use a hot burn-in knife to melt the tip of the wax stick, dripping wax into the defect. (See "Electric Appliances," page 37, for information about burn-in knives.)

2 Level the repair. When the defect is filled with the colored wax, wrap a soft rag tightly around a sanding block, rubbing back and forth over the wax filler until it's level with the surrounding surface. Keep changing the rag to a clean area, and continue rubbing until you've removed all the excess wax on the surrounding surface.

1 To fill a defect using a wax stick, rub the stick across the defect, forcing the wax into it (top), or use a hot burn-in knife to melt the wax, dripping it into the defect (above).

2 Use a soft rag wrapped around a sanding block to rub over the filled defect, leveling the wax with the surrounding surface.

CIGARETTE BURNS AND GOUGES

On some pieces of furniture, a cigarette burn or gouge could be considered part of the piece's natural character. An example of this kind of furniture is a piece with a lot of wear and distress, to the point that one more spot doesn't detract from the overall look. On most furniture pieces, however, it appears as simply unwanted damage. If the gouge is objectionable, you can do a simple repair using a touch-up pen or artist's brush and oil stain. You can also repair the gouged area by filling it with a wax stick as described on page 179.

If the gouge is in a conspicuous area, such as a table top, however, or if you're dealing with a cigarette burn, the best method of repair may be to burn-in the defect, using hot-melt finish resin sticks (burn-in sticks) and a burn-in knife. (See "Electric Appliances," page 37, for information about burn-in knives and resin sticks.) Nicks, dents, and scratches can also be repaired using this burn-in method.

The basic steps for burning-in a defect are almost the same whether the defect is a dent, scratch, cigarette burn, or gouge. The only differences are in the first step of preparing the defect surface for the melted stick.

Burn-in sticks have a limited shelf life: If you've had one longer than six months, check it before applying the stick to the finish. If it gets rubbery or gummy when melted with the proper heat, the stick is bad; if it liquefies when melted, it's good.

Because the burn-in process may take some practice to perfect, work on a few practice pieces before jumping to the real thing.

Repairing Damage with a Burn-in Knife

Difficulty Level: 🔨 🔨 🔨

Tools and Materials

Utility-knife blade	Burn-in knife and resin stick
Touch-up stain and finish	Artist's brush
Soft cotton rag	#0000 steel wool
Various grades of wet-or-dry sandpaper	

1 Dig out the defect. For cigarette burns, use a utility-knife blade edge to scratch out all charred surfaces, removing only what's necessary to reach a solid clean surface (finish or wood). For gouges, use a utility-knife blade to remove any ragged or loose finish or

1 *Before burning-in a damaged area, you may need to remove any loose finish or wood fibers with a utility knife.*

2 *When the burn-in knife gets hot enough to melt the lacquer stick, transfer a small amount of the stick to the knife tip.*

wood fibers in the gouge and around the edge. For scratches, nicks, or dents, begin with Step 2.

2 Melt the resin. Heat up the burn-in knife, and choose a resin stick that matches the surrounding finish color as closely as possible. For defects that have not lost their finish color, use a transparent amber stick or a transparent clear stick for a natural finish over light wood. If the finish color is lost and you need to use a colored stick, usually it's best to match the background color with the idea of adding grain lines over the burn-in after it's sanded. When the knife gets hot, touch the tip to the burn-in stick and see if it begins to melt. If not, heat the knife again until it melts or liquefies the stick when touched. If the liquid resin bubbles or blisters, the knife is too hot and needs to cool. Maintain knife temperature as much as possible so the burn-in resin melts on its tip.

Note: to prevent the spread of resin to areas where it's not needed, apply "burn-in balm." This will prevent the resin from sticking to undamaged finish, and save sanding and color-blending time.

3 Apply the resin. Transfer a small amount of the stick onto the knife tip, immediately pressing it into the defect, melting it in place. Make sure that the resin is still in liquid form when you press it into the defect so it fuses well to the surface. Continue to transfer enough of the stick to the defect until it's just a fraction

3 *Press the melted lacquer into the defect until it is fused with the surface. Build up the damaged area until it's slightly higher than the surrounding surface.*

4 *Use fine-grit wet-or-dry sandpaper with mineral spirits or soapy water to block-sand the burn-in.*

higher than the surrounding surface. Holding the burn-in knife as you would a pencil, use the bottom convex surface of the knife tip to pass over the burned-in defect surface, smoothing and flattening it as much as possible. Keep your knife tip at the right temperature during this step.

4 Sand the resin. Sand the burn-in surface using a felt block and 600-grit wet-or-dry sandpaper. Use soapy water or mineral spirits as a lubricant. The idea here is to level the burn-in surface smooth with the surrounding surface without cutting through the existing finish. You might be able to use 500-grit or even 400-grit wet-or-dry paper during this step, but be careful or you'll cut through the finish surface and possibly lose the finish color in this area. It's better to use finer-grit paper unless the finish film is exceptionally thick.

5 Touch up the repair. After you have leveled the burn-in, wipe over the area using a rag dampened with water or paint thinner to clean away sanding residue and to look at the repair color. If necessary, use a fine sable touch-up brush to paint in grain lines over the burned-in area, matching them to the surrounding wood. Use a pigmented oil stain for this and work off a palette surface such as a paper plate or the back of a piece of wet-or-dry sandpaper. Graining pens and pencils are also available from touch-up supply houses. Use your creativity on this step; use whatever color or grain figure you think you need to blend the repair to the surrounding wood. Often you can continue existing grain lines and figure through the repaired area to fool the eye.

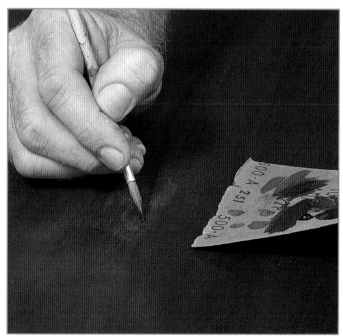

5 *After sanding, use a fine sable brush and pigment from a pigmented oil stain to paint grain lines across the repair area.*

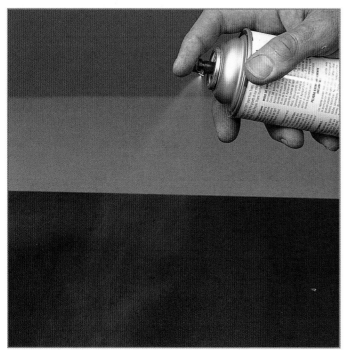

6 After the stain dries, spray finish over the touched-up area.

7 Rub the area down going with the wood grain. Use #0000 steel wool to blend the sheen with the surrounding finish.

6 Spray the repair area. Allow the touch-up stain to dry. When used for touching up in this manner, most oil stains will dry in about 5 to 10 minutes. Spray the dried spot with an aerosol can of the appropriate finish.

7 Rub out the repair with steel wool. Let the finish dry. (Read the label of the finish you're using to determine how long to allow it to dry.) Rub the area down with the grain, using #0000 steel wool to blend the sheen with the surrounding finish.

CRUSHED CORNERS AND CHEWED WOOD

Crushed corners and chewed wood are common problems: A piece of furniture can appear to be ruined by a corner crushed during a moving accident or a leg or pedestal used as a chew bone by the household puppy. This type of damage may look bad and seem tough to fix, but repair is entirely possible, and there are tricks to make it easier.

Using auto-body filler is the easiest way to fix both problems. In most cases, you can shape and finish auto-body filler to look like the surrounding wood. (See "Repairing Chewed Wood with Filler," page 185.) The filler is hard like wood and will last indefinitely. In some cases, however, you might not want to use filler material. If you have a high-quality, old piece of furniture, for example, you'll need to patch the area with matching wood and finish to match.

Repairing a Crushed Corner with Wood

To repair a crushed corner with wood, you must prepare the damaged area before applying the wood patch. You then apply the patch, shape it to form, and finish it to match.

Difficulty Level: 🔨 🔨 🔨

Tools and Materials

Dovetail saw or backsaw	Artist's brush
Matching wood scrap	Soft cotton rag
Touch-up stain and finish	#0000 steel wool
Wood glue and palette knife	Block plane
Sandpaper and sanding block	
Tack cloth and wood filler if necessary	
Clamps (hammer, nail, and drill if necessary)	

1 Cut out the damaged area. Using a dovetail saw or backsaw, cut away only the rough, damaged area with a straight cut, going with the grain.

2 Plane the corner. Plane the corner's cut surface flat and smooth using a sharp block plane. Don't take off too much wood, and make sure the cut is as plumb as possible.

3 Cut and plane the patch. Cut a piece of similar wood large enough to patch the area. Make the patch a little larger than necessary; you can shape and sand it after you apply it. Plane the joining surface of the patch completely flat and plumb to match the planed surface of the corner.

1 Make a clean straight cut as much as possible in the direction of the wood grain to remove the damaged wood.

2 Use a sharp block plane to smooth the wood surface where you made the saw cut.

3 After cutting a piece of similar wood for the patch, use the block plane to smooth the surface of the patch that will be joined to the corner until you have a good fit.

4 Test-fit and clamp the patch to the corner without glue. Once you're sure you have a good fit, apply glue to both joint surfaces and re-clamp the patch.

4 Clamp the patch in place. Test-fit and clamp the patch to the corner. If necessary, tap a small nail or brad through the patch into the corner to keep the patch from sliding on the diagonal surface when you clamp it. Predrill the nailhole to avoid splitting the wood. Drive the nail only as far as necessary to hold the patch and leave the nailhead extending. You'll remove it later. Remove the patch with the nail in it for gluing.

Apply glue to the joining surfaces, spreading it with a palette knife. Put the patch in place, lining up the nail (if you're using one) with the matching nailhole, tap the nail to seat it, clamp the patch as before, and allow the assembly to dry for at least 4 hours.

5 Shape the edge. Remove the clamps and any nails or brads used to hold the patch in place. Using a

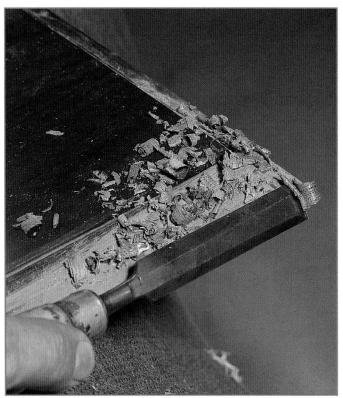

5 *When the glue is dry, remove the clamps and shape the patch to conform to the surrounding surface.*

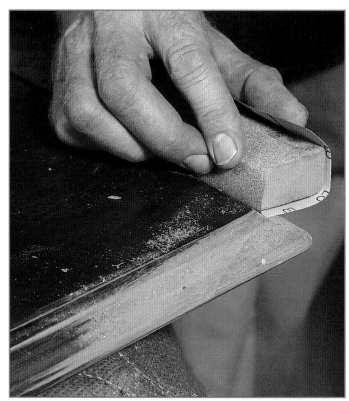

6 *Block-sand the patch smooth with the adjoining surfaces.*

sharp block plane or belt sander, carefully shape the patch to match the existing surface. Fine-tune the shaping with a sharp chisel, especially for rounded surfaces.

6 **Sand the patch.** Block-sand the surface using 120-grit sandpaper, again fine-tuning the shape of the patch to the surrounding wood. Finally, block sand the surface with 180-grit paper, making sure you remove all coarse sanding marks or plane- and chisel-blade marks.

7 **Touch up the patch.** Remove surface dust using a tack cloth, and fill the wood with paste wood filler if it needs one. (See "Filling Open-Grain Wood," page 203.) Stain the patch and any sanded wood to match the surrounding finish color. After the stain is dry (according to label instructions), apply a coat of finish. Let the finish dry, again according to the label instructions. Light-sand the area using 320-grit paper. If the patch needs additional touching up, use a pigmented wiping stain to do finer color matching. Use touch-up brushes and a soft rag to blend the color on the wood's surface. You can also use aerosol shading stains, available from finishing supply and touch-up supply houses. Apply another coat of finish, and let it dry. Use 280- to 320-grit sandpaper or #0000 steel wool to smooth the surface. Apply as many coats as necessary to build up the new finish to the existing one. Rub the final finish coat down with #0000 steel wool, blending the sheen to the surrounding finish.

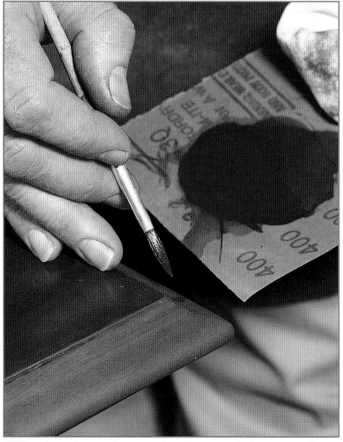

7 *Touch up the patch using oil stain to match the surrounding wood color. When the stain is dry, apply finish.*

Repairing Chewed Wood with Filler

Difficulty Level:

Tools and Materials

Wood chisel	Auto-body filler and dry stain
Grain filler (if necessary)	Touch-up stain and finish
#0000 steel wool	Soft cotton rag
Sandpaper (80- to 120-grit, 180-grit, and 320-grit)	

1 Clean the damaged area. Use a wood chisel to cut out all loose or damaged wood from the area. Do not smooth the damaged area, because a rough surface provides better adhesion for the filler material. If the damaged wood is too smooth, use the chisel to make some cuts in the wood into which the filler can bite.

2 Apply the filler. Put auto-body filler on a mixing board surface—a piece of cardboard will work fine. You can add dry pigmented stains to the body filler to match the wood color more closely, although this isn't necessary because you can touch up the filler during fin- ishing. Add cream hardener according to the label directions and mix it into the filler thorough- ly. Apply the putty to the damaged area using a palette knife to force it into the rough surface so it will stick. Fill the entire damaged area. If the area is too large, it may require another mixture and appli- cation of the filler, building up the material so that it can be shaped to the original surface form.

3 Rough-shape the repair. When the auto-body filler is dry (usually after 5 or 10 min- utes), use a wood chisel to sculpt the patch close to the desired shape.

1 Use a wood chisel to cut out any loose wood fibers from the damaged area.

2 Mix the body filler, and apply it to the damaged area, forcing it into the damaged wood surface so that it will adhere well.

3 When the filler is dry, use a wood chisel to shape the filled area to the desired shape.

4 Sand the repair. Next, use 80- to 120-grit sand-paper (with a block if you're sanding flat surfaces) to fine-tune the putty's shape, sanding the edges smooth and flush with surrounding wood. Once you're satisfied with the repair, sand the surface with 180-grit paper to remove course sanding marks.

5 Stain the patch and sanded area. If any of the surrounding wood was sanded and it's open-grain wood, fill the sanded wood and patch area with paste wood filler. (See "Filling Open-Grain Wood," page 203.) Stain the patch and sanded area to match surrounding wood.

6 Apply the finish. Let the stain dry according to the label directions, and then apply a coat of finish. When the finish dries (again, according to the can), light-sand the surface with 320-grit paper, and do any necessary touching up with artist's brushes using pigmented oil stains. You can also use aerosol shading stains to shade the repaired area, blending it into the surrounding finish. Apply as many coats of finish as necessary, using 320-grit paper or #0000 steel wool between coats. Be careful not to cut through the stain color. Rub down the final coat with #0000 steel wool to blend the sheen with the surrounding finish.

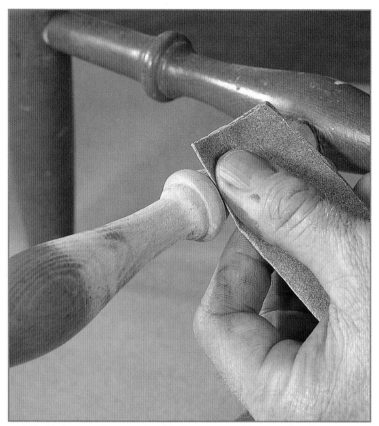

4 Sand the repair smooth with the surrounding wood surface.

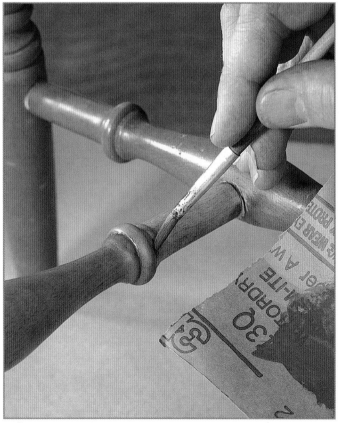

5 Stain the repaired area to match the surrounding wood as closely as possible.

6 Apply as many coats of finish as necessary to blend with the surrounding finish.

PART IV
REMOVING AN OLD FINISH & PREPARING WOOD

10

STRIPPING AND
BLEACHING FURNITURE

S tripping, or removing the old finish, is usually the messiest part of furniture restoration. If you don't want any mess at all, you might want to consider having the finish removed by a professional furniture stripper. But because some stripping processes can actually harm furniture, read through this chapter to learn about furniture stripping before making a decision. You can do your own stripping if you have the right materials and supplies, and save money in the process.

Removing the old finish from a piece of furniture is a drastic step in the restoration process. Before deciding to strip a piece, make sure you can't preserve and renew the original finish. Remember, stripping and refinishing an antique or collectible can greatly reduce its value.

WHEN TO STRIP THE FINISH

If you've scrutinized the finish and learned it's not original or if the refinishing job is a bad one, you may want to strip and refinish the piece. (See "Is the Finish Original?" page 164.) Another prime candidate for stripping and refinishing is a piece that was originally finished in a wood finish but has since been painted over. Usually you'll find that the paint was applied directly over the original finish, making it easier to strip because the paint pigments have not been able to penetrate the wood grain. Stripping and refinishing this kind of piece often exposes beautiful wood hidden under an opaque finish.

Keep in mind, however, that some pieces were made to be painted; stripping them usually uncovers inferior or unmatching wood pieces that will not finish well. If the paint has been applied to raw wood, it's usually an indication that the piece was meant to have a painted finish. In such cases you may still want to strip the paint to repaint the piece, or you may be able to simply repaint over the old color. To find out whether the paint is directly on the wood surface or atop another finish, scrape the paint or apply solvent to it in a small, inconspicuous area. If the paint pigment remains in the wood grain, it was probably painted originally; if not, the paint is over a natural wood finish and refinishing may be in order.

Another case for stripping is if the finish is so far gone or damaged that it simply cannot be renewed. Old finishes can become brittle or flaky as a result of age and mistreatment. Finishes can also be damaged by water or fire and often can't be restored without stripping and refinishing. Water can make some finishes lift and discolor permanently, while heat and smoke can blister or blacken finishes.

Some finishes, like this one, have been damaged to such an extent that they will need to be replaced.

These chairs originally had a clear finish over wood *but were painted sometime in the past. Note the chipping, which is common on furniture that wasn't meant to be painted. Stripping these chairs will likely reveal attractive wood.*

Yet another reason to strip and refinish a piece: You don't like the finish color or shade. For example, if you're putting a piece in a particular room or with another piece of furniture, you may want to blend or match the room's other furniture or the area's decor. But again, before deciding, consider the piece itself: If it's a valuable piece blessed with an original finish, you'd be better off saving the finish and buying another piece of furniture to fill your need.

STRIPPING METHODS

Once you've decided to strip and finish, what's the best method? Generally speaking, there are three ways to strip wood: with heat, with chemicals, or by sanding. Although each method will work, they are not all necessarily appropriate for stripping most furniture.

Heat-Stripping the Finish

Stripping with heat means using a propane torch, a heat gun or an infrared stripper. You hold the heat source to the finish to bubble and lift it; then scrape the finish or paint off with a scraper. The idea is to heat the surface enough to loosen or lift the finish but not enough to burn or scratch the wood underneath.

Although this method of stripping may work fine for some situations, such as stripping household exterior wood-

work that will be repainted, it's much too risky for furniture. If you choose to strip any wood using a heat gun, torch, or infrared stripper, keep a fire extinguisher close by, and wear an organic vapor mask, goggles, and heat-resistant gloves.

Note: Infrared strippers are safer (and faster) than traditional heat guns, because they work at a relatively low temperature that doesn't vaporize lead and other harmful chemicals, while quickly breaking the bond between paint and the surface to which it's applied. And while they can produce burns, it is less likely than with traditional heat guns or torches.

Stripping the Finish by Sanding

Sanding a finish off may seem like a logical approach to stripping, but it turns the job into a laborious, time-consuming task when it doesn't have to be.

Usually a belt sander or some other type of power sander is used to sand a finish off, and much of the wood is also removed in the process. Belt-sanding can leave an uneven wood surface, and it completely destroys the wood's patina, ruining—or nearly ruining—a good piece of furniture. Removing a finish by sanding also produces hazardous dust particles, requiring the use of a mask and goggles.

Chemical Stripping

Various methods are used for chemical stripping, some of which are practical for the do-it-yourselfer. Other methods, such as dipping, are commercial-only applications.

Dipping Methods. One method used by commercial shops is dipping the furniture into a tank of hot caustic solution until the finish is dissolved and then washing it with a neutralizing agent.

This process can be damaging to delicate parts and to veneer. It can also loosen joints in the furniture, raise the grain of the wood, and harm the wood's patina. For this reason I would not recommend hot-tank stripping for most furniture.

Another dipping method uses a cold chemical solution. Sometimes the stripping solution is hosed over the piece of furniture, keeping it wet until the finish is dissolved. Although this method is not as harsh as the hot-tank dipping method and will not loosen joints, it may still raise the wood grain and leave the wood gray or otherwise discolored. It's often difficult to restore the wood's beauty during the finishing process.

Hand Method. Stripping furniture by hand is perhaps the most recognizable method of chemical stripping, and it is the simplest and best method for the do-it-yourselfer. You apply a chemical solvent to the finish, dissolving and/or lifting it, and then either scrub or scrape off the finish by hand. The method requires more work and can be a little slower than commercial dipping, but it has many advantages. The most important advantage is that stripping furniture by hand won't damage furniture as easily as dipping: It doesn't destroy the beauty of the wood and doesn't loosen joints or damage veneer. Also,

most finish removers designed for use by hand will not raise the grain of the wood. All these features mean less work in the finishing process.

The supplies you need for hand stripping are readily available. You can choose from a variety of brands and types of finish removers at home centers, hardware, or paint stores. Read labels carefully to identify which stripper is best for your project.

Post-Stripping Wash-Down. Some removers contain waxes, which slow down their evaporation time, allowing them to work on the finish surface. These removers require the furniture to be washed down with a solvent such as mineral spirits or lacquer thinner after the finish is removed to clean off any wax residue left on the wood from the remover.

Other removers contain detergents, and require washing the surface with water after the finish is dissolved. Because water can raise wood grain and loosen joints and veneer, you may want to consider using a nonwater-wash remover like the ones mentioned in the previous paragraph. There are also removers, called no-wash removers, that claim to require no after-wash. Although it's not necessary to use an after-wash with such removers, a good solvent wash with lacquer thinner will often remove any stripping residues or finish traces that still may be left on the wood. This will save you both time and trouble in the next step of preparing the finish.

Chemical stripping by hand is the simplest and best method for the do-it-yourselfer. The chemical dissolves or lifts the finish, allowing you to scrape or scrub the wood surface clean.

Stripping Safety Precautions. Many removers contain chemicals that can burn or irritate your skin and give off toxic fumes. Other strippers are also flammable. When using finish removers, always read label warnings and precautions and follow directions carefully. Removers containing methylene chloride, for example, are not recommended for use by people with a heart condition as they could trigger a heart attack.

Stripping with flammable or toxic chemicals should always be done in a well ventilated area, either outdoors or someplace with a good cross-ventilation system. You can open a window and put an exhaust fan in a second window to remove fumes and pull fresh air across the work area. Wear a carbon filter respirator, and don't strip in an area with any type of open flame or where someone is smoking. Always wear protective clothing, including chemical-proof gloves and an apron. Always wear eye protection to protect yourself from chemical splashes.

Reduced-Hazard Strippers. Besides conventional chemical finish removers, you can buy reduced-hazard, or so-called safe, strippers. These formulations are non-flammable, nontoxic, and won't burn or harm your skin. They emit little or no odor; a few produce a slight, pleasant fragrance such as citrus. Some major name brands use large amounts of water in their formulations, so they are not particularly good for use on furniture. Check the label for specifics concerning the type of finish a particular product is designed to strip. Some, such as those containing N-methyl pyrrolidone, are better on furniture finishes like shellac and lacquer than others.

The trade-off for being safer is that the removers are usually slow-working and expensive. If you're concerned with any problems or hazards related to the use of harsh solvents or chemicals and you don't mind spending a little extra time and money, however, reduced hazard strippers may be the way to go.

Wood Refinishers. Wood refinishers are solvents meant to be used to dissolve a finish enough to partially remove it while leaving a thin film of the original finish on the wood. Doing this preserves the original color and patina of the wood and eliminates many of the steps involved in refinishing. They will work only on shellac and lacquer.

The difficulty in this method is being able to remove only part of the finish while leaving enough of it on the wood surface to provide a thin, even coat. Wood-refinisher solvents will also work to remove the finish totally, leaving the surface clean and ready to coat if you use enough of the solvent and scrub the wood enough. These solvents are slower-acting than full-fledged finish removers, produce strong fumes, and are extremely flammable. Unless you plan to leave part of the original finish on the wood, a finish remover, rather than a refinisher, may be your best choice.

HOW TO REMOVE A FINISH

Stripping paint or finish does not require a great deal of skill or training; what it does require is preparation. Without the proper work area, safety practices, tools, and materials, you'll end up with a mess at best and a disaster at worst. Put some time, effort, and thought into preparation for your project, and it will pay off later.

Preparation

The work area and safety are the first considerations before you begin stripping. The best place to strip furniture is outdoors. Set up an area in the shade, so the stripper does not dry out before it has time to work. If you are unable to work outside, set up a work area that's well ventilated with a fresh-air supply. Two open windows, with an exhaust fan in one, will keep a flow of fresh air through the room so fumes don't build up. Basement workshops may not be well suited for stripping because of limited ventilation. Basements also often contain heaters with pilot lights or open flames—hazardous for working with flammable products.

Wear a charcoal filter respirator, particularly when stripping indoors, but keep in mind that wearing a respirator does not negate the necessity of cross ventilation and fresh air. Cover the floor with a drop cloth (plastic or canvas) and plenty of old newspapers to catch drippings; stripper solvent can dissolve some floor materials. Don't allow smoking in or near your work area, and always read and follow label instructions for any stripper product you use.

Protect your eyes and skin with safety glasses, chemical-resistant gloves, and protective clothing—long pants, a long-sleeved shirt, and a thick work apron. When working on smaller items, such as chairs, set them up on a workbench so you don't have to bend over and work in awkward positions. This will make your work easier and prevent back strain and accidents.

Tools and Materials. The tools used for stripping are fairly simple, and chances are that you may already have some of them on hand. (See "Stripping and Finishing Tools," page 38.)

For materials, first choose a stripper for your project, and decide what solvent, if any, you need to use to wash the surface after stripping it. Have two large-mouth containers on hand for the stripping process: one into which you can pour clean stripper for brushing onto the finish surface and another into which you can scrape finish after it's dissolved. Large coffee cans, old metal saucepans, or small pails work well. Don't use glass containers because they get slippery when wet and are easily dropped. Plastic containers aren't appropriate either, because harsh solvents can soften or dissolve them.

You'll also need either coarse steel-wool pads (#1 or #2) or coarse nylon abrasive pads for scrubbing the wood surface after scraping off the majority of the old finish. Some parts of furniture, such as spindles, carvings, or wood turnings, are difficult to scrape with a putty knife and will need to be scrubbed with an abrasive pad to remove the old finish. Nylon abrasive pads are preferable to coarse steel-wool pads because they are less damaging to the wood surface.

Be sure to have some old rags on hand to soak up any excess stripping residue or remover. You'll also need rags for clean-up and the final solvent wash-down.

Using a Chemical Remover

After you've set up the work area, assembled the tools and materials needed, and read all product instructions, you're ready to begin the stripping process. Don't forget to use the recommended safety equipment and follow all precautions for the products you'll be using. Be sure to allow enough time to complete the stripping process you are starting, based on the size of the piece.

Difficulty Level:

Tools and Materials

Screwdriver and other disassembly tools
Protective gloves, clothing, and equipment
Old newspaper
Stripper and proper containers
Old bristle brush
Scraper#1 or #2 steel wool or abrasive pad
Brass brush
Lacquer thinner or other solvent
Cotton rags

1 **Apply the stripper.** Remove all hardware from the furniture. If the hardware has been painted, submerge it in a container of stripper to dissolve the paint. Disassemble the furniture where possible by taking out removable shelves, removing doors and drawers, taking out table leaves on drop leaf tables, and the like. Place everything to be stripped over a layer of old newspapers.

Some removers require shaking, so read the label and shake only if necessary. Remove the top of the stripper container carefully, as some removers can build up pres-

sure in the can or bottle. Pour a healthy amount of stripper into a wide-mouthed can or pan, and then lay a heavy wet coat on the finish surface by brushing in one direction. Don't brush over the surface once it's wet, as this will pull the stripper off the surface and cause it to evaporate quickly.

Note: To help keep the stripper from evaporating too quickly, apply layer of plastic wrap on top. (Some of the stripper will likely adhere to the plastic, making cleanup easier.)

2 **Scrape off the stripper.** After the entire surface is wet, allow it to soak for 10 to 20 minutes, giving the chemical time to soften and lift the finish. Don't allow the remover to sit so long that it dries up. Check the finish with a scraper to see whether it has been lifted or softened enough to expose the raw wood. Some finishes will bubble and wrinkle, which will be obvious, but others will only soften, and you'll have to check

1 *Lay a heavy coat of remover on the finish surface by brushing in one direction.*

2 *After the finish has dissolved or lifted, carefully scrape it into a wide-mouthed metal container.*

them with a scraper to see whether they're dissolved. If the finish doesn't seem ready to come off, let it soak a little while longer. Carefully scrape the old dissolved finish from the surface, pushing it into a wide-mouthed can, saucepan, or small pail. If the furniture has intricate turnings, carvings, or other areas that are difficult to get at with a scraper, go over those areas with a

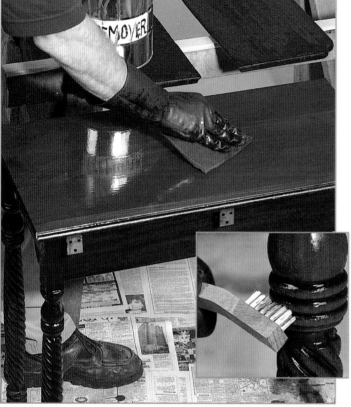

3 *After recoating the surface with stripper and allowing it time to work, scrape the remaining finish from the surface, and use an abrasive pad to scrub the surface. You can use a brass-bristle brush (inset) to scrub softened finish from carvings and crevices.*

4 *Do a final wash-down of the wood's surface using a clean rag dipped in lacquer thinner.*

brass brush or abrasive pad to get at the nooks and crannies.

3 Rub with an abrasive pad. If undissolved finish remains on the surface, recoat it with the remover as before and allow it to sit again, giving the chemical time to work. Scrape the remaining dissolved finish into the can you're using for waste. Use an abrasive nylon pad or a #1 or #2 steel-wool pad dipped in the stripper to scrub the surface to remove any remaining finish. Scrub with the grain of the wood whenever possible. If necessary, use a knife, scratch awl, or pointed dowel to clean finish out of nooks, crannies, and crevices. A brass-bristle brush can also work for carvings or crevices.

Scrub down the piece with a clean abrasive pad and lacquer thinner or other appropriate solvent to remove any leftover oils, waxes, or stripping residue. Examine the piece for any remaining finish, and apply stripper to these areas again if needed to loosen the finish. Then scrub it off. It's always easier to remove the finish at this stage than to try to remove it later during the sanding stage.

4 Clean with solvent. Wash down the piece using a rag dipped in lacquer thinner or other solvent; use a clean rag and solvent for a final wipe-down. Let the piece dry overnight before sanding or finishing. Clean any old finish and stripper residue from tools using solvent. Allow the leftover stripping sludge in the waste can to dry out completely before disposing of it, and consult local waste-management authorities regarding any ordinances concerning proper disposal.

Saving the Stain or Color of the Wood

Some pieces of furniture may have a pleasing color or stain well worth saving, although the top finish may be in bad shape. In such cases, consider removing only the finish film without disturbing the existing color or stain. This will not only preserve the finish color but will save you work in the finishing process, eliminating several steps. Keep in mind, however, that this stripping process will be slower than with regular chemical strippers.

Because regular chemical strippers tend to remove not only the top finish but also the wood's stain, you must use a different solvent if you want to retain the color of the wood or stain. Wood refinishers are designed for this application. Although they won't dissolve all finishes, they will work on lacquer and shellac, the most widely used furniture finishes. Apply the solvent to the finish with a piece of #000 or #0000 steel wool, rubbing in one small area until the finish is dissolved by the solvent and removed by the steel wool. Repeat this process, working

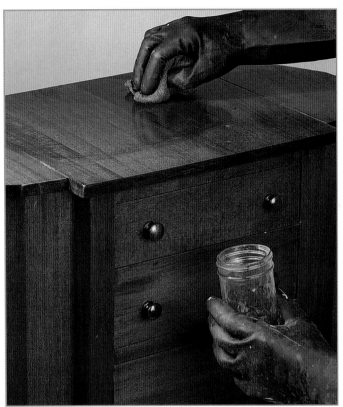

You can use wood-refinisher solvents to strip a finish from the wood without removing the existing color or stain.

in one small area at a time, until you've stripped the entire piece. Because the stain remains intact, no sanding or staining is necessary before reapplying the finish.

Removing Stains or Color in the Wood

After stripping the finish from a piece of furniture, you may discover that the wood still has unsightly stains or that the color is still not what you want. Dark water stains or ink stains are common problems in old furniture. Such stains may be considered part of a piece's charm, but you may still want to diminish them so they are less noticeable.

Other furniture, once stripped, can still contain original dye stains that have penetrated deep into the wood, leaving it too dark or splotchy looking. Unless you want to refinish these pieces in a dark finish to hide the old stain, you'll have to lighten the wood surface to a more even color. Removing these stains can be best achieved by bleaching the wood.

Ordinary liquid chlorine bleach will work for bleaching wood, but it's better to use a commercial two-part wood bleach, which is a stronger solution. You can find two-part wood bleach at a well-stocked hardware, paint store, or home center. When using bleaches be sure to

follow all safety procedures, such as wearing rubber gloves, using safety glasses, and wearing a protective apron. Remember that a strong bleach solution will not only bleach color from anything it touches but can also burn your skin. If bleach comes into contact with your skin, immediately wash it well with water.

After the wood has been thoroughly bleached, don't sand it until it has been neutralized, as sanding dust can be hazardous, acting as an irritant to your nose, throat, and lungs. It's always a good idea to wear a dust mask when sanding wood that has been bleached. Whether you want to remove individual stains or lighten an entire piece, do all heavy sanding before bleaching. (See page 199.)

To remove small stains from wood individually, apply bleach with a nylon-bristle artist's brush or a cotton-tipped swab, confining the bleach to the stained area only. Follow the bleaching procedure described below on these areas, and then bleach the entire piece to blend these lightened spots with the surrounding surface.

Using a Two-Part Wood Bleach

Wood bleaches require that parts A and B be mixed together just prior to application. Some wood bleaches also come in dry crystals (oxalic acid) and must be mixed with hot water before use. The label will give specific instructions for the mix formula and the wood bleaching process. If finishing the wood, the surface will need to be neutralized with a baking soda solution prior to finish, which is explained on the label.

When buying and using commercial wood bleaches, read and follow the instructions carefully for the particular product you are using. The following general instructions are for using a two-part wood bleach that must be mixed together prior to applying it to wood. The instructions can also be followed when using regular household bleach to lighten wood, excluding the mixing of part A and part B.

Difficulty Level: 🔨 🔨

Tools and Materials

Wood bleach
Protective gloves, clothing, and equipment
Synthetic sponge
Vinegar and water
220-grit sandpaper or finer
Dust mask

1 Scrub the surface. After checking label directions to be certain parts A and B are to be mixed together before using, pour equal amounts of the solutions into a plastic container. Wearing gloves, protective glasses, and an apron, liberally apply the bleach solution to the

1 Liberally apply the bleach solution to the wood's surface using a synthetic household sponge. Make sure the bleach saturates the wood's surface.

wood's surface using a synthetic household sponge. Make sure that any area of the wood that needs bleaching is saturated. If possible, turn the surface to be bleached horizontally to avoid runs. Be careful not to let the bleach run onto or make contact with any part of the wood that you don't want to bleach to avoid light spots or streaks. Try to wet the area to be bleached as evenly as possible and let it soak for at least 4 hours. Check back over the first 5 minutes or so to clean up any drips or runs.

2 Neutralize the bleach. After the bleach has worked and the area has dried, examine the wood to see whether it's sufficiently lightened. If not, apply another coat of bleach and allow it to work for another 4 or 5 hours. After completing the bleaching process, use a white vinegar-and-water solution to neutralize the bleach. Mix one part white vinegar with three parts water, and apply the solution to the bleached surface using a clean sponge.

3 Sand the area. After the wood is completely dry, light-sand the surface with fine sandpaper (220-grit or finer). Make sure you wear a dust mask. Don't sand heavily, or you might cut through the bleached surface to darker wood below. The purpose of sanding is just to smooth any wood grain that the bleaching process has raised. All heavy sanding should have been done prior to bleaching. (See "Sanding the Wood," page 199.)

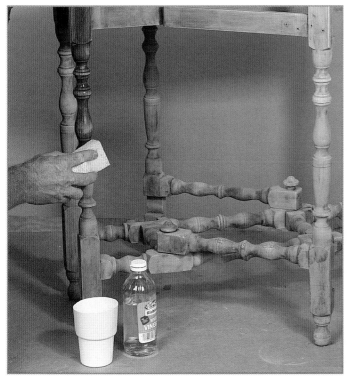

2 After the bleach has worked (about 4 or 5 hours) and has sufficiently lightened the wood, apply a vinegar-and-water solution with a clean sponge to neutralize the bleached surface.

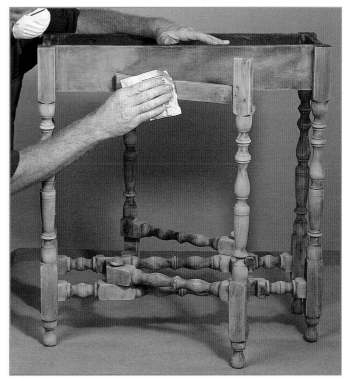

3 Allow the wood to dry, and smooth the raised wood grain by sanding the surface lightly with fine sandpaper (220- to 320-grit).

11

FIXING MINOR WOOD DAMAGE

As any experienced furniture refinisher knows, a good finish requires a good foundation. That's because furniture finishes enhance the natural wood surface rather than hide it. If the wood surface is attractive, the finish will complement it. If the surface isn't prepared properly, however, the finish will highlight the lack of preparation. For this reason, it's important to give attention to detail during the preparation for wood finishing. It's much easier to deal with surface problems before you begin finishing rather than after you've applied the finish.

Preparation involves not only sanding the wood but removing any contaminants that may remain on the wood's surface, repairing surface damage, filling open-grain woods, and changing the wood color by staining or bleaching.

CONTAMINANTS IN WOOD

Raw wood is not contaminated with wax, oil, or silicone, the culprits that create fish eye and other problems in some kinds of wood finishes. Wood in furniture that is being refinished, however, may have been subjected to many kinds of contaminants. Any waxes, polishes, or oils applied to the piece over the years may have worked their way through cracks and openings in the finish and into the wood. Although stripping the finish and sanding the wood can remove contaminants, it doesn't always succeed in totally removing them.

Note: Some tropical hardwoods, including teak and rosewood, are naturally oily and may require special treatment before finishing or refinishing. For such exotics, consult specialty finishing guides or a professional.

These contaminants do not affect most oil-based finishes, but they can ruin a lacquer or water-based finish. If you suspect contaminants in wood, you can deal with them in several ways. The first way is to seal them in by applying a coat of shellac. Shellac is an excellent sealer and will prevent these contaminants from making contact with successive finish coats. Another method to deal with contaminants in a lacquer finish is to use an additive called fish-eye eliminator. (See "Lacquer," page 58.)

A third way to deal with contaminants and prevent problems is to remove them totally by thoroughly cleaning the wood surface before finishing.

Removing Contaminants

Difficulty Level:

Tools and Materials

Cotton rags	Ammonia and water
200-grit sandpaper or finer	Mineral spirits
Protective gloves, clothing, and equipment	
#000 or #0000 steel wool or abrasive nylon pad	

1 Scrub the surface. Using mineral spirits (paint thinner) and an abrasive nylon pad or fine steel wool (#000 or #0000), scrub the stripped wood surface, going with the grain of the wood as much as possible. Wear gloves, eye protection, and a respirator because you'll be using a large amount of mineral spirits over an extended period of time during this procedure.

As an alternative to using mineral spirits, water-based degreasers are available at paint, hardware or home improvement stores. Follow label directions, but also be sure when cleaning unfinished wood to light-sand the wood to smooth out raised grain caused by water-based materials. To do this, use 280 or similar grit sandpaper.

2 Wipe down the surface. Wipe up the liquid with a clean cotton rag to remove dissolved contaminants from the wood. Repeat the scrubbing process with mineral spirits, again wiping up the liquid with a clean rag.

3 Rub the surface with ammonia. Rub down the surface with a solution of ammonia and warm water (1 cup of ammonia to 1 gallon of warm water) using a

pad made from a cotton rag. Wipe the wood surface with a clean cotton rag, and let it dry.

4 Sand the surface. Once the wood is dry, check it to see whether the grain is raised and the surface is rough. If so, light-sand the wood surface with fine sandpaper (220-grit or finer) before applying any stain or finish.

DENTS AND GOUGES

Part of the process of preparing wood for finishing involves repairing damaged wood surfaces. Some minor defects may be acceptable, but more serious ones, such as a gouge in an otherwise perfect, or almost perfect, table top, need to be repaired before you finish the furniture. Objectionable nicks, scratches, and dents also can be repaired more easily before wood is finished. You can remove some of these defects by a reasonably good sanding, but others may be so deep that you can't remove them by normal sanding alone. In such cases it's better to remove the defect by steaming it out of the wood or by filling it with putty. Examine the wood surface before sanding to decide which defects can be removed and which ones need to be filled.

1 Rub down the surface in the direction of the wood grain using paint thinner and an abrasive nylon pad.

2 Mop up the liquid using a clean absorbent rag before repeating the scrubbing process.

3 Wash the wood surface with a solution of ammonia and warm water, and then wipe it dry.

4 When the wood dries, smooth-sand the surface using fine sandpaper (220- to 320-grit) before finishing.

Steaming Out a Dent

A dent is an indentation in the wood surface where the wood fibers have been crushed or compressed. Gouges are places where the wood surface has been deeply scarred and torn, with the wood fibers broken. If dent is in a veneered surface, use wood putty as opposed to attempting to steam it out or this may lift the veneer from the substrate surface.

Often, you can remove dents by steaming them out of the wood. Steaming sometimes works with scratches and nicks, too, although they may still leave a bruise in the wood surface. By applying water and heat to the dent, nick, or scratch, steam is forced into wood fibers, swelling the wood and leveling the indented area. Before steaming, make sure you've removed all finish and contaminants from the wood so the steam can penetrate the wood grain fully.

Difficulty Level: 🔨

Tools and Materials

Household iron or burn-in knife
Palette knife and water   Damp cotton rag

1 **Drop water into the dent.** Heat an iron or burn-in knife to operating temperature, and apply a drop or two of water to the indented area using a palette knife or other flat-bladed tool to control the application.

2 **Apply heat.** Lay a clean damp rag over the dent, applying the hot iron or knife to the spot long enough to produce steam (usually a few seconds). Lift the rag, and check the dent to see whether the wood is sufficiently raised; if not, apply more water to the area, again covering it with a damp rag and applying heat. Check the spot yet again to see whether the dent has leveled. If several steam applications do not sufficiently raise the

wood, you may need to fill the area with wood putty.

Filling Wood Defects with Putty

Not all wood-surface damage can be remedied by steaming. Defects like gouges or deep scratches, where the damage is deep and the wood fibers are torn, will have to be filled with putty and sanded level with the surrounding surface.

Wood putty is available in a number of types, brands, and colors. (See "Wood Putty," page 51.) Keep in mind that staining the wood before finishing may change the way the putty matches the wood, depending on how the putty takes the stain. If the putty absorbs the stain more readily than the wood, it will probably show up a little darker; if it does not absorb the stain as much as the wood, it will be a little lighter.

Difficulty Level: 🔨

Tools and Materials

Mineral spirits   Cotton rags
Palette knife   Wood putty
Powdered pigment   120-grit sandpaper

1 Apply a drop or two of water to the damaged area. Use a palette knife or other flat blade to control dripping.

2 To raise the wood, apply heat to the area for a few seconds by laying a hot iron or burn-in knife over a damp rag

1 Prepare the area. Before filling a scratch, nick, or gouge with wood putty, make sure you clean out any loose particles such as sanding dust or loose wood fibers. Remove them using a utility-knife blade, or wash them out using mineral spirits on a clean rag.

2 Mix color in the putty. Use the back of a piece of sandpaper cut into one-quarter sections (wet-or-dry works well), a piece of cardboard, or a paper plate as a palette to mix dry pigment into a small amount of putty. Try to match the putty to the wet color of the wood, which is closer to the finished wood color.

This step may not be necessary. This is only necessary if using a neutral colored auto body type two-part putty. If you want to add color (dry pigment) be sure to add before adding the hardening agent to the mix.

3 Apply the putty. After the area to be patched has dried, use a palette knife to apply the putty to the defect, pressing it into the damaged surface. Be sure that the putty goes deep into the gouge so that it adheres well. Leave the patch slightly higher than the surrounding wood. If the area is large, it may require two applications.

4 Sand the patch level. Let the putty dry until it's hard. If you're using a two-part putty that dries by adding a hardening agent, leave a small amount of the mixed putty on the piece of sandpaper after filling the defect. When this putty is hard, the putty used for repairing the wood surface will be ready to sand. Check ready-to-use putty for hardness by pressing your thumbnail into the putty; when no impression is left, the putty is ready to sand. Sand the patch using 120-grit sandpaper until the putty is level with the surface of the wood. If the patch is on a flat area, use a sanding block with the sandpaper.

SANDING THE WOOD

After taking care of any obvious wood defects, the next step is sanding. Although you may consider sanding a tedious task, it's important. This part of the preparation process can make or break your finished product.

Inspect the wood surface carefully, paying attention to any areas that may need extra attention, such as inside corners, moldings, or joints with old excess glue on them. Remember that whatever is noticeable at the unfinished stage of the wood will be amplified once you apply finish.

Which Sandpaper Should You Use?

The objective in sanding is to remove any surface scratches and to smooth the wood sufficiently in preparation for the finish application. Ironically, the process of sanding wood to get rid of surface scratches produces surface scratches of its own. The difference is that the intentional scratches either run in the direction of the wood grain, rendering them invisible, or (in the case of the marks produced by a random-orbit sander) are so small that they are not noticeable.

Because most hand sanding of wood is done in the direction of the wood grain, 120-grit paper is usually sufficient. You can use a garnet, aluminum oxide, or stearated paper. (See "Sandpaper," page 49.) If you want to get a smoother surface, you can graduate to 150-grit or possibly even

1 Before filling a wood defect, clean out sanding dust or loose particles using a utility-knife blade or mineral spirits on a clean rag.

2 Mix the wood putty's color to match the wet color of the wood, which more closely resembles the wood color after it's finished.

3 Apply the wood putty to the defect, being sure to press it well into the damaged surface so that it will hold.

4 After the putty is dry, sand the area level with the surrounding surface using 120-grit sandpaper.

180- or 220-grit sandpaper. Keep in mind, though, that if you make the wood surface too smooth before finishing it, you could prevent it from adequately absorbing your stain or finish. This degree of smoothness could better be achieved after you've applied the sealer coats of finish to the wood.

There are some cases when it's absolutely necessary to sand with 180-grit or finer paper to eliminate sanding marks. Some woods, such as burl or crotch veneers, have irregular grain patterns, making it nearly impossible to follow the direction of the wood grain when sanding. Using 150-grit paper will usually leave sanding marks that can only be eliminated by graduating to a finer grit of paper. Some hardwoods, such as maple, can also show sanding marks easily because they're exceptionally dense with little grain pattern to hide the marks. A finer-grit paper can solve this problem.

Power sanders can leave vibrator or swirl sanding marks in the wood's surface. For this reason, when using a power sander you can often begin sanding with a slightly finer grade of paper. Instead of beginning the sanding process with 120-grit paper, for example, begin with 150-grit. Then you can move to a finer grit on the final sanding, which will help get rid of sanding marks left by the previous coarser grade of paper.

Preparing for Finish Sanding

When sanding to prepare a piece for finishing, consider several things before you begin. Try to achieve a fairly even color over the entire piece. Avoid sanding too heavily in one area and not heavily enough in another, as this can create light and dark areas in the wood surface, particularly if the old stain color stays in the wood. If the piece only needs a light sanding to avoid cutting through the original color or patina, be sure to do this over the entire piece. Once you cut through in one area, it will be difficult to blend this area into the rest of the piece.

Be sure to examine the wood to determine which scratches or defects you want to eliminate. On some older furniture you may want to leave certain age or distress marks while removing other more objectionable defects or scratches. Once you have decided this, it will help you to determine how much sanding is necessary.

Lastly, pay attention to the smoothness of the surface when sanding. Make sure all surfaces have been sanded smooth and there is no raised grain or rough surfaces. Knock off any sharp edges or corners so they will accept stain and finish. (See "Sanding Tips," page 51, for more on sanding.)

THE PROS KNOW

HOW TO COLOR PUTTY

To match the wood more closely, use dry powdered coloring pigments. You can buy these as touch-up stains through finishing supply companies. Because these dry pigments are concentrated, you'll need only small amounts to change the color of the putty.

To do this, mix only the amount of putty you need with the dry powdered stain until you achieve the desired color. If you add too much colorant, the putty may become too thick and dry; to take care of this, add a little solvent to the putty. Some brands of wood putty also sell a solvent to thin the material; if not, read the label so you can decide what to use as a solvent.

If the putty contains petroleum distillates, lacquer thinner will work as a solvent. If the label says the material is flammable or contains alcohol, you can use denatured alcohol. If the putty is nonflammable and has little smell, it's probably water-based latex, and you can thin it with water.

While most putty comes in a ready-to-use form, others, such as water putty, come in dry powdered form and need solvent mixed with them before you can use them. Wood putty is also available with a catalyst that you add to the material to dry and harden it. Auto-body filler works just as well as two-part wood putty and is less expensive.

The advantage to using a two-part putty is that it does not shrink, it dries quickly, and it gets extremely hard and solid, making it good for

building up large areas. Its greatest disadvantage is that it doesn't absorb stain as well as wood. You can, however, use dry powdered stains, as with other kinds of wood putty, to help you match the wood color. With this type of putty, add the stain and get the putty color as close as possible before adding the hardening agent.

Difficulty Level: 🔨 🔨

Tools and Materials

Sanding block with 120-grit sandpaper or power pad
Sander with 150-grit sandpaper
180-grit sandpaper   Mineral spirits
Cotton rag

1 Sand flat areas. Sand all flat areas of the piece using a sanding block (cork, felt, or rubber) and paper or a power pad sander. If you are hand sanding with a sanding block, use 120-grit paper and sand with the grain. If you're using a power pad sander, use 150-grit paper and be careful not to damage any edges, corners, or other delicate areas on the piece. It's a good idea to wear a dust mask.

2 Sand detail areas. Hand-sand all irregular areas, such as inside corners, moldings, turnings, carv-

ings, and the like. Fold the paper to reach into cracks and crevices, and use special sanding blocks, such as a piece of dowel, to sand contoured surfaces. Don't forget to knock off any sharp edges at this stage, softening them slightly so they'll be ready to accept finish and stain more easily. Graduate to a finer grade of paper, such as 150-grit for hand sanding or 180-grit for power sanding, and repeat the flat and detail sanding.

3 Wet and examine the surface. Before beginning the finishing process, wet all wood surfaces with mineral spirits or paint thinner. You don't need gloves or other personal protection because you're just giving the piece a quick wipe with the mineral spirits. While the wood surface is wet, look closely for any cross-grain scratches, machine sanding marks such as swirls, or defects that might have been missed during the sanding process. Sand these areas out before you begin to finish the piece.

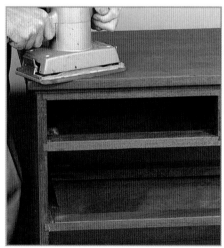

1 Sand all flat areas first, using a power pad sander (150-grit) or a sanding block with sandpaper (120-grit).

2 Hand sand all irregular areas such as moldings, turnings, carvings, and inside corners.

3 Before applying finish, wet the surface with mineral spirits to reveal any defects that may need attention.

THE PROS KNOW

RAISING THE WOOD GRAIN

One method for putting a finishing touch on the wood-sanding process involves raising the grain by applying water and then sanding the grain smooth. This process is not necessary in most refinishing work, but it's helpful if you plan to use any water-based products in the finishing process. Because water raises wood grain, finishing products such as water stain and water-based polyurethane and paint will raise the grain after you start to finish if you haven't gone through this process. Then during finish sanding, you'll be more likely to cut through the finish or stain color. These cut-through areas can then require difficult touch-up work, adding time to the project and possibly compromising its appearance.

To raise the grain, wipe the entire wood surface down thoroughly with a wet rag, making sure that all surfaces are wet. Wipe off any excess water, and let the wood dry overnight. After the grain has been raised, causing the wood to feel rough, sand it with a fine paper (220-grit). This type of sanding can be done quickly. The sandpaper should only be passed over the surface enough to make it feel smooth again. All heavy sanding—with 120-grit paper—should have been done before wetting the wood.

12

FILLING WOOD GRAIN AND STAINING

After you've sanded wood you've been working on and eliminated various imperfections, you may be eager to jump right into the finish application. Before applying the finish, however, there are other preparatory steps to consider. If you are using an open-grain wood, for example, you should apply a paste grain filler before applying the finish. On open-grain woods, paste filler produces a smooth nonporous surface upon which to build the finish. Staining the wood is another step to consider. Although some woods have natural beauty without being stained, most need some type of stain to enhance their appearance. You may also want to stain the wood simply to change its color to match another piece of furniture. This chapter explains both filling and staining the wood.

OPEN-GRAIN WOODS

Amateur refinishers often overlook an important step in the finishing process: filling wood that has open grain. Though not absolutely necessary, this step can greatly improve the appearance of the final finish.

Some open-grain furniture woods that commonly get a filler treatment include mahogany, walnut, oak, ash, rosewood, chestnut, butternut, and elm. If you're finishing with a film finish like lacquer, shellac, or varnish (polyurethane), fill any of these woods before you apply the finish. Without filler, the wood will generally appear grainy and porous. The only time filling is not recommended is when you're finishing open-grain woods with oil or wax.

Paste Wood Filler. Wood filler, or grain filler, is a paste-like substance that can be applied to open-grain woods after sanding and before finishing. (See "Paste Wood Filler," page 53.) Because filler is not meant to stay on the wood's surface but only in the open grain crevices, you must remove excess filler before it hardens. After the material dries, sand the surface smooth with fine sandpaper. This process provides a smooth, level, non-porous surface for finish application.

Oil- or Water-Based? Wood filler is available in both oil-based and water-based forms, and either type will do the job. There are a few differences between the two, primarily in the consistency of the filler and the amount of drying time needed before you can apply the finish.

Oil-based filler is thicker than water-based filler and, because of its oil content, requires at

Grain Not Filled

Grain Filled

Wood *is composed of innumerable channel-like fibers packed together. With open-grain wood, the upper fibers form crevices that must be filled for a smooth surface.*

least overnight—and possibly longer—to dry. Water-based filler dries more quickly, and that means you have less working time with the material: It can be finish-coated in as little as two hours.

Another small but potentially important difference is that oil-based filler may not be compatible with water-based finishes, while water-based filler, once dry, is compatible with both water and solvent-based finishes. Whichever filler you decide to use, be sure to read and follow label directions closely.

Filler Color. Wood filler is available in a variety of colors, including natural. While wood filler is not meant to add a lot of color to wood, it will have some effect, primarily in the open grain of the wood because this is where most of the filler stays. If you want the grain to look darker, use a dark-colored filler; if you're trying to de-emphasize the wood grain, making it more subtle, use a lighter-colored filler. Most woods will look better when filled with a filler that is a little darker than the wood itself, as this will enhance the grain rather than blend it in with the surrounding wood color.

Staining before Filling

After stripping and sanding an open-grain wood, the next step is usually to fill the wood. There are some exceptions, however. When you're going to use a dye stain to color the wood, for example, you might want to stain the wood before filling it. The reason for staining before filling in this case is that dye stains must penetrate the wood to color it, and wood filler can hinder this penetration. This is not true when using pigmented stains, because they add color primarily on top of the wood.

One drawback to staining the wood before filling it is that you can cut through the stain color when you sand the wood filler, the last step in the filling process. Such cut-through areas can be difficult to blend in with the surrounding color. Using a water-soluble aniline dye can diminish this difficulty. Use the dye to stain the wood before filling it. You can then use the dye to restain the cut-through surface after you've completed the filling and sanding steps. A water-soluble dye stain will more easily blend the cut-through areas with the surrounding color.

Sealing before Filling

Sealing the wood before filling may be necessary if you want to use a dark-colored filler but you don't want to darken the overall wood color. Sealing the wood first prevents the dark filler from significantly darkening the wood surface while still allowing it to fill and add prominence to the wood grain.

If you decide to seal the wood surface before filling it, use a thinned coat of lacquer for spray sealing and a thinned coat of shellac for brush sealing. After the sealer coat dries, sand the surface lightly using extra-fine sandpaper (280-grit). After tacking the surface to remove sanding dust, proceed with the filling process.

Filling Open-Grain Wood

Difficulty Level: 🔨 🔨

Tools and Materials

Wood filler	Latex gloves
Paintbrush	Coarse rags
220-grit stearated sandpaper	
Rubber squeegee or plastic scraper	
#0000 steel wool or nylon abrasive pad	

Because wood filler is so thick, you must thin it down to a brushable consistency before applying it to wood. Use mineral spirits to thin oil-based filler (or naphtha if you want a solvent that's a little faster drying) and water to thin water-based filler.

1 Apply filler to the wood. Mix filler (enough to do the job) in a separate container, and be sure to mix the thick pigment well into the solution so it has a thin, creamy consistency. If you're changing the filler color, add the necessary tinting color. Put on a pair of vinyl or latex dishwashing gloves, and use a regular paintbrush

1 Use a brush to apply the wood filler to the wood. Make sure you cover the entire surface, including cracks and crevices.

2 As the filler begins to dry and thicken, use a coarse rag to remove the excess by wiping across the wood grain.

3 Pack the wood filler into the open grain by rubbing in a circular or cross-grain motion with the palm of your (gloved) hand.

(natural bristle for oil-based or synthetic for water-based) to apply the filler to the wood. It's not important how you brush on the filler as long as you cover the entire wood surface, including cracks and crevices. Apply the filler to one small section of the piece at a time so you'll have time to work it into the wood before it dries.

2 Remove excess filler. As soon as the filler begins to dry—immediately with water-based and after a few minutes with oil-based—use a coarse rag such as burlap to begin removing the excess. Wipe across the grain as much as possible so you don't pull the filler out of the grain pores. You can also use a rubber squeegee or a plastic scraper with a broad blade to force the filler into the wood pores while at the same time scraping off the excess. If you use a scraper, be careful not to scratch the wood.

3 Pack the filler. After you've removed the majority of the excess filler from the surface, use the palms of your gloved hands to pack the filler down into the wood grain, rubbing in a circular or cross-grain motion. As you do this, the friction from your hands will cause the filler to dry more quickly, so you should go immediately to the next step.

4 Wipe across the grain. Using a clean rag, wipe over the wood surface to remove all excess filler. Wipe across the grain as much as possible to allow the filler to remain in the pores. Also at this point, clean excess filler from any corners, cracks, or crevices. You can use the point of a sharpened dowel to get at the filler, or use a screwdriver tip with a rag pulled over it. Be sure to get the wood surface as clean as possible without removing the filler from the wood grain.

5 Sand the surface. After the filler is completely dry, use 220-grit stearated paper to sand all flat wood sur-

4 Use a clean rag to wipe the wood surface, removing any remaining excess filler. Remove filler from corners, cracks, and crevices.

5 *When the filler has dried completely, sand flat areas with 220-grit sandpaper to smooth the surface.*

faces. Sand in the direction of the grain. It's not necessary to sand heavily, only enough to smooth the surface. Rub out all turned or irregular areas with nylon abrasive pads or #0000 steel wool.

STAINING WOOD

Just as mother always told you, "the clothes make the man," so also can a finish make a piece of furniture. An otherwise unattractive piece of furniture can be greatly improved by an attractive finish. Conversely, a good-looking piece can be ruined by a bad finish.

Because wood color is such a crucial part of the final look of furniture, decisions concerning stain are important. Should the wood be stained in the first place? What type of stain should you use? If you do stain, what color will give you the look you're after?

Some of the answers to these questions can be a matter of personal preference, but others can make your work easier and allow you to get the best look for your particular piece.

When to Stain

When refinishing furniture, staining the wood isn't always necessary. Some woods, such as walnut or mahogany, have a natural beauty that is revealed by simply applying a clear coat of finish. There are other naturally light woods, like pine or maple, that you may want to keep that way— to stain them would make them too dark. You should consider staining, however, if any of the following is true:

• The wood is ugly and lifeless. It's been said that no wood is unattractive. This sentiment may be true when the wood is in its natural state. But many times I've

seen wood that is unattractive and lifeless after it's been stained, finished, and then stripped in preparation for refinishing. The right choice in stain color can greatly improve the look of a piece in this condition.

• The piece is made up, either partially or totally, of inferior wood. Many pieces of furniture have been constructed using plain-looking woods, such as birch or poplar, only to be stained and finished to look like more expensive woods, such as cherry, mahogany, or walnut. Prominent parts, like tops, drawer fronts, door panels, and chairback splats, were often constructed using attractive wood veneers, with a secondary wood used for the other furniture parts. The secondary wood was then stained and finished to match the attractive primary wood. To achieve professional-looking results when refinishing this type of piece, you'll need to stain the secondary wood parts to match the better, more attractive wood. To determine the natural color of the primary wood, wet it down with mineral spirits or put a coat of finish only on that part of the piece. You will get an accurate color to which you can refer when staining the rest of the wood to match.

• The piece needs to match a particular finish or color. If your piece needs to match another piece or if you want to achieve a particular look, such as dark walnut or brown mahogany, you may need to stain the wood to achieve this goal. If you're trying to match pieces, such as a desk chair to a desk, wipe the chair down with mineral spirits to wet the wood, and then compare the chair with the finished desk. This procedure will give you an approximate idea of the stain color you must use on the chair to match the desk. Turn the chair upside down, and use an inconspicuous area like the seat bottom to test the stain you choose for a color match. Compare the stain color while the stain's still wet, or let the stain dry and apply a coat of finish before comparing the color.

• The piece is constructed of high-quality wood but needs to be revitalized or enhanced. Sometimes even though a piece is constructed from quality furniture wood, the wood may have lost its vitality. An example of this loss of beauty is when walnut or mahogany has been bleached by sunlight, which robs wood of its natural color. You might be able to revitalize the wood by staining it with a thinned reddish-colored stain. Other situations may require using stain at full strength to restore the original wood color.

Types of Stain

There are a variety of brands and types of stain on the market today. It can be confusing deciding which one to use. Understanding a little more about them will help you make a choice.

Wood stains fall into two basic categories: pigmented stain and dye stain. Both types are usually thin and runny, making them difficult to work with; however, both types are also available in gel form, making them almost foolproof. Manufacturers also offer stains combining both pigment and dye.

Pigmented Stain. Pigmented stains contain thick color pigments that are suspended in the stain solution. (See "Pigmented Stain," page 54.) The amount of stain color left on the wood can usually be controlled by how the stain is wiped after application. To remove more of the stain color, simply wipe the surface more thoroughly immediately after applying the stain.

There are several reasons to choose a pigmented stain. A variety of pigmented stains are available at paint or hardware stores and home centers, and manufacturers have designed them to be user-friendly. The directions for use are easy to follow and often yield optimal results. When buying wood stain, you can't always tell what type of stain you're getting by reading the label. Adding to the confusion, different manufacturers use different names to describe their products. Pigmented stains can be called wiping stain, pigmented oil stain, or penetrating oil stain. The best way to identify the type of stain you're getting is to read the directions for use on the label. For example, water-based pigmented stains will be indicated by label instructions to clean up with water rather than paint thinner or mineral spirits.

Dye Stain. There are three types of dye stain, each determined by its solvent: water soluble, alcohol soluble, and oil soluble. (See "Dye Stains," page 54.) Dye stains are particularly good for coloring wood evenly and enhancing otherwise subtle grain patterns in figured woods like curly maple or fiddleback cherry. A disadvantage of dye stain is that it fades when exposed

Dye stains are particularly good for enhancing otherwise subtle grain patterns like the pattern in this maple board.

to sunlight. Some dye stains can be more difficult to use than pigmented stains, and they're usually harder to find when you try to buy them.

Gel Stain. Gel stains can be classified under either pigmented or dye stains. (See Gel Stains," page 55.) Thicker in consistency than other kinds of stain, gel stains are easy to apply, produce no drips or runs, are easy to clean up, and provide even color. Just about anybody can use them with satisfactory results.

Pigment-Dye Stain. Some stains contain both pigment and dye. In these stains the dye colors the dense parts of wood that the pigment can't. You can tell a stain contains both pigment and dye if, after all the pigment has settled to the bottom of the container, the liquid part of the stain can still color a light piece of wood.

Stain Application

Although there are certain variations in application methods for different brands and types of stain, the basic idea is the same: Saturate the wood with stain, and wipe off the excess. Differences in drying and penetration time required for various stains can determine how quickly you must work or how large an area you can stain before wiping, but the process itself is similar.

Regardless of the stain you use, make sure you've prepared the surface properly before committing the stain to the wood. Once the stain is on, it's difficult to go back and try to deal with surface problems like cross-grain scratches, orbital sander swirl marks, and other blemishes. These problems are best dealt with before you begin staining.

To check the wood for problems before staining, wet it down with mineral spirits and look at the wood closely while it's wet. You should be able to detect any problems that might show up during finishing. Make sure all old finish or glue is removed, as old residue will prevent the stain from penetrating the wood. Make sure the wood is free from dust and dirt, and wear gloves and a respirator while staining.

NOTE: After the stain dries, the color may appear dull or faded. Some stains can even appear to change color once dry. Don't let this fool you; remember how the stain looked when it was wet, and you'll have a better indication of its true color. The color will return as soon as you apply the finish over the stain.

Washcoat. Before you actually apply stain, there is one more element to consider: the washcoat. When you stain wood using a liquid stain, some woods may need to be preconditioned with a washcoat. (Staining with gel stains will not require this step.) A washcoat partially seals the wood to control stain penetration. You might want to washcoat wood for any number of reasons:

• Resin-rich woods like pine or cherry may absorb stain unevenly, resulting in a blotchy appearance. A washcoat will give you a more even appearance.

• If a piece has a lot of end grain exposed where the stain will penetrate deeply, causing these areas to get too dark, a washcoat will limit that stain penetration.

• You might want to keep the color lighter, fine-tune a color, or match a color to another one by reducing stain penetration.

• You might want to play down the impact of a wood's grain or figure.

Because it's hard to know how wood will take a stain until you apply it, try to test it on an inconspicuous area of furniture first to find out whether you need to precondition the wood before staining.

Applying a Washcoat. Washcoating can be done several ways. You can apply a pre-mixed wood conditioner, available in hardware stores and home centers. Oil-stain manufacturers offer these products for just this purpose, and they are easy to use by simply following label directions. Some professionals mix their own washcoat solution by adding two cups of boiled linseed oil to a gallon of mineral spirits. The solution is then liberally applied to the wood, making sure that all areas, especially porous ones, are saturated. Allow the solution to

soak into the wood by letting it sit a few minutes before wiping it off, and then proceed with staining.

Another way to washcoat wood is to apply a coat of thinned shellac. Thin the shellac to about a ½-pound-cut mixture, and use a brush or rag to apply the shellac to the wood. Before it can dry, wipe off the excess with a clean rag. You may have to do one section of the piece at a time to be able to wipe the shellac off before it dries. After the shellac dries, scuff-sand the surface with very fine stearated sandpaper (280-grit), and then tack the surface to get rid of dust before proceeding with the staining process.

Applying Pigmented Stain

Difficulty Level: 🔨

Tools and Materials

Stain	Latex gloves
Respirator	Paintbrush
Cotton rags	

These steps for stain application are general and subject to label instructions for the particular stain you are using.

1 Mix the stain. Stir stain thoroughly until the color pigment is distributed throughout the solvent. It's a good idea to wear protective gloves and a respirator, especially if you're working in less than ideal ventilation conditions.

2 Brush on the stain. Using a natural-bristle brush, flood the wood surface with stain, and let it pene-

1 When using a pigmented stain, be sure to stir thoroughly to distribute the pigment throughout the solvent.

2 Use a natural-bristle brush to cover the wood surface completely with the stain.

3 Use a clean, soft rag to wipe off any stain that hasn't penetrated the wood surface.

trate into the wood for the prescribed amount of time. If necessary, stain one section at a time.

3 Wipe excess stain. Using a clean rag, wipe off the excess stain, wiping with the grain when possible. To allow the stain to add more color to the wood, use a lighter wiping action, smoothing out the color pigment on the wood surface with a soft rag. To keep the stain from affecting the wood color as much, use a heavy wiping action to remove more of the stain pigment from the wood's surface.

Applying Dye Stain

If you're using a water-based dye stain, wet the raw wood with water first to raise the grain. After the wood dries, light-sand the surface using 280- to 320-grit sandpaper to smooth the surface and begin the staining procedure. If you're using alcohol- or oil-based stain, begin as follows.

Using a brush or rag, flood the wood surface with stain, making sure the stain penetrates all areas well. Wipe off any excess stain with a clean rag.

To darken the color of the wood even more, you can mix a darker color of dye stain and apply it over the first stain. With dye stain, restaining the wood can be done right after the first application. To remove dye stain from wood, use bleach. (See "Removing Stains or Color in the Wood," page 194.)

Applying Gel Stain

Because of gel stain's consistency, you apply it using a rag instead of a brush. It's a good idea to wear protective gloves. Apply the stain to cover the wood surface completely, and then wipe off any excess. Gel stains add color more slowly and evenly than other types, so you don't have to worry about lap marks and other inconsistencies. Read label directions for specific instructions.

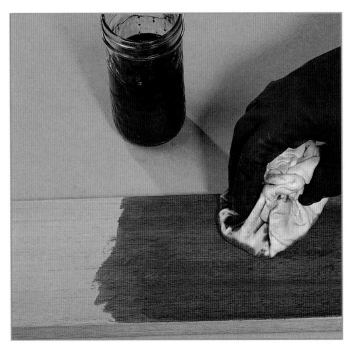

To apply a dye stain, *use a brush or rag to flood the wood surface, and then wipe off the excess with a clean, soft rag.*

Apply gel stain *by using a rag instead of a brush, covering the wood surface, and then wiping off any excess with a clean rag.*

PART V
FINISHING FURNITURE

13

APPLYING A FINISH

For someone who's restoring furniture, the refinishing process is usually the most rewarding part of the work. After all, the finish coat can make all the difference in the appearance of a piece of wood. Even after hours of preparing, stripping, sanding, filling, and staining, wood can still look dull and lifeless. As soon as the finish makes contact with the wood, however, the wood jumps to life, revealing otherwise subtle beauty. In addition to beautifying wood, the finish protects it.

FINISH BASICS

The search for the ideal finish has continued for centuries, and although many finishes have been developed, none is perfect. Because no finish will suit every situation, you'll have to make compromises when you choose one. Keep this fact in mind when you make your decision.

The finishes covered in this book are

- Shellac

- Lacquer and its variations

- Varnish and its variations

- Oil finishes

- Waterborne finishes

- Paint

- Wax

All these finishes have strengths and weaknesses. (See "Finishes," page 56.) Some finishes are easy to apply and maintain but offer little protection; others give excellent protection but can be difficult to apply or keep up. Some finishes penetrate the wood more deeply than others. Some finishes can be wiped on; some can be brushed; and others are better sprayed.

Whatever finish and application method you use, you must make sure conditions are as favorable as possible for you to achieve good results. Minimize dust as much as possible. Use a tack cloth on the surface of the piece before applying, dust all surfaces, and sweep or vacuum the floor well. After cleaning, use a spray bottle of water to mist the floor if possible to help hold down any additional dust kicked up by movement. You can also reduce the possibility of air-borne dust particles by waiting until the end of the day to apply your finish.

Next, make sure you have adequate ventilation. Also, try to establish a stable temperature and humidity level in the finish area. Most finishes work best at room temperature with a low relative humidity level. Although it may be hard to control temperature conditions totally, try to have conditions as favorable as possible.

Finally, set up the work-space lighting and the finishing project in such a way as to allow light to fall across the surface so you can see how the finish is going on. Put the piece you're finishing between you and the light. As the light reflects across the surface you're finishing, it will show clearly how the finish is going on and let you deal with any problems or missed areas.

Choosing a Finish

Even though you might not come up with a finish that meets all your demands, you can certainly find one that meets the most important ones. Ask yourself the following questions as you decide on the right finish for your piece:

• What will the finish look like? One of the main reasons you're finishing is to beautify the wood. Consider whether the type of finish you'd like to use is appropriate for your piece. A traditional-style piece, for example, may look better with a traditional-looking film finish, such as shellac, lacquer, or varnish. Other pieces might lend themselves more to a penetrating finish like tung oil or Danish oil. The bottom line is, will you be satisfied with how the finished product looks after all your work is done?

• What kind of protection will the finish provide? Do you need maximum protection, or is that a minimal consideration for the piece? To decide, consider where and how the piece will be used. If the piece will be placed in a room mainly for decoration and will receive little use, protection is not a primary consideration. Pieces like cabinets or wall curios might fall into this category. But if the piece is used frequently, protection is vital. Table, chest, and dresser tops, for example, usually need a tough, durable water- and alcohol-resistant finish.

• How difficult is the finish to apply, and do you have the right equipment? (See the application section for each type of finish.) Even though this question doesn't have anything to do with the purpose of a finish, it can

be an important one to answer before beginning your project. Count the cost in terms of ability, time, and equipment before using a particular finish.

• How repairable is the finish? Oil and wax finishes are easy to fix, usually by just adding more finish, but film finishes are more tedious to repair. If there's a good possibility of damage or wear on your particular piece, then this is an important factor to consider when choosing a finish.

WIPE-ON AND PAD-ON FINISHES

If you want the easiest finishing job and you're not concerned with protection and durability, use a wipe-on finish such as paste wax or one of the oil formulations. French polishing, which involves applying shellac with a padded cloth, is considered a pad-on finish. The technique is extremely tricky to master, and the film-building finish is much more durable than wax or penetrating oil.

Applying a Paste Wax Finish

You can apply a wax finish directly to raw unfinished wood or wood that's been sealed with a thin coat of shellac. Good furniture paste waxes are available in clear and darker tinted forms. (See "Wax," page 63.) Depending on the look you want, you can use either kind.

Be sure the wood surface has been prepared. If you want to seal the wood before applying the wax, put on a thin coat of shellac first. After the sealer coat is dry, rub the surface down with #0000 steel wool to smooth it. Remove all steel-wool residue and dust using a tack rag, and then apply the wax. (See "Applying Paste Wax," page 168.)

Maintenance. You can usually repair a wax finish by simply applying another coat of wax. But to maintain a wax finish, it's a good idea to wash off the old wax every year or so and reapply the finish. This will prevent wax buildup and discoloration of the wax over time.

Applying an Oil Finish

Because you can apply different types of oil finishes by following the same basic finishing procedures, they are all included here in the same step-by-step instructions. The main difference in applying various oil finishes is the drying time required; this specific information should be listed on the container label.

You can apply oil finishes using a brush, roller, or lint-free cloth. Some manufacturers even suggest using your hands to apply it. If the piece you're finishing is large, you may need to complete several of the finishing steps on one section before moving on to the next so you have plenty of time to work before the finish begins to dry. When finishing with oil, it's also helpful to warm the oil before application because warm oil penetrates wood better. Place the container of oil in a pan of hot water for a few minutes to warm it.

Difficulty Level: 🔨

Tools and Materials

Oil finish	Cotton cloths
#0000 steel wool	Tack rag

1 Apply the oil. Be sure the wood is prepared for finishing, including staining if necessary, and that the surface has been dusted with a tack rag. Apply the oil liberally to the wood's surface, letting it penetrate for

the prescribed amount of time (usually about 15 minutes). If the wood surface does not appear uniform after the oil begins to penetrate, apply more oil to dry areas.

2 Wipe the surface dry. Allow the oil to penetrate into the wood for a few minutes. Wipe away any excess oil with a clean soft cloth before the finish totally dries.

3 Rub the finish with steel wool. After allowing the oil to dry for the prescribed amount of time—usually 1 hour to overnight—rub the surface down using #0000 steel wool. The finish must be thoroughly dry before you begin this step.

4 Rub the finish with a tack cloth. Dust the surface with a tack rag, and repeat Steps 1, 2, and 3 as many times as necessary to get the look you want. Most problems in an oil finish (nicks, scratches, etc.) can be covered by simply applying another coat of oil finish. Oil

1 Use a cotton cloth to apply the oil finish liberally to the wood's surface.

2 After the oil has had time to penetrate into the wood, use a clean cloth to wipe away any excess.

3 When the oil has dried, use #0000 steel wool to rub the surface down.

4 Tack the surface, and repeat Steps 1, 2, and 3 until you are satisfied with the final look.

finishes can be renewed about once a year or so by applying more of the same finish

French Polishing

French polishing is the process of building up a finish by padding on many thin layers of shellac. This method originated hundreds of years ago and has produced some of the most beautiful furniture finishes ever seen. When done properly, the finish produces unusual depth and richness in the wood, almost impossible to create with other finishes. If enough steps are taken, it can be built up to a glass-like finish while maintaining a soft natural luster. Because French polishing could almost be considered an art, it will take practice to perfect the skill before committing to use it on a good piece of furniture.

The shellac mixture for padding—the polish—should be a 1- to 2½-pound mixture. The thinner the mixture, the easier the application, but the more coats it will require to build up the finish. While learning the padding method, start with a thin mixture (1-pound cut) until you get the hang of it; then you can progress to using the thicker cut.

Before you start, prepare the wood for finishing. When working on new wood, seal it with a coat of boiled linseed oil or tung oil. This isn't necessary when you're refinishing wood—you can begin by applying the shellac. The first shellac coat can be applied by pad or brush, as long as it's sufficiently thinned so it won't leave brush marks. Put the shellac mixture in a plastic squeeze bottle or a small-mouthed jar so you can control the amount dispensed onto the pad. While there are some variations in French polishing methods, you can follow the basic steps outlined here to achieve a fine finish.

Difficulty Level: 🔨 🔨 🔨

Tools and Materials

Thinned shellac	Cotton cloths
Latex gloves	320-grit stearated sandpaper
#0000 steel wool	Tack rag
Mineral or linseed oil	

1 Make the pad. The shellac is applied with a special pad called a "tampon" by the French and a "rubber" by the English; this pad is made up of a wad of absorbent material (soft wool or cotton) wrapped in a lint-free bleached cotton cloth. The interior wadding can be of the same material, as long as it's absorbent. To form the pad, ball up the wadding and wrap it inside the lint-free cotton cloth to form a pear-shaped pad about the size of a large egg. Pull the cloth tight around the wad to form a wrinkle-free pad surface.

When holding the pad, the loose ends of the cloth, which are pulled together around the absorbent wadding, should face up into your hand while the smooth portion of the pad faces down away from your hand. This smooth portion will be the part that makes contact with the wood as you pad on the shellac finish. It needs to be clean, smooth, and wrinkle-free; otherwise defects will show up in your finish. When you're not using the applicator pad, store it in an airtight container, such as a small jar with a screw-on lid. The pad will not dry out, and you'll be able to use it whenever you need it.

2 Disperse the finish. Before you actually apply the shellac, dampen the applicator with denatured alcohol and then with the shellac mixture. Add shellac to the part of the pad that will make contact with the wood surface, and disperse it by tapping the pad into the palm of your other hand several times. (During this process it may be a good idea to wear gloves to protect your hands from the chemical. Wearing gloves is espe-

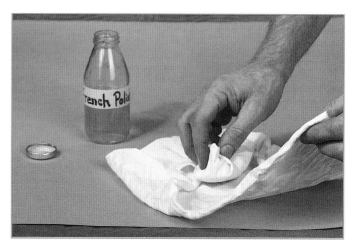

1 *The French polish pad is made up of a wad of absorbent material wrapped inside a lint-free cotton cloth.*

2 *Dampen the pad with finish, and disperse the finish by tapping the pad into the palm of your other hand.*

cially important if you are not used to working with your hands on a daily basis.)

3 Apply the finish. Pad the shellac onto the wood surface in the direction of the grain. The applicator should always be in motion when it comes in contact with the wood, otherwise it will leave print marks wherever it stops. The padding motion should be like a pendulum, swinging down to the wood surface, making contact, moving across the surface, and lifting off the other side, all in one sweep. Continue back and forth with this padding motion, working over the entire surface. If the pad begins to get too dry, recharge it with the shellac.

Once you have covered the entire surface, begin the process again. Continue padding the shellac until the surface becomes tacky and the applicator pad begins to stick when it comes in contact with the surface. Seal the applicator pad in an airtight container, and let the finish dry for at least an hour.

After the finish is dry, use 320-grit stearated aluminum oxide paper to scuff-sand the surface. Scuff sanding means to sand lightly and only enough to smooth the surface. Follow the sandpaper by rubbing over the surface with #000 or #0000 steel wool or a fine nylon abrasive pad. Wipe the surface with a tack cloth, making sure it's free of dust or steel-wool particles. Apply shellac as before by padding it on. As the applicator pad begins to dry, change the direction of the padding motion

> ### AN ALTERNATIVE TO FRENCH POLISH
>
> A modern alternative to French polish is padding lacquer. Padding lacquer can be bought from finishing supply companies under a variety of names (Rapid Pad and Lacover, among others). Padding lacquer is actually a misnomer. It's really a premixed shellac-based finish especially formulated as a pad-on finish. The material works well, is easy to use, and produces results similar to those of shellac. Padding lacquer can also be used to pad over existing finishes if you're recoating and touching up an area. Applied like French polish, padding lacquer dries and builds up quickly.

from straight pendulum-like strokes with the grain to small circular strokes. Next go to figure-eight strokes and then back to straight-with-the-grain strokes. Changing the padding motion helps to spread out and level the finish, preventing it from forming ridges that you'll have to sand out later. To lubricate the pad, dip your finger in linseed oil or mineral oil, and rub the oil onto the pad. Use only a tiny amount of lubrication.

Continue adding shellac to the applicator pad and padding it onto the surface. Don't make the pad too wet or apply the finish with too much pressure, as this could begin to dissolve and cut through the previous shellac coat. The idea is to pad the shellac onto the surface in such a way as to build up each coat on top of the previous one. As the finish begins to get tacky, stop and let it dry overnight.

3 *Pad the shellac onto the surface by using a pendulum motion, keeping the pad constantly moving (above, left to right). Apply repeated coats until the finish is built up sufficiently. Scuff-sand between coats with 320-girt stearated sandpaper. Lastly, rub the surface down with #000 or #0000 steel wool dipped in paste wax followed by a good buffing with a soft clean cloth.*

At this point the finish should be smooth enough to apply the next coat without sanding or rubbing. Apply the finish again as above, and allow it to dry overnight. This step can be repeated as often as necessary to build up the finish to the desired thickness.

After the final application there may be some oil residue on the surface. To remove any oil, make a new, clean applicator pad and slightly dampen it with denatured alcohol. Use light, straight, with-the-grain strokes to whisk the pad across the surface, picking up the oil and producing a gloss surface. If a satin sheen is desired, let the finish dry for several days and either rub it down with the grain using #0000 steel wool or apply a coat of paste wax with the steel-wool pad followed by a good buffing with a soft clean cloth.

BRUSHED AND SPRAYED CLEAR FINISHES

Brushing Shellac

Brushing on a shellac finish is a simple method that can produce excellent results with a minimum of work and trouble. When applying shellac with a brush, work over one area at a time before moving on to the next. Use the brush to lay the shellac on the surface, overlapping the strokes and brushing with the direction of the wood grain if possible. Don't try to brush over areas once they have been coated because the finish usually will have already started to dry.

Thin the first coat of shellac to about a 1-pound cut to act as a sealer coat; this means if you buy premixed shellac, you may have to thin it by adding denatured alcohol. To get a 1-pound cut of shellac from a 3-pound mixture, for example, you'll need to mix one part of the 3-pound shellac to 1⅓ parts of denatured alcohol. Most shellac containers provide mixing formulas.

It's not crucial that the first coat be a 1-pound cut mixture as long as you thin it to about half the thickness of successive coats. The thinner the mix, the easier it will be to work with but the more coats will be required.

Difficulty Level: 🔨🔨

Tools and Materials

Thinned shellac	Cotton cloths
Latex gloves	#0000 steel wool
Tack rag	Pure bristle brush
280- to 320-grit stearated sandpaper	

1 Brush on the shellac. Prepare the wood surface for finishing, and clean off all dust, tacking the surface. Apply the first coat of shellac with a brush after thinning it with denatured alcohol.

2 Sand the surface. After the first coat is dry—about ½ to 1 hour—scuff-sand the surface with very fine (280- to 320-grit) stearated sandpaper. If you've shellacked over a stained surface, be careful not to cut through the finish when sanding and thus remove the stain color. Keep in mind that shellac, even after it's dry, has a tendency to clog sandpaper, so you may need to change the paper often. Wipe a tack cloth over the surface to remove dust, and then brush on a coat of unthinned shellac. Let the second coat dry for an hour or longer; then scuff-sand the surface with the same-grit sandpaper as before. Continue coating and sanding until the finish is sufficiently built up—this usually will mean a total of three or four coats.

1 *Apply the shellac with a pure bristle brush. Make sure to brush in the direction of the wood grain when possible.*

2 *.When the shellac is dry, use 280-grit stearated sandpaper to scuff-sand the surface.*

3 After applying the last coat, rub the surface down with #0000 steel wool for a satin sheen.

Allow more drying time between each succeeding coat (for example, first coat: ½ to 1 hour; second: 1 to 2 hours; third: 2 to 3 hours; fourth: overnight).

3 Finish the last coat. Rub the last coat down with #0000 steel wool for a satin sheen. If you want a semi-gloss or gloss sheen, wait one or two days for the finish to cure after the last coat, and apply paste wax with a #0000 steel-wool pad. Buff it with a soft cloth. For a gloss sheen, allow the wax to completely harden (about 1 hour), and polish the surface using a lamb's-wool pad.

Applying a Lacquer Finish

Because lacquer is fast-drying, it's easier sprayed than brushed and thus may not be the best choice for the do-it-yourselfer. This fast-drying characteristic can be a definite advantage, however, in that the finish will pick up few airborne dust particles before it dries, making for less work when trying to achieve a smooth, professional-looking finish. If you are willing to practice with lacquer to get the knack of applying it, you may find that you like using it better than other, slower drying finishes. Since lacquer is available in various sheens, decide which is best for your piece before applying it.

Note: Shellac can also be sprayed, but care must be taken to avoid runs.

Preparing to Spray Lacquer. If you plan to spray lacquer, remember that it's important to have the proper equipment, including a quality spray gun, an air compressor with hoses and air gauge, a safety-approved exhaust system with an explosion-proof fan and lights, and a good-quality organic-cartridge respirator mask. Don't spray near open flames or sparks to avoid explosion or fire. When spraying, place the object between you and the exhaust fan, allowing you to spray in the direction of the fan. The spray gun should be aimed at the surface at a 90-degree angle from about 7 or 8 inches away. Keep the gun moving at a consistent speed while spraying, and keep it parallel to the surface being sprayed.

The spray gun will have several adjustment knobs; use them to adjust the spray (fan) pattern and the volume of fluid coming through the gun. For most finishing jobs you'll need a rather wide fan pattern to cover the surface quickly. Test the fan pattern and the amount of finish being sprayed on, using scrap wood or a piece of cardboard. Make the adjustments so that the gun produces a full, wet coat when you're moving it across the work at moderate speed. This adjustment may require some trial and error to get it right.

The air cap on the nozzle of the gun can be turned to produce a vertical spray pattern for spraying horizontal surfaces or a horizontal spray pattern for spraying vertical surfaces. When spraying lacquer, look closely at how the finish is going on the wood, and allow each pass to overlap the previous one by one-half. This will prevent any dry areas and ensure an even, wet coat of finish.

Spraying Lacquer. Prepare the wood for finishing. Tack the surface to remove dust particles, and spray a coat of lacquer sanding sealer on the piece. Allow the sealer to dry thoroughly; then sand the surface using 280- to 320-grit stearated silicone carbide paper. (If you're trying to get a slick, poreless lacquer finish, repeat this step to build up the sealer in the open grain until it's level with the surrounding surface. Sanding with 280- to 320-grit stearated paper after each sealer coat allows the sealer to build up in the open grain.) Tack the surface to remove dust; then spray a coat of lacquer onto the surface.

Allow the finish to dry at least 1 hour, and rub the piece down with #000 steel wool, smoothing the surface. Tack the piece again to remove all dust, and spray on another lacquer coat. After the finish dries for 1 to 2 hours, rub it down—if you desire—with #0000 steel wool, and then spray on another coat. After applying the final lacquer coat, allow the surface to dry overnight, and use #0000 steel wool to rub down the finish with the grain. For a waxed finish, allow the finish to dry for several days, and apply the wax with #0000 steel wool, rubbing with the grain, followed by a buffing with a clean soft rag. To increase the shine, polish with a lamb's-wool attachment on an electric drill. (For other final finish treatments, see Chapter 14, "Finishing Touches," beginning on page 222, and follow specific instructions for desired sheens.)

Controlling Runs. Lacquer doesn't run easily because it dries quickly; however, it is not impossible to get runs. For example, if you stop moving the gun across the surface while depressing the trigger, too much finish could build in one spot and cause a run. Also, if you pass over the same spot too many times, such as on crosspieces or corners, the finish could run. You can control run problems by releasing the trigger whenever the gun is stopped or when it passes over previously sprayed areas.

When you begin spraying a piece of furniture, start with the less visible areas first, such as inside cabinets and drawers or under shelves. When spraying tops, spray the edges first. This strategy will keep any overspray to a minimum on the most visible parts of the furniture by coating them last. Before spraying lacquer, it might be necessary to add retarder solvent and a fisheye eliminator to prevent problems before they begin. (See "Lacquer," page 58.)

You should strain the finish through a paint strainer/filter before spraying it; these filters are available at paint stores. When you finish spraying, run some lacquer thinner through the gun to clean it. Occasionally you may have to take the gun apart to clean it.

Brushing Lacquer. To brush a lacquer finish, buy lacquer formulated especially for brushing and, because the solvents are so strong that they can melt a synthetic-bristle brush, use a natural-bristle paintbrush. The strong solvents can also have an adverse effect on pigmented wiping stains or oil-based fillers, causing them to partially dissolve, particularly as the lacquer is brushed on. The solvents can also cause natural oils in some woods, such as rosewood or dark mahogany, to bleed. To prevent problems like these, seal the wood surface with shellac before applying lacquer.

When applying multiple coats of brush lacquer, allow each coat enough time to dry completely before applying the next coat. Otherwise, each successive coat will have a tendency to soften and dissolve the previous one. The longer you let the previous coat dry, the less likely you are to experience this problem. One hour is usually sufficient unless the label instructs otherwise. Once you've sealed the surface, lightly scuff-sand it using 280- to 320-grit stearated silicone carbide paper, being careful not to cut through the shellac to the raw wood surface beneath.

After tacking the surface to remove dust, lay the piece to be finished horizontally if possible. Using a natural-bristle brush, apply a brush coat of lacquer with long, straight, slightly overlapping strokes. Don't try to brush the finish out like varnish or paint. Apply the finish by laying it on, working over one section at a time without rebrushing areas already coated. Allow the finish to dry at least for the amount of time prescribed by label directions, and then scuff-sand it with 280- to 320-

grit stearated silicone carbide paper to remove any dust or rough areas.

Rub the surface down with a tack cloth; then apply another brush coat of lacquer and let it dry. If the finish is built up sufficiently at this point and it has dried overnight, use #0000 steel wool to rub it down in the direction of the wood grain to produce a satin sheen. To produce a gloss sheen, wait a few days, rub the surface down with paste wax on #0000 steel wool, and buff it using a soft, clean rag followed by a lamb's-wool attachment in an electric drill. If more finish is needed, brush on another coat before the final rubdown or waxing.

Applying a Varnish Finish

In the same way that lacquer can be considered a finish made for a spray gun, varnish is a finish made for a brush. Even though some modern varnishes like polyurethane have reduced their drying times considerably from old-time varnishes, they're still slow drying compared with lacquer. This slowness to dry allows the finisher ample working time during brush application. If you want a tough film finish and all you have to apply it with is a brush, consider a varnish finish.

Varnish is a high-solids finish that will build on wood surfaces fairly quickly. But because it's slow drying, you'll have to deal with dust and debris that settles in the finish as it dries. To address this problem and guarantee good adhesion, you must sand between finish coats and sand, rub, or polish the final coat. Although varnish, like lacquer, is available in various sheens, you can also control the sheen via the final rubbing or polishing process. (See "Finishing Touches," beginning on page 222.)

Preparation. If you're preparing to apply a varnish finish, it's important to have as dust-free an environment as possible. Turn off any blowers or fans, and don't work in an area where air is moving. Dust the entire work area, including the workbench and floor. Also, dust the piece you'll be finishing, and make sure that cracks, crevices, and even the wood grain are dust-free. If you have an air compressor with an

When working with varnish—*or any slow-drying finish—view the surface in reflected light (above) so you can easily see any problems in the finish. Try to place the work horizontally to reduce the risk of runs, sags, and drips.*

air nozzle, you can get rid of dust from the area by blowing it out; if not, a vacuum cleaner with a brush attachment will work. You can also spray a mist of water on your bench and floor to hold the dust down.

After cleaning, give any airborne dust time to settle before you start finishing. A good time to apply a varnish finish is just before you leave the workroom for the day. This gives the finish time to dry without additional dust being kicked up by movement in your work area.

Lighting is also important when applying a varnish finish. Place the piece you're finishing between you and the light source so you can see the light reflecting across the finish surface. This will reveal how the finish is going on the piece. If possible, always place the work to be finished horizontally to reduce the possibility of runs, sags, or drips. Horizontal placement also gives the finish opportunity to flow out and level itself while drying; this may require partial disassembly, such as removing doors and drawers to lay them in a horizontal position.

THE PROS KNOW

VARNISHING IRREGULAR SURFACES

When applying varnish to irregular areas, use a fairly dry brush and follow these instructions:

• Turnings (round legs and spindles). Apply the varnish by brushing across the turning and then by brushing lengthwise to smooth out the finish.

• Carvings. Apply varnish to the carved area, making sure to get it into all cracks and crevices. Unload the brush of finish, and use it to brush out excess finish from the carving.

• Moldings. Moldings usually can be finished by simply brushing the varnish lengthwise in the direction of the molding.

• Door panels. Brush varnish first on the panel and then on the panel edge, the inside frame edge, the frame itself, and the outer edges.

• Inside corners and edges. When finishing an inside corner on a panel, start the brush stroke in the corner and work outward. Avoid dragging the brush over panel edges, as this will cause drips and runs, and excess finish will form along the edge. Begin the brush stroke on the flat part of the panel away from the edge and brush toward it. Lift the brush just as it reaches the edge.

When mixing varnish, stir it rather than shake it, because shaking varnish can produce bubbles that will remain in the finish when it's applied to wood. The best brush to use is a good-quality china bristle brush; the finer the bristles, the less you'll have to contend with brush marks. Make sure the brush is clean and that it does not have old paint particles in it, which could ruin your finish. Make sure there are no loose bristles by flexing the brush on your hand a few times and then by vigorously brushing a clean surface with it.

Soak the brush briefly in the correct finish solvent, and remove the excess from the brush before dipping it in the varnish. Soaking helps condition the bristles to accept the varnish and makes cleanup easier. When you load the brush with the finish, dip the bristles about one-third to one-half way into the finish, and then flex the brush on the inside of the can to work the varnish into the brush. Don't drag the brush across the rim, which can produce bubbles. Use a 2- to 2½-inch brush for large flat areas and a smaller brush for detailed or irregular areas. To get rid of dust particles, hair, or lint from a freshly varnished surface that has not begun to dry, use a pointed artist's brush that has been made tacky with varnish. Lightly touch the particle with the brush's tip to remove it.

Application. Initially, apply the varnish to a prepared surface by brushing diagonally across the grain in short strokes to help spread the finish. Then brushing with the grain, hold the brush almost perpendicular, and drag it lightly across the surface in the direction of the grain. Work over one area at a time until the entire surface is done. Before the varnish begins to dry, unload the brush of varnish, and tip off the finish by again holding the brush at a right angle to the surface. Lightly drag the tip all the way across the surface in the direction of the grain. Begin your strokes in the air before lowering the brush onto the surface, and lift the brush off the surface immediately when reaching the other edge.

When you apply varnish, *hold the brush almost perpendicular, and line up the brush strokes so they are disguised by the wood grain.*

Allow the first varnish coat to dry, usually for 24 hours. Sanding varnish before it's dried sufficiently can damage the finish coat and may require refinishing. Scuff-sand the finish with 280-grit stearated silicone carbide paper to remove any roughness or dust and to provide inter-coat adhesion. Use a tack rag to remove all dust, and then apply a second coat of unthinned varnish.

After allowing the varnish to dry for 24 hours, again sand the finish with 280-grit paper. Use a felt sanding block on flat areas. Continue applying varnish for up to four coats, depending on the amount of film buildup you want. On the last coat, don't sand the varnish with 280-grit paper; instead, let it dry for 72 hours, and then sand the finish with 600-grit wet-or-dry sandpaper, using soapy water or mineral spirits as a lubricant. Give the surface a good rubdown with #0000 steel wool in the direction of the grain; then wipe the finish down with a clean, soft cloth. (Other final rubbing/polishing methods can also be used to produce a variety of effects; see Chapter 14, "Finishing Touches," beginning on page 222.)

PAINT FINISHES

Application methods for a paint finish vary, depending on the type of paint used. A variety of paints, including opaque lacquers, are suitable for painting furniture. Oil and latex paints can be applied by brush. Colored lacquers usually will need to be sprayed on.

No matter which paint you decide to use, preparing the wood surface beforehand is just as important as it is with transparent finishes. Although paint can hide objectionable stains or unwanted color variations, it won't hide dents, nicks, gouges, or scratches that mar the wood surface. (See "Dents and Gouges," page 197.)

If you're painting an open-grain wood like mahogany or oak and you don't want open pores to show up in the final finish, use a paste wood filler. (See "Filling Open-Grain Wood," page 203.) Most manufacturers of sol-vent-based paints also recommend using an undercoat-ing, or primer, before applying the top color coat or coats. A primer is an opaque version of the clear sealer used for transparent finishes. Primers are usually white but can be tinted to match the top-coat color more closely, making them easier to cover. Because primers are easy to sand, you can build them up in several coats, sanding the final coat to provide a smooth foun-dation for the top coats.

As with brushable transparent finishes, a paint finish is only as good as the brush with which it's applied, so be sure to use one of good quality. Use a synthetic-bristle brush to apply latex paints and a natural-bristle brush for solvent-based paints. Presoak the brush briefly in the

OTHER PRIMERS FOR A PAINT FINISH

Thinned shellac can be used as an undercoat for any paint, accomplishing several things. Shellac seals the wood surface while slightly raising wood grain for a final preparatory sanding with fine sandpaper. Shellac also acts as a good bar-rier coat to prevent any contaminants or resins from wood knots, as in pine, from bleeding into the finish. Thinned shellac can provide a barrier coat if you're painting over another finish or paint that may not be compatible with the paint you are using. Sealing the wood with shellac is also helpful if you think you may want to refinish the piece in the future in a natural wood finish: The shellac undercoating will pre-vent paint pigments from penetrating the wood grain, which could make them difficult or impossible to remove later. There are two other primer alternatives. Alkyd enamels can be thinned like varnish and used as their own undercoating before applying the paint full strength. Latex paint can also act as its own primer—but without being thinned. When the first coat is applied to raw wood, the grain will usually become raised, requiring a good sand-ing with fine paper before recoating.

appropriate solvent, and brush out the excess on clean paper or wood before dipping it into paint.

Applying Alkyd Enamels

Difficulty Level: 🔨 🔨

Tools and Materials

Thinned shellac	Alkyd enamel
Natural-bristle brush	#0000 steel wool
Tack cloth	Soft cotton cloth
Primer	280- to 320-grit sandpaper

1 Apply a shellac coat. Prepare the wood for finish-ing. (See "Preparing for Finish Sanding," page 200.) If you're painting over an existing finish or paint, use the deglosser solvent recommended on the paint label directions to wash the surface. Apply a thinned brush coat of shellac, and let it dry.

2 Sand the shellac. After the shellac is dry, sand the surface with 280- to 320-grit stearated silicone car-bide paper.

1 Apply a coat of shellac as a barrier coat between an old finish or raw wood and the new paint.

3 Apply primer. Dust the surface with a tack cloth, and brush on a coat of the recommended undercoating (primer) or a thinned coat of enamel. Allow the undercoating to dry fully.

4 Sand the surface. Sand the surface with 280- to 320-grit stearated silicone carbide paper, and remove all dust with a tack cloth. If you're using a primer or undercoating, brush on another coat, sanding after it dries with 280- to 320-grit stearated paper.

5 Apply a top coat. After the primer is dry, brush on a coat of enamel by first brushing across the grain and then with the grain, as with varnish. Continue the same brushing procedure as you would with varnish. (See "Applying a Varnish Finish," page 217.) Let the enamel dry for about 30 hours. If the enamel covers the surface well and there appears to be a sufficient amount of top coat, go to the next step. If not, repeat Steps 4 and 5 to build up the top coat sufficiently.

2 When the shellac dries, sand the surface using 280- to 320-grit stearated sandpaper.

3 Rub the surface with a tack cloth, and apply the primer for the paint you will be using.

4 Sand the surface with 280- to 320-grit stearated sandpaper. You can then apply another primer coat.

5 Apply the top coat first by brushing across the grain and then with the grain, just as with varnish.

6 *After the last top coat is thoroughly dry, wet-sand the surface using 600-grit wet-or-dry paper and soapy water.*

7 *After sanding, use #0000 steel wool to rub down the entire surface, giving it a glassy finish.*

6 **Wet-sand the surface.** Using 600-grit wet-or-dry sandpaper, wet-sand the surface using soapy water as a lubricant. Don't rub so vigorously that you'll cut through the paint surface. Also, be careful on ridges and edges so that you don't cut through the paint. For uneven or irregular areas, you may want to rub the painted finish with #000 or #0000 steel wool rather than sandpaper.

7 **Rub down the surface with steel wool.** When you've finished sanding, rub down the piece well with #0000 steel wool. Wipe the surface with a soft clean cloth. You should now have a smooth, glass-like finish, with no rough spots or brush marks apparent when you run your hand over it.

Spraying Solid-Color Lacquer

Spraying a lacquer paint finish is much like spraying a transparent lacquer finish. All the same wood-preparation steps should be followed, with the exception of staining the wood. A shellac barrier coat is a good idea to seal in contaminants or wood resins and oils before application.

THE PROS KNOW

FINISH ALTERNATIVES FOR PAINTED SURFACES

To get an even better final painted finish, use one of the rubbing and polishing methods described in the last chapter, "Finishing Touches," starting on page 222.

As another alternative, you can wet-sand the surface with 400-grit wet-or-dry sandpaper and soapy water until it has a uniform matte appearance when dry. Clean off all sanding dust, and brush on a full coat of clear interior varnish—not polyurethane—according to the instructions "Applying a Varnish Finish." (See page 217.) Let the finish dry for 30 hours, and then rub it down with #0000 steel wool or with pumice, rotten-stone, and automotive polishing compound. (See "Finishing Touches.") This clear coat gives the paint additional protection as well as providing it with a rich, deep luster.

Although clear lacquer sanding sealer can be used as a sealer coat for opaque lacquer, opaque primer under-coatings are also available. Opaque automotive lacquers, for example, provide a primer that can be used under the finish. Opaque primers provide a superior foundation for the top coats. If you are using a primer under-coating, apply and sand it as you would a sealer coat under clear lacquer. If you're spraying a lacquer paint finish, refer to the finishing instructions for spraying a transparent lacquer finish. The steps for applying the sealer also apply to primer coats.

As with alkyd enamel paint, lacquer paint can also be coated with clear coats of lacquer to produce a deeper luster. To coat lacquer paint, allow the finish to dry overnight after the last coat of paint, and wet-sand the surface using 400-grit wet-or-dry sandpaper and soapy water or mineral spirits as a lubricator. For irregular areas or ridges, use #0000 steel wool to prevent cutting through the color. Clean and dry the surface completely. Spray on two coats of clear lacquer, rubbing the surface down with #0000 steel wool between coats. Allow the coats to dry for 72 hours, and then do a final rubbing with #0000 steel wool. You can leave the surface as is or follow with a coat of paste wax, buffed and polished with a lamb's-wool electric drill attachment. (Other final finish treatments can be followed. See the next chapter.)

14

FINISHING TOUCHES

Although finishing the wood can be considered the last step in restoring furniture, there's also a final step in finishing the wood: the process of rubbing out the finish to eliminate surface imperfections and produce a particular sheen. Although there are a few finishes, particularly fast-drying lacquers, that don't require this step, most will need some kind of rubbing technique to produce a professional-quality look. Slow-drying finishes in particular will pick up dust particles and other contaminants while drying. Even though you may not want to alter the sheen after your final coat, you'll still need to rub out the finish to remove these surface imperfections.

FINAL SHEEN

A finish's final sheen is determined by two things: the type of finish material used (satin, semigloss, gloss) and the process used to rub out the finish on the final coat. To alter a finish's sheen, manufacturers add varying amounts of finely ground pigments to the mixture. Called flatting agents, these pigments work in the dried finish film to deflect rather than reflect light, causing the finish to appear duller or flatter. The more flatting agent added to a finish mixture, the flatter the sheen will be. So when deciding on the finish's final sheen, consider the type of material you're using.

For example, a satin, or matte, finish material will not produce a gloss sheen, even though you may use a gloss rubbing schedule on your final coat. But a glossy finish material can be rubbed down to create a variety of final sheens, including gloss, semigloss, and satin. For that reason, remember you're not limited when rubbing a final finish down to a duller sheen. But you do have limitations when trying to rub a dull or matte finish up to a higher sheen. The best choice when selecting a finish material is to use one with a sheen closest to the final look you want.

Creating a Sheen

Rubbing out a finish can be done with a variety of materials. These rubbing materials work by abrading the surface with tiny scratches of varying size and depth. (See "Pumice and Rottenstone" and "Rubbing Compounds," page 64.) The smaller the scratches, the glossier the surface; the larger the scratches, the flatter the sheen. A high-gloss finish is achieved by following a step-by-step process of working through a series of finer and finer rubbing materials, winding up with an abrasive so fine that the scratches produced are not visible to the naked eye. A satin sheen can be produced through a process that uses a coarse abrasive to create visible scratches in the finish. Although the scratches are visible, they're small enough to give the surface an overall matte appearance rather than looking like individual scratches.

Because rubbing materials are abrasive, there's always a chance of cutting through the finish coats when using them. The more rubbing a finish requires to achieve a sheen, the greater the chance of cutting through the finish. So rubbing out to a gloss sheen will require that you build up the finish material on the wood to a sufficient degree of thickness that you won't cut through it.

Remember that some finishes, like varnishes, form individual layers with each coat rather than melting together to form one single layer as solvent-based lacquers do. So if you cut through the top layer of a varnish finish, a subtle line will appear outlining the cut-through area. These marks are called witness lines, and once they appear they cannot be rubbed out of the finish. When rubbing out a finish, then, try to be even-handed—not staying in one place too long—and be sure to build up the finish as needed for the rubbing process you intend to use. Use only the grade of rubbing materials necessary to produce the desired sheen, and be careful of cutting through on edges, corners, or other irregular areas.

Rubbing Materials

Pumice. One of the oldest materials used for rubbing out a finish is pumice, a hard volcanic stone ground into a light-colored powder. (For this and the other abrasives, also see pages 63–64.) Pumice is available in varying grades from F to FFFFF, the latter grade being the finest. The powder is mixed with water or oil to produce an abrasive slurry, which is then rubbed on the finish surface in the direction of the wood grain with a thick piece of felt to produce a flat sheen. The degree of flatness is determined by the grade of pumice selected; FF or FFF grade is used to create a flat or satin sheen.

Rottenstone. Another ground stone used in the same way as pumice is rottenstone. Rottenstone is dark gray in color and finer than pumice. When used as a follow-up to rubbing with pumice, rottenstone will produce a semigloss to gloss sheen.

Wet-or-Dry Sandpaper. Ultra-fine wet-or-dry sandpaper can also be used as an abrasive rubbing material after the final finish coat. The grades suitable for this purpose are 400-grit and higher. Wet-or-dry paper should be used with water, oil, or mineral spirits as a lubricant. Coarser papers (in the 400- to 500-grit range) produce flatter sheens, while finer papers (above 500-grit) can be used in conjunction with polishing compounds to create higher glosses. These extremely fine papers are usually available wherever auto paint is sold.

Steel Wool and Nylon Abrasive Pads. Two other rubbing abrasives that can be used on finishes are steel wool and nylon abrasive pads. (See page 48.) Steel wool is used in its finest grades of #000 and #0000 to produce a satin, hand-rubbed effect. This same effect can be produced with very fine nylon abrasive pads, rubbing with the wood grain. Although very fine steel-wool pads usually already contain light oil for built-in lubrication, additional lubricants—paste wax, a light oil such as mineral oil, or even soapy water—can be used with either steel wool or nylon abrasive pads. Paste wax will produce a little higher luster than the others. A special "wool wax," or "wool lube," which produces a satin, low-luster effect when used as a rubbing lubricant, is also available from some finish-supply companies.

Rubbing Compounds. Premixed rubbing and polishing compounds are also available from finish-supply companies or auto-paint suppliers. These compounds, when used after the finish surface is properly prepared with other abrasives, will produce varying degrees of gloss that can be difficult or impossible to get by other means.

Buffing and Polishing. Rubbing or polishing compounds can be applied by hand, using a soft clean cloth, or by machine, using a power buffer or electric drill equipped with a lamb's-wool pad. Buffing and polishing a finish is hard work. If you're working on a small item you can probably do it by hand, but if you want a high gloss on a large table top, using a power buffer will save you hours of work, not to mention gallons of sweat. It's important to note that rubbing and polishing compounds contain a variety of solvents in their mixtures. To avoid damaging the finish, be sure to test them on an inconspicuous spot before using them.

RUBBING TO VARIOUS SHEENS

Because there is often a variety of methods used to achieve a particular finish sheen, the following procedures may not include all of them. They do, however, include at least one way to achieve each type of sheen. As you work on your particular finish, use these instructions to guide you—but don't let them restrict you. As you familiarize yourself with the way various rubbing materials work and the effects they produce on the finish, you may even want to develop your own rubbing schedule to accomplish a satisfying sheen.

Creating a Satin Finish

A smooth satin sheen can be achieved by following the rubbing schedule presented in the following steps. The first step may be omitted for finishes that go on extremely smooth and dry quickly, such as sprayed lacquer.

Difficulty Level: 🔨🔨

Tools and Materials

FF or FFF pumice	Mineral spirits
Soapy water or mineral oil	Felt block or pad
Clean cotton cloth	400-grit wet-or-dry sandpaper

1 **Wet-sand the surface.** Rub down the surface with 400-grit wet-or-dry sandpaper backed with a felt block, using slightly soapy water or mineral oil cut 10 to 20 percent with mineral spirits. Sand in the direction of the wood grain if possible. Sand every square inch of the surface to produce a consistent dull appearance.

2 **Cover the surface with pumice.** Sprinkle FF or FFF pumice over the finish surface, and wet the powder with a little soapy water or mineral oil cut with 10 to 20 percent mineral spirits to produce a slurry. To wet the powder, use a plastic spray bottle for water or a sprinkle can or jar for mineral oil.

3 **Rub with a felt block.** Use a felt block or 1/4-inch-thick felt pad to rub the pumice mixture in the direction of the wood grain. Rub over the entire surface, being sure to cover every square inch while applying firm, even pressure. Pay attention so that your rubbing strokes are as straight in one direction as possible.

1 To produce a satin finish, begin by wet-sanding the surface with 400-grit wet-or-dry sandpaper backed with a felt sanding block.

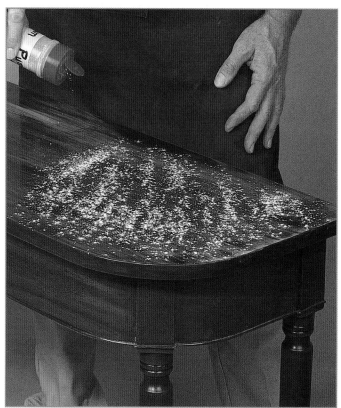

2 After sanding, cover the finish surface with FF or FFF pumice, wetting it with soapy water or thinned mineral oil.

3 Using a felt block or pad, rub the pumice mixture firmly in the direction of the wood grain.

4 Clean the finish surface by using a soft cotton rag dipped in water or mineral spirits, again rubbing with the grain.

4 Rub the finish with a rag. Wipe the surface with a clean rag dipped in clear water or mineral spirits, again rubbing with the grain. Check the surface sheen to make sure it's consistent; if it's not, repeat Steps 2 through 4.

Creating a Semigloss Finish

Difficulty Level:

Tools and Materials

#0000 steel wool or nylon abrasive pad
Paste wax   Clean cotton cloth
Drill with buffing attachment

1 Go over the surface with steel wool and wax. The easiest way to achieve a semigloss finish is to rub the finish surface in the direction of the wood grain with #0000 steel wool or an extra-fine nylon abrasive pad using paste wax as a lubricant. Apply firm, even pressure and straight strokes. Cover the entire surface. An alternative method is first to sand the surface with 600-grit wet-or-dry sandpaper, and then use steel wool and wax. Use soapy water or mineral oil cut 10 to 20 percent with mineral spirits as a lubricant with the sandpaper. Clean the surface with clear water or mineral spirits before applying the wax.

2 Buff the finish. Use a soft clean cotton cloth to buff the surface in the direction of the wood grain. Allow the wax to set for about 30 minutes. Use a soft cloth to polish the surface by hand or a lamb's-wool attachment to polish it with an electric drill.

1 A semigloss sheen can be achieved by first dipping #0000 steel wool in wax and rubbing the finish surface firmly in the direction of the grain.

2 Next use a clean soft cloth to buff the surface. Allow the wax to set, and then polish it by hand or machine.

Creating a High-Gloss Finish

Before deciding to rub a finish to a gloss or high-gloss sheen, be forewarned: This process requires more steps and harder work than any of the other sheens. Even if you have a power buffer for the final polishing steps, there's still plenty of handwork involved in the preliminary steps, and you can be assured of a thorough aerobic workout. But with hard work and patience, a beautiful high-gloss finish can be achieved that will more than reflect the effort required to accomplish it.

There are some important factors to consider before beginning the rubbing/polishing schedule needed to get a high-gloss finish. First, do you want the finish to be a filled-pore finish, meaning that the grain of the wood has been filled completely with paste wood filler and finished so there are no visible pores in the finish surface? (See "Filling Wood Grain and Staining," beginning on page 202.) If these open pores are visible before beginning the rubbing schedule, they'll become even more evident when the surface is polished to a high gloss.

To produce a filled-pore finish (in addition to filling open-grain woods with paste wood filler), you must build up the finish sufficiently, sanding it thoroughly between coats. Do this until all the grain pores are completely filled up and the finish is completely leveled. Note that achieving this result requires extra steps during the finish process and great attention to detail.

Before you begin the rubbing/polishing process, it's crucial that the finish have enough drying time—especially for a high-gloss finish because of the vigorous rubbing and polishing that are required. (If you use a buffing machine, the buffer can cause enough friction to heat a fresh—or uncured—finish until it becomes soft and easily damaged.) Even when they seem dry, finishes can require additional curing time to reach their maximum level of hardness. For most finishes, you'll need to allow a curing time of approximately two weeks before beginning a vigorous high-gloss rubbing schedule.

Difficulty Level: ⚒ ⚒ ⚒

Tools and Materials

Felt block   Soft cotton cloth
Soapy water or mineral spirits
Rubbing compound
600-, 1000-, and 1500-grit sandpaper
Polishing compound
Buffing machine with lamb's-wool pad(s)

1 Rub the finish using fine sandpaper. Sand the surface thoroughly, using 600-grit wet-or-dry sand-paper lubricated with soapy water or mineral spirits (paint thinner). Sand in the direction of the wood grain if possible, and cover every square inch of the surface. Use a felt block to back the sandpaper. Clean the surface with mineral spirits or clear water, and check to be sure the surface is thoroughly sanded. If there are any shiny areas, repeat the sanding process until the entire surface has a flat appearance. Sand the finish thoroughly with 1000-grit wet-or-dry paper just as you did with the 600-grit paper. One of the purposes of sanding with 1000-grit paper is to remove any scratches left by the 600-grit paper, so you must do a thorough job, covering the entire finish area. Clean the surface again with clear water or mineral spirits, and check to make sure it's been thoroughly sanded with the 1000-grit paper. If not, sand the surface again. At this point, you can graduate to an even finer grit wet-or-dry paper (1200-grit to 1500-grit) or you can go to the next step with little difference in the final results.

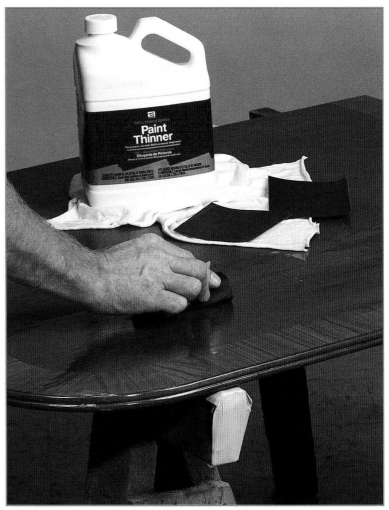

1 *Begin by sanding the surface first with 600-grit wet-or-dry sandpaper backed with a felt block and then with 1000-grit paper.*

2 Apply fine rubbing compound. Wipe fine rubbing compound onto the finish with a soft cloth, and rub the surface with a clean soft rag or with a lambs-wool pad or a foam buffing pad. You may need to use water as an additional lubricant to this process. Put water in a pump spray bottle and add as needed. If you're rubbing by hand, use a small circular pattern to work over the entire surface a little at a time. Remember that you're using a super-fine abrasive to remove any previous scratches left by sandpaper, so you must give the surface a thorough rubbing. If you're power buffing, be careful not to cut through on the edges of the piece or burn the finish by allowing the pad to stay in one spot too long.

2 *Apply fine and extra-fine rubbing compounds to the surface using a lamb's-wool pad on a power buffer.*

Wipe down the surface completely using a clean soft cloth, and then apply an even finer polishing compound to the finish, again rubbing with a clean soft cloth. If you use a lamb's-wool pad, be sure to wash it thoroughly or use a new pad so you don't mix the previous rubbing compound with the finer polishing compound. These compounds can usually be washed out of the pad by using soap and water. Rub over the entire surface thoroughly. Clean off the surface using a soft cotton cloth. If you did all the steps properly, you should have a beautiful high-gloss finish.

THE PROS KNOW

ANOTHER WAY TO A GLOSS FINISH

To achieve an understated low-luster gloss finish, follow these steps:

• Sprinkle FFF or FFFF pumice over the finish, and wet it with a little soapy water or mineral oil cut with 10 to 20 percent mineral spirits to produce a slurry. Use a plastic spray bottle to apply water or a sprinkle can or jar to apply mineral oil.

• Use a felt block or ¼-inch-thick felt pad to rub the pumice mixture in the direction of the wood grain. Use firm, even pressure to rub in a straight motion with the grain over every square inch of the surface.

• Clean the finish surface completely using a soft cotton cloth dipped in water or mineral spirits, again rubbing in the direction of the grain. Completely remove all the pumice powder from the surface before beginning the next step. Use reflected light to be sure the surface sheen is consistent; if it isn't, repeat the first two procedures.

• Sprinkle rottenstone over the finish, and wet it with soapy water or mineral oil cut with 10 to 20 percent mineral spirits to produce a slurry on the finish surface.

• Use a clean felt block or ¼-inch-thick felt pad to rub the rottenstone mixture in the direction of the wood grain. Use firm, even pressure, rubbing in a straight motion with the wood grain and thoroughly covering the whole surface.

• Clean the surface with a soft cotton rag dipped in clear water or mineral spirits, and check the surface to see whether the sheen is consistent; if it isn't, repeat the previous two procedures.

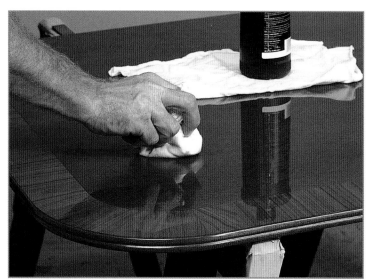

3 Apply a glazing liquid using a soft cloth. Allow the surface to haze before buffing it with a cloth to produce a mirror-like finish.

3 Apply glazing liquid. For a final touch to the high-gloss finish, use a glazing liquid, available at auto-paint suppliers. Apply the liquid polish using a soft clean cloth and working in a small circular pattern. As soon as the polish starts to haze on the surface, you can buff it with a soft cloth to produce a polished, mirror-like finish.

FURNITURE HARDWARE

After you've finished the wood-restoration and finishing processes, you should be ready to reinstall cabinet hardware. If any hardware is missing, you'll need to find replacements. Old hardware can be hard—or impossible—to match. In addition to searching furniture and cabinet hardware websites for matching replacements, check with local antique dealers or furniture-restoration shops. Although it's a shot in the dark, most furniture dealers and restorers have accumulated a variety of odd pieces of old hardware that just might include what you need.

It's best to keep as much of the original hardware as possible, of course, but if you can't find matching replacements you may have to

swap all the hardware so that everything matches. When replacing hardware, consider the style of the furniture as well as the quality of the hardware. If you have some of the original hardware, you'll be able to tell what the new pieces should look like. Hardware quality can also be improved on when it's replaced. For example, brass-plated steel hardware can be replaced with solid brass to give the furniture a quality look.

Cleaning and Polishing Hardware

Most furniture hardware is either solid brass or brass-plated and can be cleaned and polished by hand or by machine using a buffing wheel. You need to know which type the hardware is before you clean it.

Solid or Plated? To determine whether the hardware is solid brass or brass-plated, check it with a magnet: If the magnet sticks, the hardware is plated; if not, it's most likely solid brass. If your hardware is solid brass, either hand or machine cleaning will produce satisfactory results, although machine buff-

***Solid or Plated?** Most fine-quality furniture uses solid-brass hardware. Use a magnet to check hardware; if it doesn't stick, the metal is probably brass.*

ing gives a higher luster. If the hardware is brass-plated, clean it by hand because buffing by machine can cut through the plating material to the underlying steel.

Lacquered Hardware. Some brass has been lacquered to slow the tarnishing process or to produce an antique brass effect. In this case, you may need to strip the finish from the brass before trying to polish it. A lacquer coating will usually become evident when you begin to polish the brass because lacquer is harder to remove than the effects of tarnish. If you need to strip the brass, put some finish remover in an open container and submerge the hardware in the solution. Let the pieces soak for 10 to 15 minutes, and then take them out and rub them with #0000 steel wool to remove the lacquer

Machine Polishing

To polish hardware by machine, use a buffing wheel on a bench grinder along with a buffing or polishing compound available for use with the wheel. (See "Bench Grinder," page 37.) These compounds come in stick form in various grades to produce different types of luster. If you use a coarse compound, it will clean quickly but will produce a duller sheen. If you use a very fine compound, it may work a little slower but a brilliant luster will be produced. Read the labels of the material, and choose the compound that will produce the look you want.

When using a buffing wheel to polish hardware, wear safety glasses, and hold the hardware firmly so the wheel doesn't pull it from your hand and shoot it across the room. You may want to keep a container of water at the wheel so you can dip the metal to cool it. This is necessary because of the friction produced by the buffing wheel on the metal.

Difficulty Level: 🔨

Tools and Materials

Water	Soft cotton cloth
Bench grinder with buffing wheel	
Stick of polishing compound	

1 **Prepare the buffing wheel.** Apply polishing compound to the buffing wheel by firmly holding the end of the stick on the moving wheel.

POLISHING HARDWARE BY HAND

To clean and polish the hardware by hand, use a brass cleaner, and follow label directions. Good-quality brass cleaners are available at hardware stores and home-supply centers. For tough cleaning jobs, you can make your own brass cleaner by mixing one part water with two parts ammonia and adding some baking soda (about two tablespoons per pint of liquid). Here's how to use the cleaner solution:

• Using an open coffee can or a saucepan, submerge the hardware completely in the liquid, making sure that none of it extends above the surface, as this can leave a permanent waterline mark on the metal. Let the brass soak for about 15 minutes.

• Remove one piece of hardware at a time, cleaning it as you go by scrubbing with a rag or #0000 steel wool. (If you use steel wool, the brass will have a slightly duller appearance after it's cleaned).

• As you clean each piece, submerge it in clear water to rinse it, and then dry it with a clean rag.

• To increase the metal's luster, apply commercial brass cleaner and let it haze. Then buff the piece using a clean soft cloth.

1 To apply finishing compound to the buffing wheel, push the stick into the turning wheel.

2 While holding the brass hardware firmly, apply it to the moving wheel, slowly working over the entire piece until it is polished.

3 Use a soft cloth to clean any compound residue from the hardware and buff the metal to a bright luster.

2 Apply the hardware to the wheel. Hold onto the brass hardware firmly, and apply it to the rotating buffing wheel, applying just enough pressure to polish it. Slowly work the entire piece of brass over the wheel until it's completely polished, dipping it in water to cool it if needed. Repeat Step 1 when the buffing wheel begins to lose its effectiveness to polish the brass.

3 Buff the hardware. Clean any polishing-compound residue from the hardware using a clean soft cloth. Buff the piece to a high luster

Lacquering Cabinet Hardware

As previously mentioned, some brass hardware is lacquered to prevent or slow tarnishing. Although this may sometimes be a good idea, it has some negative aspects. If the lacquer gets scratched, for example, the exposed brass will begin to tarnish, and the finish will then have to be stripped off before you can clean the piece. Brass that hasn't been lacquered is much easier to clean and polish.

Because much of the hardware on furniture is either drawer or door pulls, which tend to get constant handling, there's a greater chance of scratching or wearing through the lacquer coating. Some manufacturers use a process to bake on the lacquer finish, making it tougher. Although not as good, an alternative is simply to spray on a lacquer coating. The easiest way to do this is by using a good grade of aerosol spray lacquer.

To coat cabinet hardware with lacquer, follow these steps:

• Cover a flat surface with kraft paper or some other medium-to-heavy grade of paper. Lay the hardware out on the paper so it can be sprayed. Be sure that the surface is dust-free (using a tack rag) and that the hardware is clean and dry.

• Follow the directions on the can to spray a coat of aerosol on the hardware. Hold the can about 7 inches from the hardware surface as you spray on a full, even coat of lacquer. Let the finish dry, about 15 to 30 minutes.

• Repeat the previous step, and let the hardware dry for about 1 hour before installing it on the furniture.

AND IN CONCLUSION...

Although many years have passed since I began restoring furniture, the challenge of taking a piece from worthless to beautiful and useful remains satisfying. Many people may have passed by the old Victorian rocker I discovered in pieces in a cardboard box and pronounced it valuable only for firewood. But it only took one person to see the chair's potential and restore it to its original beauty. (See "Introduction," page 8, for a photo of the chair.)

Now that you've likely completed or are about to complete whatever furniture project you began, you can judge for yourself whether your journey into furniture restoration has been worthwhile. At this point you should be able to look—with a sense of satisfaction and accomplishment—at the piece of furniture that first inspired you to make the journey. Not only do you have a tangible reminder of all your hard work, but you've also gained the knowledge and experience to pursue future projects.

It is my hope that, like the Victorian rocker that reminds me of my earliest work, your first repair and refinishing project is only the beginning of many exciting adventures in the creative world of furniture restoration.

G L O S S A R Y

Abrasive Any material used to wear away, smooth, or polish a surface; for example, sandpaper that is used to smooth wood.

Alligatored finish Any finished surface that shows numerous cracks caused by aging and drying.

Aluminum oxide A long-life grit for abrasive wheels and sandpapers.

Aniline dye A synthetic tinting medium made from coal-tar products, which can be dissolved in water or alcohol and used to change the color of wood.

Apron The board between the tops of a table's legs that supports the top or, in the case of a chair, the seat. Also called the "skirt."

Backsaw A saw with a back, or spine, used for small work on the benchtop.

Block plane A small hand plane used on end grain.

Blotching A staining problem in which the stain is unevenly absorbed, causing light and dark areas. This is caused by a swirly grain or uneven density of a piece of wood.

Burn-in knife Electrically heated tool with a curved spoon-like tip that is used to melt lacquer or shellac sticks for repairing finish surfaces.

Burn-in stick Stick of filler material used in the repair of surface damage to furniture. The filler must be melted onto the damaged surface and then trimmed smooth. Also called lacquer or shellac stick.

Butt joint A joint in which two pieces of wood are joined lengthwise without overlap or tongue.

C-clamp Used for small clamping work, these clamps get their name because of their shape.

Carcase The framework or body of a cabinet or piece of casegood furniture.

Carpenter's glue See "Polyvinyl glue."

Casegood furniture Furniture such as bureaus and cabinets (casegoods) designed to contain things in drawers or behind doors as opposed to furniture that stands, such as tables and chairs.

Chamfer A square edge cut equally on one or both sides of a piece of wood so as to form a bevel.

Clamp A tool that holds pieces of wood or other items together.

Clear finish Any of a number of wood finishes that allow the wood grain and color to be seen.

Closed-grain wood Wood such as maple and birch that has small, tight pores and a smooth surface when sanded.

Coarse-grain wood See "Open-grain wood."

Contact cement A rubber-based liquid glue that bonds on contact; often used for applying veneers.

Crazing A mild form of alligatoring, characterized by small cracks in the finish.

Crosscut saw A saw used for cutting across the grain of wood.

Cyanoacrylate A strong and fast-acting adhesive with industrial, medical, and household uses. It is also known as CA glue, instant glue and super glue.

Dado A type of groove that runs across the grain.

Danish oil See "Oil finish."

Denatured alcohol A solvent used to thin shellac.

Distressing A finishing process that adds dents, scratches, burns, and other indications of wear and age to furniture for decorative purposes.

Dovetail joint A joint formed by one or more tapering projections (dovetails) on one board fitted tightly into mortises carved into another.

Dovetail saw A small backsaw usually filed for rip cutting.

Dowel A wood pin frequently used to join two pieces of wood. The dowel fits into holes drilled in each piece; this creates a dowel joint.

Dust mask A disposable device to cover the nose and mouth and prevent inhalation of dust or other material in the air. Compare with respirator.

Epoxy adhesive Adhesive based on an epoxy (or epoxide) resin or several such resins. They are of limited use in furniture-making but come in handy for quick repairs.

Fasteners Nails, screws, brads, and other items that are used to join two components or to secure hardware to furniture.

Fish eye Small craters in a new finish that are the result of an adverse reaction between the finish and substances such as wax or oil on the surface.

Flush-cut saw A small saw with a flexible blade and no back/spine.

French polish A solution of shellac in alcohol used to give furniture a shiny finish. The alcohol evaporates to leave a thin coating of shellac on the piece.

Gent's saw A small backsaw with a straight handle.

Grain The direction and arrangement of wood fibers in a piece of wood. Grain reflects the growth-ring pattern in the tree. The grain will look different in different woods and as a result of different sawing techniques.

Grain filler See "Paste wood filler."

Grit A measure of the roughness of an abrasive paper. The lower the figure given for the grit size, the coarser the paper.

Hardwood Wood that is cut from deciduous (leaf-shedding) trees. Although all such wood is designated as hardwood, some types are actually physically soft and easy to dent.

Hide glue The traditional glue used by cabinetmakers. It comes in toffee-like sheets, in pearls, or as a premixed liquid. Hide glue is reversible by applying heat and water.

Jack plane A general-purpose bench plane used to smooth rough stock. The bed is commonly 14 inches long with a 2-inch cutter.

Lac beetle An insect that secretes a fluid that is made into lac flakes, the basic ingredient in shellac.

Lacquer A clear or colored finish material that dries to a hard, glossy finish. Usually applied with a sprayer, lacquer dries too quickly for smooth application with a brush, unless it is specially formulated.

Lacquer stick See "Burn-in stick."

Linseed oil A finishing oil made from pressed flax seeds. An ingredient used in paint (oil-based) and varnish.

Methylene chloride A chemical used as the active ingredient in some paint and varnish removers.

Mineral spirits Volatile solvent for oil-based finishes. Also called turpentine or paint thinner.

Miter joint A corner joint formed by cutting the ends of two pieces of lumber at an equal angle—usually 45°.

Mortise A (usually) rectangular slot or recess cut into a piece of wood and designed to receive a male part, or tenon.

Mortise-and-tenon joint A joint in which one piece has a square or rectangular projection (tenon) that fits snugly into a similarly shaped hole (mortise) in the second piece.

Mortise chisel A strong chisel designed specifically for cutting mortises.

Oil finish A clear finish produced by rubbing an oil, such as linseed or tung oil, on bare or stained wood. The oil is rubbed to a soft, glowing finish. Also called Danish oil.

Oilstone A fine-grained stone, lubricated with oil, which is used for sharpening cutting edges. Also called sharpening stone.

Open-grain wood Wood such as oak, mahogany, and walnut that has large, obvious pores. Also called coarse-grain wood.

Paint A pigmented opaque material that completely covers and hides the surface to which it is applied. Paint is available in oil-based and water-based formulas.

Paint thinner See "Mineral spirits."

Paste wood filler Liquid or paste mate-rial designed to fill in holes or grain lines so that final finishes may be applied to a smooth surface. Also called grain filler or pore filler.

Patina The overall effect of the aging process on wood or a finish, generally characterized by a muting of the colors and a satin finish.

Polyurethane A varnish to which plastics have been added. It creates a durable finish.

Polyvinyl glue A frequently used wood glue that has as its base a synthetic resin called polyvinyl acetate. Also called wood glue (white) and carpenter's glue (yellow).

Pore filler See "Paste wood filler."

Pumice A lava-rock abrasive ground into a powder as a polish.

Rabbet A notch-like cut made on the edge or end of a frame or board to receive a sheet of glass, a wooden panel, or another piece of wood to form a rabbet joint.

Rail The horizontal member of a frame or carcase.

Raising the grain A process of damping the surface of wood with water to bring up or lift small fibers for final smooth sanding.

Rasp A rough-sided tool designed to dig into and wear away material such as wood.

Reamalgamated finish A previously alligatored or roughened finish that has been made level by rubbing the surface with solvent that melts the finish and allows it to dry smooth.

Respirator A filter device with a replaceable cartridge worn over the nose and mouth to remove irritants—dust and toxic pollutants—from the air.

Rottenstone A fine powder abrasive made from crushing decomposed limestone. Rottenstone and oil are used as a fine finishing polish.

Router A wood-machining tool with a small vertical high-speed cutting blade.

Sanding block A padded wood block around which a piece of sandpaper is wrapped for hand sanding a surface.

Sanding sealer A thinned shellac or other lightweight clear finish applied to wood to prevent the raising of wood grain by stain, filler, or final finish material.

Sandpaper A coated abrasive—usually flint, garnet, or aluminum oxide—glued to a paper, cloth, or plastic backing. It is used for smoothing or polishing woods.

Sawhorse A stand used to hold wood while it is being cut. Two sawhorses can hold plywood to form a work surface.

Sharpening guide A device used when sharpening the blades of chisels or planes. It holds the blade against the oilstone at exactly the correct angle.

Sharpening stone See "Oilstone."

Shellac A clear finish material created by dissolving lac flakes in denatured alcohol. A 5-pound cut of shellac is made by dissolving 5 pounds of lac flakes in 1 gallon of denatured alcohol. A 1-pound cut is 1 pound of flakes in a gallon of alcohol.

Shellac stick See "Burn-in stick."

Softwood Wood that comes from logs of cone-bearing (coniferous) trees.

Spline A thin piece of wood used as a wedge or as a joint reinforcement. A flat strip of wood may be glued into slots cut into two boards to be butt- or miter-joined. The spline increases the glue surface and the strength of the joint. In a worn joint, a spline may be inserted into the end of a cut dowel or tenon so that the section will fit more tightly into the joint hole or mortise.

Spontaneous combustion A fire caused by the heat generated by oxidizing oils in rags thrown in a pile rather than laid out to dry.

Stain Any of various forms of water- or oil-based transparent or opaque coloring agents designed to penetrate the surface of the wood to color (stain) the material.

Stain controller Slow-evaporating petroleum-distillate solvent that is applied to hard-to-stain wood like pine as a washcoat. It works by filling up the pores and less-dense parts of the wood so the stain takes on a more even appearance. Also called wood conditioner.

Tack rag A piece of cheesecloth or other fabric treated with turpentine and varnish to create a sticky or tacky quality so the rag will pick up and hold all the dust that it touches.

Tenon The male part of a motise joint.

Toxic Poisonous.

Tung oil A water-resistant finishing oil or varnish ingredient made from crushed tung-tree seeds.

Turpentine See "Mineral spirits."

Varnish A durable clear finish made of a mixture of resins, oil, and turpentine or other volatile spirits.

Veneer A thin sheet of wood applied to a piece of inferior wood or plywood. Fine wood veneer is used in furniture. This allows you to use rare and exotic woods, which either are not available in solid form or would be too expensive.

Vise A device, usually having a pair of jaws, designed to hold wood or other material while work is being done on it.

Warp The twisting of wood as it dries.

Washcoat Application of a wood conditioner, thinned linseed oil, or thinned shellac to wood prior to staining. You would apply a washcoat to wood that might blotch when stained with a liquid stain. See also "Stain controller."

Wax stick A colored wax crayon that hides small defects in finished wood.

Wet-or-dry sandpaper A type of abrasive paper that can be used with lubrication. The grit is of silicon carbide, and the paper and glue are waterproof. Lubrication may be water or mineral spirits.

Wood conditioner See "Stain controller."

Wood glue See "Polyvinyl glue."

Wood putty Any of various paste- or dough-like materials used to fill holes and other defects in wood.

INDEX

METRIC CONVERSION TABLES

Sizes: Metric cross sections are so close to their nearest U.S. sizes, as noted at right, that for most purposes they may be considered equivalents.

Lengths: Metric lengths are based on a 300mm module, which is slightly shorter in length than a U.S. foot. Check your requirements accurately to the nearest inch, and consult the table below to find the metric length required.

Areas: The metric area is a square meter. Use the following conversion factor when converting from U.S. data: 100 sq. feet = 9.29 sq. meters.

METRIC LENGTHS

Meters	Equivalent Feet and Inches
1.8m	5'10⅞"
2.1m	6' 10⅝"
2.4m	7' 10½"
2.7m	8' 10¼"
3.0m	9' 10⅛"
3.3m	10' 9⅞"
3.6m	11' 9¾"
3.9m	12' 9½"
4.2m	13' 9⅜"
4.5m	14' 9⅛"
4.8m	15' 9"
5.1m	16' 8¾"
5.4m	17' 8⅝"
5.7m	18' 8⅜"
6.0m	19' 8¼"
6.3m	20' 8"
6.6m	21' 7⅞"
6.9m	22' 7⅝"
7.2m	3' 7½"
7.5m	24' 7¼"
7.8m	25' 7⅛"

Dimensions are based on 1m = 3.28 feet, or 1 foot = 0.3048m

METRIC SIZES (Shown before Nearest U.S. Equivalent)

Millimeters	Inches	Millimeters	Inches
16 x 75	⅝ x 3	44 x 150	1¾ x 6
16 x 100	⅝ x 4	44 x 175	1¾ x 7
16 x 125	⅝ x 5	44 x 200	1¾ x 8
16 x150	⅝ x 6	44 x 225	1¾ x 9
19 x 75	¾ x 3	44 x 250	1¾ x 10
19 x 100	¾ x 4	44 x 300	1¾ x 12
19 x 125	¾ x 5	50 x 75	2 x 3
19 x 150	¾ x 6	50 x 100	2 x 4
22 x 75	⅞ x 3	50 x 125	2 x 5
22 x 100	⅞ x 4	50 x 150	2 x 6
22 x 125	⅞ x 5	50 x 175	2 x 7
22 x 150	⅞ x 6	50 x 200	2 x 8
25 x 75	1 x 3	50 x 225	2 x 9
25 x 100	1 x 4	50 x 250	2 x 10
25 x 125	1 x 5	50 x 300	2 x 12
25 x 150	1 x 6	63 x 100	2½ x 4
25 x 175	1 x 7	63 x 125	2½ x 5
25 x 200	1 x 8	63 x 150	2½ x 6
25 x 225	1 x 9	63 x 175	2½ x 7
25 x 250	1 x 10	63 x 200	2½ x 8
25 x 300	1 x 12	63 x 225	2½ x 9
32 x 75	1¼ x 3	75 x 100	3 x 4
32 x 100	1¼ x 4	75 x 125	3 x 5
32 x 125	1¼ x 5	75 x 150	3 x 6
32 x 150	1¼ x 6	75 x 175	3 x 7
32 x 175	1¼ x 7	75 x 200	3 x 8
32 x 200	1¼ x 8	75 x 225	3 x 9
32 x 225	1¼ x 9	75 x 250	3 x 10
32 x 250	1¼ x 10	75 x 300	3 x 12
32 x 300	1¼ x 12	100 x 100	4 x 4
38 x 75	1½ x 3	100 x 150	4 x 6
38 x 100	1½ x 4	100 x 200	4 x 8
38 x 125	1½ x 5	100 x 250	4 x 10
38 x 150	1½ x 6	100 x 300	4 x 12
38 x 175	1½ x 7	150 x 150	6 x 6
38 x 200	1½ x 8	150 x 200	6 x 8
38 x 225	1½ x 9	150 x 300	6 x 12
44 x 75	1¾ x 3	200 x 200	8 x 8
44 x 100	1¾ x 4	250 x 250	10 x 10
44 x 125	1¾ x 5	300 x 300	12 x 12

Dimensions are based on 1 inch = 25mm